The Storm at Kalidjati

Gateway to disaster after the fall of Singapore

Francis Hansen

Matthew

This book will be of interest to you!

Poppa Ralphs was in the
        48th LAA Regiment RA
        Gunner
        Army No 906837.

In memory of the officers and men of the British and Allied armed forces in Java, February-March 1942

especially
49th Battery, 48th LAA Regiment RA

Kalidjati airfield, Java, 21st February-1st March 1942

[Author's collection]
Bombadier Jack L L Gunn, 49th LAA Bty, 1914-1994

Acknowledgements

With many thanks to the officers and men who served in Sumatra and Java whose reports, journals and correspondence post-war are preserved in archives, allowing me to write this book. A full list is given in the bibliography and all warrant a 'thank you' for the fascinating light they throw on this campaign. Read them if you can.

It seems wrong to pick out individuals but I must mention Lt-Col Saunders with his acid pen and Brigadier Blackburn's clear report, but above all the journals of Lt-Col J V O Macartney-Filgate and Rev R C R Godfrey. These are contemporary accounts of inestimable value. Finally, thank you also to Jack Gunn, whose stories got me interested in this campaign.

As an expression of gratitude, I shall donate a percentage of any profits from this book to charities that work with Far East veterans and their families.

About the Author

Francis Hansen is the pseudonym of a history graduate and ex-archivist who has been researching this topic for years. Now retired, Francis lives in the Thames Valley with a partner who also has devoted their life to history, close to younger daughter Soph, her husband and five children, and very convenient for the National Archives. But not so convenient for elder daughter Elly, her husband and son in the United States.

Contents

One: an unknown conflict and an acceptable loss

This book is about the Java Campaign, which partly coincided with and partly took place after the fall of Singapore on 15ᵗʰ February 1942. While little-known in Britain, this debacle has several interesting aspects. It was probably, in fact, one of the worst military fiascos that the British armed forces were involved in in the whole World War II. Firstly, the military command structure was never filled and never became operationally capable. Secondly, the only land and air units allocated to it were ones already in the area that could be deployed there in time. And thirdly, it had no logistical support of any kind. There were a few other problems associated with fighting there but these will be dealt with later.

You would be forgiven for thinking that after Singapore fell to the Japanese there a solemn hush, an intake of breath and a respectful pause in the Far East before battle was resumed in the jungles of Burma and the myriad islands of the Pacific as the immediate aftermath is ignored in much British literature. Yet no such vacuum existed, as the Japanese forces that had pushed so suddenly and so aggressively southwards since early December continued to move onward and outward in the manner they had meticulously planned months before.

It was obvious to the Allies in the region - the British, the Dutch, the Australians and the newly-combatant Americans who were all struggling to stem the tide - that Singapore was probably for the chop some weeks before it actually fell. And not just Singapore: the Philippines were similarly doomed. To prepare for those eventualities, they reached agreement at the end of December 1941 to form a combined Allied defence force to stop further enemy expansion in the south-west Pacific, an organisation known to history by its telegraphic address: ABDACOM. The loss of Singapore was not an end: it was the end of a British and Australian campaign.

To agree the constitution and find spare senior officers to man some of the positions in the new command was one thing: to find the necessary forces to fight was completely another. There was precious little to spare when battles were being fought in other parts of the globe and national defences were already nearly overwhelmed by the victorious Japanese in other parts of this war zone. But there were some army units, a few squadrons, a warship or two that might be close enough. There were a few ships in transit with troops bound for Singapore and some RAF and RAAF squadrons that would escape before it fell. The powers-that-be, far from the battlefield, were not sure exactly *what*, but these forces would be put at the disposal of ABDACOM to form a strong defensive line to hold the Netherlands East Indies (modern-day Indonesia and surrounding islands) and prevent the Japanese reaching Australia.

It took only a few weeks to demonstrate quite clearly to all involved that this line could neither be held nor reinforced. By now all that was left to ABDACOM was Java, the main island of the Netherlands East Indies (NEI). But neither could the defending forces, especially the land forces, be withdrawn. They had to be seen to stand and fight, to the last man and the last bullet if necessary, to prove that the senior partners amongst the Allies, particularly Britain, were serious in their intention to protect Australia, especially after the loss of Singapore. The Dutch homeland in Europe had fallen to the Nazis yet young Dutchmen were still fighting in the Allied cause. Defending part of their empire recognised their sacrifice. It was one of those situations in warfare where one side has to take a hit, an 'acceptable loss', as someone described it to me with reference to this particular campaign.

There was a partial withdrawal. The senior officers who had staffed ABDACOM generally departed, and officers and men with particular skills or abilities that the Allies desperately needed were shipped away as the Japanese net closed around Java. There were notable exceptions, but generally those left behind were those who were 'expendable'. These were left under the command of the colonial Dutch commanders, men who had never expected nor been trained to deal with such a situation. They in turn constructed a defence plan for the island. This had two basic parts, the first of which was to try to use what ships and aircraft they had to stop the Japanese landing on Java in the first place. The second was a post-invasion plan, based on the assumption that there were only two beaches where the Japanese might land. Given this, the Allied forces would undertake a fighting retreat to delay the invaders, so that any relief force that might be around would have time to turn up. Failing this, the 'last stand' would be around the city of Bandoeng in the mountainous central spine of the island.

As plans go it was not particularly ambitious but, given the circumstances and the forces at their disposal, it was the best they could do. Speaking with hindsight, there was a very obvious flaw in this. It relied on the Japanese landing on one or both of two beaches. Unfortunately, they also landed on a third. And this third was only forty miles away by good roads from one of the two major airbases on the island, Kalidjati.

Kalidjati had been the main Dutch air force training base and also boasted a major repair centre. It was big. Its runways may have been grass but in the week leading up to the Japanese invasion it was home to Dutch bomber and fighter squadrons plus all the remaining RAF and RAAF bombers on Java. It should not have taken a military mastermind to work out that such a facility so close to the coast would be a prime target for the enemy. If the

Japanese took Kalidjati, the whole defence plan would be in ruins. There was plenty of room there for their fighter and bomber aircraft and they could destroy the puny defence forces on Java within days. And the airfield was also only a few miles from a road leading to Bandoeng; a shorter if more difficult route to the one the Dutch commanders hoped the invaders would take. It was certainly practicable for the invading force that landed on 1ˢᵗ March 1942.

Kalidjati did have defences. 49ᵗʰ Light Anti-Aircraft Battery (LAA), RA, had turned up with its ten Bofors guns on 21ˢᵗ February to reinforce the two Bofors guns on the airfield manned by Dutch veterans. There was also a small Dutch colonial army presence for ground defence which was relieved late on 28ᵗʰ February by a British force that had, until four days before, been the remains of a heavy anti-aircraft battery that had lost its guns following action in Sumatra. That they were hardly trained infantry was not as important as the fact that they had no armoured vehicles and arrived in the dark the very night before the enemy attacked. In the chaos that followed, the Japanese won a fully-provisioned and fully-functioning airfield in a couple of hours. And that airfield was in easy striking distance of the appointed final redoubt.

The death toll at the airfield was the greatest loss of life the British suffered in any one action in the fighting on the island. The British and Australians alone lost around 120 officers and men. Air force losses are difficult to pin down exactly but 49ᵗʰ Battery (Bty) lost one officer and 59 Other Ranks, while 12ᵗʰ Heavy Anti-Aircraft Battery, (HAA), RA, the airfield defence force, lost two officers and 41 men. Not all of these died during the capture of the airfield. Others were victims of the Japanese front-line troops' habit of killing prisoners rather than following the provisions of the Geneva Convention. When the wounded and the lost guns were also accounted for, the 49ᵗʰ ceased to be an active anti-aircraft battery. Its survivors became infantry like the survivors of 12ᵗʰ HAA Bty. The RAF had not lost many men but its bomber force had been destroyed.

It is not enough to say that the Japanese conquered Java and the other islands of the NEI. The Allies also lost them by their own actions or lack of them. The seeds of the disaster had been sown from the very beginning of ABDACOM. In the chaos following the decision to set it up, many things had not been done that should have been done and many important problems had been overlooked at senior level. At regimental, battery and squadron level the officers in command struggled to make their own solutions to these, with varying amounts of success.

I have made the loss of Kalidjati the centrepiece and climax of this book. Kalidjati was where it all went wrong and with Kalidjati lost, Java was doomed. What happened there on 1ˢᵗ March 1942 was a 'perfect storm' when everything that could go wrong, did go wrong. It was a microcosm of the chaotic campaign that followed the fall of Singapore: a hostile climate, no knowledge of the local language, no orders or intelligence from above, lack of essential equipment, stores and ammunition, and incompetence, indecisiveness and inadequate communications at all levels. Many men paid a terrible price for their superiors' failings in the flash-flood that swept through the airfield that day. Even luck was not on their side. The sheer speed and chaos of it all is captured beautifully in Gnr C H C North's letter accompanying his form giving details on the missing:

'I have tried to help you on this matter with what I know and what I think happen, I know that you must know if possible what did actually happen, but failing this you have to have what people think happen, that is the persons who were there, so I have include in my statement what I thought happen to these men.'[1]

The story of exactly what happened at Kalidjati that day and why will unfold later. This book follows the course of the post-Singapore campaign from its beginnings to the bitter end, woven around the story of 49th Bty and other RA units, to show how politics and military commands affected both ends of the scale, top to bottom, from the General to the Gunner, from the Brigadier to the Bombadier. Politically and militarily, besides destroying the Dutch defensive plan for Java at a stroke, the loss of Kalidjati had the potential to cause a deep rift among the newly-formed Allies in the Pacific and beyond. There was nearly an international incident over the loss of the airfield in 1942.

In the days that followed, before the formal Allied military surrender on 12th March 1942, the Dutch waged a bitter but futile two-day battle against the invader in the Tjiater Pass, while two Australian battalions of infantry under Brigadier A S Blackburn, VC, fought so hard that the Japanese refused at first to accept that his force was so small. The courage of all the defenders was pointless. The Japanese were too strong and too well-prepared.

You will not discover much about the fall of Java from British history books, though the Australians and the Dutch are much more forthcoming. Yes, it was a small campaign – so small in post-war military eyes that Major-General H D W Sitwell, nominally in charge of British land forces, was not required to write a despatch for publication. He did write one, however. There are two versions of it in the National Archives. Officers commanding regiments appear to have been required to write reports and some have survived in the same place, though not one for 48th LAA Regiment (Regt), of which 49th Bty was part. However, the regiment's last

---

[1] TNA: WO 361/342: letter dated 18th January 1946

commanding officer, Lt-Col J V O Macartney-Filgate, wrote his own account of what happened during their deployment in the Far East and also spent several years after the war trying to trace all his men and their fates. He sent copies of all these to the Regimental Chaplain, Revd R C R Godfrey, who was actually on Kalidjati airfield when it fell and also wrote his own memoirs in captivity.[2]

These are only a few of the surviving near-contemporary accounts that I have used to write this book. Some officers' reports have been particularly enlightening. It was a chance to vent their anger at what had happened to them and their men and one or two are quite detailed. I have used later memoirs as sparingly as possible as frankly things get forgotten, misremembered or muddled with the passage of time. What you will read here was almost without exception written within ten years of the fall of Kalidjati and Java as a whole.

Which brings me nicely to why I got interested in this in the first place. When I was young, I knew a man called Jack Gunn, a veteran of 49th Bty, who was a great raconteur. Almost without exception, his stories were about his early life, his time in the Army before deployment, or his time as a prisoner of war in the Far East, but there were a couple of things he told me that actually referred to his short time in action in the NEI. One thing that stuck in my mind was his account of his airfield being overrun by the Japanese. It was very short and lacked detail but went something like this:

'One morning the Japs came over the airfield wall as we were having breakfast. We were on the far side of the airfield so we grabbed our rifles and ran into the jungle. There we were reformed by officers who led us back and we took it back again. We were taken to see the bodies of the men who had been on the other side of the airfield. They had been ripped open by the Japs and left to die. They hadn't stood a chance. Their rifles were all stacked while they had their breakfast and they didn't have a chance to get to them. The Japs had killed them even though they were unarmed. "Look at them well" we were told. "That's what'll happen to you if the Japs get hold of you." We couldn't hold the airfield so we went off into the jungle.'

Jack has been dead for many years, but I have followed up what I can remember. Oddly enough, I have found corroborating evidence for most of what he told me.

Jack was just an ordinary bloke, like so many of his contemporaries in his battery or his regiment or on Java. When he and the survivors talked, they talked of themselves as ex-FEPOWs[3]. When they wrote their memoirs, it was memoirs of being a FEPOW. Their post-war life was defined by this, by

---

[2] IWM Documents.7879: Private papers of Canon R C R Godfrey
[3] FEPOW: Far East Prisoner of War.

this defeat and this captivity. Perhaps it was the result of a helplessness they felt that came from the way they were left to defend the un-defendable with no chance of escape. They didn't know what was going on and were pushed from pillar to post without the proper supplies and support in a foreign land far from home. The men who fought and died or became prisoners here were ordinary everyday men, the man in the street. The 'best' or the 'special' had mostly been evacuated. This was the reality of the 'acceptable loss'.

This book covers the British involvement in the land warfare in the NEI after the fall of Singapore, often through the eyes of these men. What they did before they became prisoners. They were soldiers and they did their best under the circumstances they found themselves in. But the ones who got the truly dirty end of the stick were those who ended up at Kalidjati.

Two: 48ᵗʰ LAA Regiment prepares for war

Jack Gunn was annoyed and a little surprised when he was called up in the autumn of 1940. He was not one of those young men who instinctively volunteered the moment war was declared; in fact, given his own choice, he would not have gone to war at all. Less than six months before, he had married Sue, his fiancée and business partner. This up-and-coming 'Oil and Hardware Merchant', as his Army records have it, was doing well, travelling with his own van round rural Cambridgeshire selling whatever necessities of life his customers needed, from oil to soap powder to chamber pots and saucepans and anything else in between. He and Sue had a Grand Plan; they would work hard at 'The Business', as they called it, not have any children and retire at forty with a fortune which would allow them to do what they liked. One of his friends in the same line of business as him was excused military service and he thought the same would apply to him. In short, in the spring of 1940, the world still seemed to be his oyster in spite of the war.

But it was not to be and, whether it was by sheer chance or someone had an evil sense of humour, Jack was conscripted into the Royal Artillery. Gunner Gunn joined 49ᵗʰ Bty, 48ᵗʰ LAA Regt, in September 1940 a week after his twenty-sixth birthday. He is described in his Army records as having fair hair and hazel eyes, being 5ft 8¾ins tall and weighing 203lbs. At 14½ stone he would not be considered particularly fat by today's standards but people were more slender then and his Army nickname was 'Tubby'. His weight would fluctuate between 12-17 stone throughout his life. The only time he was thin was when he was a prisoner of war.

He did not take easily to the discipline of military life. Being his own boss had made him used to taking orders from no-one but himself and anyway, he judged men by what they were like, not by what titles or rank they might have. This is not a good attitude in the military. He was put on charges for things like wearing plimsolls on parade (he did not like Army boots) and cleaning his kit with his wife's silk underwear - and narrowly missed being caught AWOL on at least one occasion. Luckily, the last lift he got back to camp was with an off-duty officer who was also a little late back! He liked the camaraderie of the Battery and being stationed on the East Coast around the Felixstowe area meant he did not have far to travel home on leave, though he swore that the Germans always bombed Cambridge whenever he did so.

He enjoyed being in the Royal Artillery. It meant seeing new places and he found this fascinating. He had probably rarely left Cambridgeshire for more than an odd day or two before he joined the Army but it would not have been unusual then for a working class man to have lived most of his life around the same place. What he and most of his contemporaries amongst the rank and file knew of the world would have come from reading books or newspapers or from watching cinema newsreels. Remember, growing up in a world without television and computers, what these men were confronted with in the Far East – climate, food, local people, other languages, geography, vegetation, etc - was far beyond their knowledge and came as a terrific shock. And that was even without going to war there.

Men in his regiment came from all parts of the British Isles and had many different professions. A few would have been 'regulars', some would have volunteered and others, like Jack, would have accepted conscription when it came. They tended to be older on average than those in the infantry and many were married, but generally they were a fairly average cross-section of the male population of fighting age. Jack was different from most of his contemporaries in one way: he could drive.

There was a real problem with producing trained drivers for the Royal Artillery regiments that went overseas at the time that his did. They were essential to drive the trucks that towed the guns once the batteries were mobile, besides the other transport for the unit in the field, yet very few people knew how to drive at the start of World War II. Lt-Col M D S Saunders, a Regular Army officer who assumed command of 21st LAA Regt, RA, on 31st October 1941, pulled no punches in his report to the War Office[4] on his return from captivity in the Far East either about his experiences at home or abroad. He was furious about the standard of drivers provided to his regiment, given the vital role they would play once the unit was operational and cites the experience of one of his batteries:

'33 drivers joined the Battery six days before it proceeded to Blandford [for mobile training]. Of this number only three were fit to drive. In order to move the Battery to Blandford, it was necessary to borrow drivers from 44 A.A. Brigade. … Every day at Blandford, on which exercises were carried out, drivers for vehicles were again supplied by N.C.O.s'.

The new drivers were given a week's intensive individual training in driving and maintenance but as Saunders pointed out, it wasn't really good enough for any battery going on active service that their drivers should effectively learn on the job in active service conditions.

Nor, to the Colonel's fury, were they all the 'A' standard he was told his men should be before embarkation. He gave the example of one driver who could 'see only with difficulty out of both eyes, was a dwarf in size, and

---

[4] TNA: WO 106/2563: Java story of 21 L.A.A. Regt, 1941-2. Lt-Col Saunders' report

possessed such highly arched feet that he was quite unable to press in the clutch of any car of size larger than a light 8 cwt.'

Saunders claimed that this and another case of unsuitability he cited were 'by no means isolated' among the drivers he was expected to accept. His protests and demands for suitable replacements went winging swiftly back but there is no record of how successful he was. After all, someone had to take these men on their regimental strength. I imagine he would have welcomed a man with Jack Gunn's experience of driving with open arms.

I am not going to detail the moves 49th Bty made either when deployed in England or when training to go abroad. The Regimental[5] and Battery[6] War Diaries still survive in the National Archives. One thing the records do show, which is of particular interest here, is how both battery and regiment were experiencing changes to their officers and manpower right up to just before departure. This practice was standard at the time and was complained about by more than one commanding officer. As a regiment prepared for deployment overseas, it shed men who were either too young to serve abroad or not up to A1 fitness. Their places were filled by men from other regiments or by men who had only just finished training.

Saunders again pulled no punches in his report over this. 21st Regt was ordered to mobilise on 15th October 1941 for deployment overseas on or soon after 15th November. At much the same time, two of the regiment's three batteries, 80th and 136th LAA, were replaced by 48th and 79th LAA. At the same time, 48th lost many men who were Category 'B' but were very experienced. Their replacements were not. Saunders explained:

'The Regiment was brought up to full War Establishment by drafting of 420 Other Ranks. None of these had had mobile training of any kind. ... Of this total, about 90 per cent. came straight from Training Centres with their training necessarily very limited. ... these men had had no experience of corporate Battery life, and were, in consequence, pitch-forked into the vortex of mobilisation without being granted any time in which to settle down into the necessary routine of the daily life of a soldier. The last reinforcement joined the Regiment on 3rd December, two days before it proceeded to the port of embarkation. In effect, the Regiment proceeded overseas with approximately 50 per cent. of its personnel new, unknown, and only partially trained.'

We will hear more of 21st Regt later as Fate was to take them to Java with 48th Regt, which was meanwhile going through the same pre-embarkation processes. Macartney-Filgate complained in his memoirs:

---

[5] TNA: WO 166/2721: War Diary of 48th LAA Regiment; 1940-41
[6] TNA: WO 166/2796: War Diary of 49th Battery LAA; various dates in period 1939-41

'some forty per cent of the rank and file who were below the required medical category were posted away, their places being taken by new drafts who were of suitable medical category but of whom many had reached only the most elementary degree of training. At the same time the regiment which had hitherto been on a static basis was made up to full mobile establishment. The tremendous change-over in the rank and file was, of course, due to the fact that over six months the regiment had been required to provide drafts of fully trained, fully fit men for other units moving overseas and had received low category men in exchange'.[7]

During the first six months of 1941, the Regt:

'had been called upon to find a steady stream of trained officers, N.C.O's and men to fill vacancies in units proceeding overseas, to satisfy the call for Bofors detachments on merchant ships and to provide "cadres" for new batteries in process of formation. In fact, while operationally engaged as static A.D.G.B. units defending certain vital targets they were at the same time required to perform the functions of draft finding units and to train the comparatively inexperienced recruits who were posted to the batteries to replace the men drafted away.'

Again, like their sister regiment, there was a desperate struggle to train drivers who could not drive and gunners who had only a rudimentary idea of their duties.

There were major changes in the officers in the regiment too. In the senior ranks, Lt-Col S R Pearson moved from 72nd HAA Regt to take command on 11th August 1941. He was a Regular Army officer who had been with the Territorials before being commissioned as a 2nd Lieutenant in the RA in January 1919 and his promotion had followed the slow and steady path of a peacetime officer in a small army with few chances of advancement. He had reached Major by August 1938 and been promoted to Acting Lt-Colonel when he took up his posting with 48th Regt, a rank that changed to Temporary Lt-Col in the November shortly before departure. From copies of his letters to his wife now in the Imperial War Museum, London,[8] it appears that only a little while before this he had been in Malaya and was probably a little grizzled by his service here and in India. He made the extraordinary mistake of asking a number of 'intelligent looking chaps' amongst the ORs in his new regiment how old they thought he was and got answers around sixty. Being only forty-four at the time, he was horrified but fortunately some of his officers scored nearer the mark and went somewhere to salving his feelings!

---

[7] 'The 48th Light Anti-Aircraft Regiment Royal Artillery in the Dutch East Indies, February-March 1942'; Lt-Col J V O Macartney-Filgate
[8] IWM Documents 8116

Major R N Russell, who took over 242nd Bty, 48th Regt, on 9th September, and Major C P Graham, who took command of 95th Bty shortly before the regiment embarked to go overseas to allow Macartney-Filgate to assume the post of second-in-command to Lt-Col Pearson, were, like Macartney-Filgate, both World War I veterans who returned to the Army for World War II. Macartney-Filgate had been awarded the MC in 1918 for conspicuous gallantry and devotion to duty.[9] The third new battery commander, Major R J S Earle, who took charge of 49th Bty at some date after 16th September, was a much younger man. Born in 1915, he had been a Regular Army officer since January 1935. He had returned to England about September 1941 and took command of the battery after a period of leave.[10] As the date of his promotion to Acting Major is given in the Army List as 20th October 1941, he probably arrived at the battery around then. He was known personally to Pearson, who always referred to him in his letters as 'Robert' while he used surnames for the other battery commanders.

If he was younger and potentially less experienced than the other battery commanders in the regiment, he had another World War I veteran as captain in his battery. Captain R J Newman, who re-enlisted or was recalled to the Colours on 23rd June 1939 with the rank of 2nd Lieutenant and a Temporary Short Service Commission, had been a captain with 6th Battalion (Territorial) The Essex Regiment in 1916. Newman was popular with the men[11] and he must have been a steadying influence in a battery that had a large proportion of young inexperienced officers, several of who were probably new to the battery when it sailed in December 1941. Three of the six lieutenants do not appear in either the Battery or the Regimental War Diaries before they end in October 1941, so probably joined from October onwards (the October entries are only sketchy) while another, 2nd Lt R Mounsdon, joined, newly-commissioned, in August 1941. While Capt Newman and three lieutenants had been with the battery for six months or more, it was generally the case that many officers and men were new to the unit and in some cases new to soldiering.

All in all, it was a right royal shake up all round in the LAA regiments going abroad in the second half of 1941 and Jack might have missed going with his. While his battery was on airfield defence in East Anglia, the RAF asked for volunteers within their ranks to fill the role of air gunners in Bomber Command. Jack decided that from what he had seen the dice were stacked very much against air gunners surviving the war and that he would be safer where he was. Statistically this was a bad call, though no-one could have

---

[9] London Gazette, 19th March 1918.
[10] TNA: WO 361/342: J.H.J. Webster's statement
[11] Jack Gunn, always a judge of the man rather than the rank, liked and respected him above all others.

guessed it at the time, for while Bomber Command aircrew deaths were approximately 44%, the death rate for his battery once deployed in the Far East would be almost 60%[12]. But this was hidden in the future and the decision looked a sensible one. Anyway, he did survive against the odds.

The other opportunity was presented by an accident during the regiment's mobile training in Yeovil during late August and early September 1941. He was jumping down from a lorry on 9th September when his wedding ring got caught up and nearly stripped the flesh from his finger. However, on 2nd December the Casualty card in his Army records reports 'Injury not likely to interfere with future efficiency' and A/Bombardier Jack Gunn duly moved out with his battery *en route* to the Clyde a couple of days later. For the great movements in personnel in the autumn of 1941 to make 48th Regt battle-ready had led to rapid promotion for him from Gunner to Acting Bombardier between 16th September and 1st October 1941. He had a year's experience of both active service on the guns and life with the battery by then, which would have been invaluable with so many new men in the regiment. By the time 49th Bty landed in Java on 3rd February 1942, Jack would be a Bombardier.

However, Java was not the regiment's original destination. That was Singapore. At that time, there was still no war in the Far East and Malaya would be miles away from the constant attentions of the Luftwaffe in East Anglia and all the bloody fighting going on in the Western Desert. It looked a good place to be before 8th December and from the War Office's point of view it would give the unit time to shake down after all the changes. Rev Godfrey gives an insight into the way the officers saw their new posting:

'Singapore. The hot far-eastern city where life is lived leisurely and the troops knock off work at an early hour. Going to Britain's far-eastern fortress. Leaving the theatre of war altogether and saying goodbye to air-raids and things. ... in went tin trunks into the bowels of the ship, containing shot guns, tennis rackets, golf clubs, all for the time when we reached Singapore.'[13]

Unfortunately he and his fellow officers did not know the reality of Singapore. We must start by recognising that it never was an impregnable fortress and anyone who asserts this now has clearly not examined the large fund of contemporary material which shows this. Was such a thing possible there anyway given the way warfare was changing, even if economic forces had not been at work? It was scarcely a completed military

---

[12] This is calculated taking Bomber Command deaths as 55,000 on an estimated 125,000 operational aircrew and for 49th Battery, 297 officers and men deployed in the Far East with 177 deaths.

[13] Journal of Canon R C R Godfrey, amongst the papers of Canon Godfrey deposited at the Imperial War Museum, London, ref: IWM 7879

installation when war broke out in the Far East and its defences were limited to five 15-inch guns, six 9.2-inch guns and fourteen 6-inch guns fixed to fire only out to sea towards the south, south-east and south-west of Singapore Island. The reasons for this made sense if the total defence plan had been implemented, which unfortunately it wasn't.

In the early 1920s, a series of international naval conferences and agreements began, starting with the Washington Conference (1921-22), with the object of keeping the peace by regulating the size of fleets of the major powers. It also set up a zone covering most of the Pacific, except for the Hawaiian Islands, where no new fortifications or associated military building could take place – a so-called 'status quo' zone. This effectively led to a moving apart of main naval bases so that the Great Powers would not come into conflict with each other in the normal run of their activities. It was effectively a recognition of 'spheres of influence'. The line ran close to the coastline of Asia and put both Hong Kong and the American colony of the Philippines within the 'status quo' zone, resulting in the British decision to build new main naval harbour at Singapore. The move westward from Hong Kong had its advantages for the British. The balance of British trade and Imperial interests was moving more towards the Indian Ocean and the old naval base in Hong Kong was too small for the newer ships of the Royal Navy that had been developed over the last few years. It was also rather close to the home waters of the Japanese fleet, especially in the new diplomatic climate. Britain and Japan had been allies since the early years of the century but now that alliance was allowed to drop on the British side as it might have appeared counter to American interests in the area, centred around their colony of the Philippines. If a more even-handed stance was intended by the politicians in the United Kingdom, it certainly seemed more like a deliberate snub to the Japanese.

The concept of a naval base at Singapore had been sold to the Dominions of Australia and New Zealand as a policy of imperial defence known as the 'Singapore Strategy'. Briefly and crudely, the Royal Navy would retain command of the seas at all times and, with a fleet based in Singapore, would provide the first line of defence for the Empire in that area against any attack by a foreign power. The Dominions themselves would need only to raise forces sufficient for defence against local attacks or internal disorder. Not surprisingly, Australia and New Zealand wished to make economies in their military spending at the end of the First World War, which this policy allowed them to do, and they accordingly cut their forces to the bone, preferring to ignore the obvious snags. They were relying on the Mother Country on the other side of the world to provide their external defence when their most likely enemy seemed to be Japan, whose main bases were a mere 2,000 miles away. This plan did not consider the possibilities either that the Japanese might attack without giving two months warning (the earliest a fleet might be sent from Britain to relieve it) or that when the time came for action, the fleet might not be available anyway due to circumstances elsewhere.

And no one was quite clear how the new modern naval base at Singapore, one large enough to take and repair the largest vessels now in service with the Royal Navy, would be defended. The Australian Prime Minister from 1923-9, Stanley Bruce, admitted that while he was:

'not quite clear as to how the protection of Singapore is to be assured, I am quite clear on this point, that apparently it can be done'.[14]

The initial idea for the naval base was that, situated on the island of Singapore and surrounded by water, it would be defended by seaward-pointing naval guns and the British fleet against any aggressor who threatened it. It did not even begin to face the problems of providing an army or air force to defend the base but as soon as it was debated amongst the British Chiefs of Staff, someone pointed out a new reality. Whether this was Air Marshal Hugh Trenchard as is claimed by his supporters in the RAF or whether others also pitched in is neither here nor there for the purposes of this story. The fact is it was made clear that the rising capabilities of air power not only potentially made the base vulnerable to attack from another quarter but also gave it another form of defence. Billy Mitchell was experimenting with sinking battleships by bombing in the United States and the possibilities this offered were clear enough. The RAF, which was now policing the Empire in Iraq and on the Afghan border, could use its bombers to destroy an enemy fleet out at sea before it even came within striking range of Singapore.

The idea had much to commend it in theory. 'Policing the Empire' had proved a cheaper alternative to Army action over great swathes of the Middle East, where distances were huge, roads were few and the local government could be encouraged to pay for the aircraft that enforced the law for it. However, where Singapore was concerned, it was neither so simple nor so cheap. There must be sufficient aircraft of the right type. Those aircraft need airfields - or suitable harbours if they were the flying boats favoured for transport and reconnaissance in those parts of the world. They require a large number of ancillary personnel beyond the pilots themselves, with equipment and services to back them up. And when push comes to shove, they must be able to make good their boasts and actually sink large numbers of enemy shipping. I say this without being in any way critical of the abilities of the RAF aircrew, as destroying ships by aerial

---

[14] Quoted in *'Heading For Disaster? Australia and the Singapore Strategy'*, by Peter Dennis, at the 'Fall of Singapore 60th Anniversary Conference', National University of Singapore, 16-17 Feb. 2002

action was a difficult thing to do then even if no-one on the ships was firing back at the attackers. Unfortunately in Malaya, Singapore and later Sumatra and Java, none of the conditions necessary for success for the RAF were present in 1941 to 1942.

Faced with the old means of defence and the new possibilities of attack, the result was a compromise involving the two. Compromises can be a useful and even productive way of solving differences but this was sadly not so in Singapore. War weariness in the 1920s and financial meltdown in the 1930s meant there was less money for either so progress on the base itself was slow and even slower on the squadrons to defend it. The situation was bad enough without the improvements in aircraft and armaments over this period. Major problems had arisen because aircraft development in the 20s and 30s had produced faster machines with longer range and aircraft carriers were also being constructed by the major powers, particularly the USA and Japan.

Therefore whereas it was enough to have airfields on the island itself to defend it when Singapore naval base was little more than a twinkle in its commissioners' eyes, by the mid-1930s it was becoming clear that there must be airfields over the whole of Malaya to allow sufficient squadrons to deploy to defend from further away against both longer-range land aircraft and carrier-based planes. And these airfields would need ground troops to counter enemy ground forces and anti-aircraft guns to defend them against enemy aircraft - a projected eight heavy anti-aircraft guns and eight light anti-aircraft guns for each one of them - which was why 48th LAA Regt was going to Singapore and Malaya.

It would be good to be able to say that the authorities were well on track with their plans for defence in the area but this was not the case. We will deal with the shortage of land forces later but unfortunately by the outbreak of war only about 17% of the AA guns needed were in place. Some airfields had one or two, many had none. The nearest to 'establishment' was Seletar on Singapore Island, which had eight light anti-aircraft guns when hostilities started. The basic problem was that the British Empire was disastrously overstretched. Sustaining an empire requires large resources, resources that frequently are renewed and increased by expansion. By the 1920s the British Empire was on a path of decline. Part of this was due to over-expansion – her own resources could not meet the demands of running such a huge proportion of the world's surface - and there was no further expansion room even had the resources for the enterprise been available. Part also was the effect of the Great War, which had exhausted treasury, manpower and capabilities.

Prime Minister Winston Churchill's insistence that the war in Western Europe, which had broken out in September 1939 and threatened the very heart of the Empire, should be the main priority for British forces was undeniably a sensible one. However, the war had spread beyond Europe itself by the end of 1940 following Italian attacks on the British in North Africa. While these might be rebuffed, the German forces which arrived to boost the Italian effort were not as easily dealt with and, while troops had to be left in Britain in case of an invasion from Europe, it became necessary also to reinforce in Egypt and Iraq against the renewed Axis effort in those regions. Iraq, then a British protectorate following the First World War, was a vital source of oil for the Empire and could also be a back door to both Egypt and India if the German 'Operation Barbarossa' against the USSR, which started in June 1941, was successful. And of course India too would need reinforcing against that.

Therefore what there was in the way of British military capability was not only fully employed but actually overstretched. All of mainland Europe was either under Axis control or neutral and the United States had carefully avoided getting involved. When Japan entered into an alliance with Germany and Italy, the Tripartite Pact, on 27th September 1940, the problem of an undefended and indefensible Empire east of India had raised its head. Japan had spent the last fifteen years expanding her empire by force and the weakness of the other imperial powers in her back yard, so to speak, offered her an unparalleled chance to grab land and resources while the going was good. The British, however, had just the solution for this eventuality, as Air Chief Marshal Sir Robert Brooke-Popham, Commander-in-Chief in the Far East, 17th October 1940 to 27th December 1941, recalled in his post-war despatch[15]:

'it was the policy of His Majesty's Government to avoid war with Japan'.

This 'guideline' was reinforced on more than one occasion by telegrams insisting:

'Avoidance of war with Japan is basis of Far East policy and provocation must be rigidly avoided' and 'Our policy in the Far East is still to avoid war with Japan.'

Unfortunately this meant that any real efforts to improve defences in any way could be seen as provocative acts, which did not help the situation in Hong Kong, Singapore or Malaya.

And because resources were so scarce and the Japanese must not be provoked into attacking, the forces sent out to the Far East were correspondingly small. A Ministry of Shipping file on 'Shipping Plans for Future Troop Requirements', now in the National Archives,[16] has an

---

[15] Supplement to The London Gazette, 20th January 1948
[16] TNA: MT 40/45: Movement of troops and stores: estimate of future commitments, 1941

interesting list entitled 'Detail of requirements of shipping space for period 1st September to 31st December 1941'. The Middle East (Egypt and adjacent) was to get 94,900 Army personnel in all, including 10,500 in anti-aircraft units, 25,000 men as 'Drafts to complete 1st reinforcements' and 10,000 as 'Drafts to cover estimated additional wastage'. Iraq was substantially lower overall with 13,200 in total, of whom 7,500 were anti-aircraft artillery while India, with a total of 14,400, would get 8 infantry battalions over the four months with 8,000 men as 'Drafts for Indian expansion scheme'. In comparison, Malaya would receive only 6,500 Army personnel including 3,000 anti-aircraft – around three Regiments at full war strength, not nearly enough to make up the deficiencies in airfield defences. With the addition of two regiments of field artillery, 500 RASC personnel, 1,500 'Drafts' and whatever share of the 38,000 RAF and Royal Navy personnel also on the move worldwide in the four-month period were being shipped that far east, the Japanese could hardly be frightened into thinking that the British were preparing for war.

Not that they were, of course, because thanks to that incredible bad luck which was to pursue Allied forces throughout the early stages in the war in the Far East, the Japanese already knew how poorly defended and equipped for war the British Empire in those parts really was. This information was from a source a hundred times more reliable than their own excellent network of agents in the field – the Imperial Chiefs of Staff themselves. The governments and people of Australia and New Zealand looked to Malaya and Singapore as their defence against Japanese incursion from the north, a fortress to ensure that their links with India and beyond would remain unbroken. Singapore itself had a special significance: it was the embodiment of the protection the Mother Country offered to her Dominions and Colonies, the essence of the British Empire itself. Any betrayal here could, for the Anzacs, be another Gallipoli.

Fighting men from these two Dominions were absolutely vital for Britain's survival and should their governments think they should withdraw them to defend their homelands it would have a very substantial impact on the war in North Africa and beyond. And it was not just on the ground that they were important - they also supplied ships, sailors and airmen. Losing this vital input would have made the British war effort unsustainable. So it was that when the Chiefs of Staff in London drew up an 'Appreciation' of the situation in the Far East in July 1940 that set out in sorry detail how little defence was either in place or even possible in British possessions out there, they put it on a slow boat to Singapore intending it to reach Brooke-Popham after an Allied conference there at which the delegates would, if the true situation was known, undoubtedly ask for even more reinforcements than the ones they were not going to get anyway.

Unfortunately, SS 'Automedon' met up with a German commerce raider in the Indian Ocean, the report was seized and passed on to the Nazis' delighted if astonished Japanese allies. They had not realised just how bad the British defences were and were likely to remain and the information gave them the confidence to push ahead on several fronts without fear of any substantial response.

Thus they could confidently move into Thailand and then mount an attack on Malaya and the Philippines at the same time as attacking Pearl Harbor. And news of that attack was received on Convoy WS 14 as it slipped from the Clyde on 8th December 1941. Now the officers and men of 48th Regt really wondered what the future held for them. It wasn't going to be tennis parties, that was for sure. But why was it that Britain was even fighting Japan, a country with which it had had alliances in the early twentieth century and which had fought on the Allied side along with Britain and the United States in World War I?

The policy of 'sakoku' or 'closed country' had brought Japan a golden age known as the 'Taihei' or 'Great Peace' lasting for over two hundred years from 1614 to 1853, a time noted for its culture and literacy. With no need to support large armed forces, the country could afford to spend its resources on other things. Nearly every adult male in its cities could read or write – way ahead of what any western country could boast. In its attempts to preserve this situation, Japanese officials politely but firmly rebuffed any attempt by a foreign power to encourage it to open itself to the world. One visiting U.S. Navy captain received a note declining to trade and pointing out that his country was being treated no differently to any other:

'We can make no distinction between different foreign nations – we treat them all alike; and you, as Americans, must receive the same answer with the rest. It will be of no use to renew the attempt, as all applications of the kind, however numerous they may be, will be steadily rejected. We are aware that our customs are in this respect different from those of some other countries, but every nation has a right to manage its affairs in its own way.'[17]

What could be more reasonable or polite? Unfortunately it was not good enough for those who were convinced of Western or Aryan superiority to all other races or of the need to convert the world's peoples to Christianity. It was sadly inevitable that if not Admiral Perry's fleet then some other would force a change of policy. When the time came, the Japanese governing circles realised that the country could no longer live the secluded life it had done for the last two hundred years, however much it wished to: the major powers in the rest of the world simply would not allow it to do so.

---

[17] *The Imperial Cruise: a Secret History of Empire and War'*, James Bradley, Back Bay Books, Hachette Book Group, New York, 2010, p175

Nevertheless, fears that they might be dominated as a colony or fought over like a prize by these other countries led to a conscious decision to reinvent Japanese life at a superficial and political level to be as much like a Western state as possible. The Meiji Constitution introduced a constitutional monarchy, democracy and an independent judiciary while an enthusiastic programme of industrialisation was introduced. The political leaders hoped by these measures to be seen as 'honorary whites' rather than some form of barbarian prey.

For a time it seemed as though playing the game would be enough to be treated equally. In 1905 Theodore Roosevelt, President of the United States from 1901-1909, sent a high-powered delegation, including William Howard Taft, the Secretary of War, seven senators, and twenty-three congressmen (all with wives and aides) and his daughter Alice on a Pacific cruise visiting, amongst other places, Japan, where they had a rapturous welcome. Japan was at the time at war with Imperial Russia and naturally saw the visit as some sort of support for its side of the argument, a view which was strengthened when Taft, in a top-secret meeting with the Japanese Prime Minister and at Roosevelt's direction, entered a confidential pact allowing Japan to expand into Korea, quite ignoring the fact that it is unconstitutional for a US president to make any treaties with other countries without the approval of the US Senate. Sadly for the Japanese, they did not understand this and Roosevelt did not stand by his word; they had to withdraw from the disputed territories after the end of hostilities, a great humiliation which was probably not improved by Roosevelt being awarded the Nobel Peace Prize for his efforts as a peacemaker in the Japanese-Russian conflict. Naturally no outsiders had any knowledge of the secret negotiations.

The Japanese, perhaps not surprisingly, felt they had been betrayed. They had played international affairs the way the Western Powers did, they had won a war fair and square and at the end they had been forced to hand back what they had won in fair fight from their enemy - which they were sure no major Western Power would have been made to do. But besides his bad faith, Roosevelt had made another major mistake. In his communications with the Japanese he had referred to the American 'Munroe Doctrine' which had warned European Powers not to interfere with matters in the Americas as all of these areas were seen by the United States to be within its 'sphere of influence'. Unhappily for future events, he appears to have made some sort of suggestion that Japan might think in terms of a Munroe-style sphere of Japanese influence in the Far East and it is not unreasonable to see the 'Greater East Asia Co-Prosperity Sphere', as the Japanese called their World War II conquests, as a development of this.

It was not surprising that the British had a succession of alliances with the Japanese - both had strong navies at the beginning of the twentieth century and so had interests in common. Indeed, prior to World War I most Japanese warships were built in Britain. There was also co-operation between their forces; the Royal Naval Air Service, the flying branch of the Royal Navy until the formation of the RAF in 1918, gave advice and help with naval flying to the Japanese. This was continued by the RAF in its early years. The alliances and co-operation only ceased in the 1920s when the British government felt that the United States might be unhappy with these following the Washington naval conferences. It was not well received by the Japanese – it looked suspiciously like another snub by the Western Powers: they had also been expected to swallow without comment the return to China of Shantung and Kiaochow which they had gained from Germany under the Treaty of Versailles. It was a loss of face on an epic scale as no Western power had had to hand territory back like this. In addition, the Western powers, amongst which I am here including the Dominions, introduced legislation against non-white, and in some cases specifically Japanese, immigration. This was just another mighty slap in the face.

The situation was exacerbated by the fact that Japan was experiencing major internal problems. It was an industrialised country with few natural resources and a greatly increasing population. The older generation who had fronted the pro-western Meiji reforms were dying off and their policies had not brought the benefits that had been expected. Japan turned its back on the West and found its own badly-needed resources by military means. By the time its armed forces came up against the British in Malaya they had been fighting their way across Asia since the early 1930s, oblivious to the opinions of those who they felt had betrayed them. They were now seasoned and ruthless fighters. If the British, Americans, Russians, Dutch, etc, could help themselves to what they wanted round the world, so could the Japanese. None of which excuses the appalling treatment of both civilians and military forces in the lands they invaded. Not all Japanese were responsible for this but those who were committed crimes against humanity on an almost unbelievable scale.

The Japanese moved steadily into French Indo-China during 1941 and seemed to be intent on pushing on into Thailand. Oddly enough, in spite of this inexorable movement in their direction, most of the civilians in Malaya and Singapore seemed to be totally oblivious to the threat of war. The area was a hotchpotch of nationalities – European planters and traders, Chinese traders, Tamil labourers, a few thousand Japanese traders and entrepreneurs, and the native Malays, who were the only ones who truly regarded the area as their home. The others worked, took advantage of whatever the country had to offer and looked forward to the time they would go home, having made their pile, big or small, in a way like guests at a hotel. Sqn Leader F J Howell, who arrived in Singapore on HMS 'Prince of Wales' on 4th December 1941 to take over command of 243 Squadron, remarked that although all the news they had received on the way out had convinced them war was only a matter of days away, the same could not be said for the inhabitants of the Island[18]. There was no camouflage to speak of and only Air Headquarters had an air raid shelter. There were none at his airfield, Kallang, or at the naval base. Like other officers with war experience, he noted that there was no dispersal of aircraft, workshops, stores or personnel. The place was run on a peacetime basis and the locals felt that there would be no war as they didn't do things like that in that neck of the woods. The Japanese air raid on the night of 8th December 1941 was a rather nasty surprise for them.

---

[18] TNA: AIR 20/5578: Malaya operations 1941-1942: fighter operations. Sqn Ldr F J Howell's report

Three: WS 14: Convoy to chaos

Convoy WS 14[19] sailed from the Clyde in the late evening of 8th December 1941. Her ships had one of three final destinations: the Middle East, Bombay or Iraq and Malaya, the third contingent being by far the smallest at the time of sailing. Its departure was originally planned for 1st December but this was changed on 23rd November to 6th December. Further problems with assembling ships and lack of serviceability culminated in 2200hrs on 8th December being finally set as the time the convoy should cross the bar of the Clyde, which it duly did.

What the records of this convoy will not tell you about is an incident involving the troops being embarked on the 'Duchess of Atholl', known to sailors as 'The Dancing Duchess' owing to her tendency to roll alarmingly in anything other than calm seas. 48th LAA Regt had been due to sail on the 'Athlone Castle' but her engines had broken down so it was transferred to the 'Duchess', which appeared full of troops already. Rev (later Canon) R C R Godfrey, padre of the 48th, described the situation in his memoirs, written a couple of years later in a Japanese POW camp:

'a dirty looking ship and we compared her size, as an ocean going liner unfavourably with that of Athlone Castle. Once aboard we noticed the difference again. Instead of an officer to a cabin there were (except for colonels and the like) four. The men were far worse off. It was hot as hell down below and fresh air non-existent.'

Lt-Col J V O Macartney-Filgate, who became commanding officer of 48th Regt on 2nd March 1942, but was at this time Major Macartney-Filgate, second-in-command, 48th LAA, describes the conditions for the other ranks in his memoirs (also written in a POW camp) thus:

'Hammocks below decks slung side by side with not one inch between them accommodated part of the rank and file; the remainder slept in serried ranks on the deck immediately under the hammocks. The heat, when all men were assembled in their quarters, was stifling; the prospect, should rough weather be encountered bringing sea-sickness in its train, horrible to contemplate. ... the "Duchess of Atholl" was ... grossly overcrowded.'

Weeks of military training made no difference to the troops faced with this situation. Rev Godfrey tells us:

'That night there was pretty well a riot on board. A lot of the men (not ours) refused to go below decks and threatened to walk off the ship, but were finally prevailed upon, after a lot of shouting and references to the Altmark, by the O.C.Troops, to go below on the promise of things being made better on the morrow.'

---

[19] TNA: ADM 237/1600: Convoy WS 14 and DM 2.

Luckily, Rev Godfrey is no longer alive to read that he was wrong and at least one man from his regiment, Bombadier Jack Gunn, 49th Bty, was involved in this fracas. His account to me went something like this:

'We went up to Glasgow to get on a troopship and there were a lot of sergeants and others saying that we shouldn't get on it because it wasn't safe. At last there were a lot of us on the dockside refusing to get on and the blokes who'd started it all and stirred it all up were up there on the ship looking down and laughing. Because I was one of the senior men there, I was arrested as a ringleader and charged with mutiny. I was really frightened because mutiny was a capital offence, but one or two days out of port they changed the charge to 'Conduct prejudicial to military discipline' and I was reduced to the ranks. Then a couple of days later I was asked to give a lecture on gunnery. I said "NCOs give lectures, Gunners don't" and they gave me my stripes back.'[20]

At the same time as the residents of Singapore and Malaya were discovering the realities of life, 49th Bty was finding its feet on board ship. Or rather not finding them, as the 'Dancing Duchess' lived up to her name and the men on board were mostly struck low with seasickness. What it was like below decks with the ORs I cannot tell; Jack claimed to have been seasick from the Clyde to Durban and must have been feeling too rough to worry about the conditions as he didn't leave any reactions to them. Rev Godfrey, however, who was treasurer of the kitty set up by the seven RHQ officers of 48th Regt – miss a meal through seasickness and you forfeit your sixpence – did not suffer at all. He did share a cabin with a victim though and on one occasion wore his gas mask while he ran with a sick bowl to the nearest 'lats', nearly frightening the life out of someone he met on the way. When the ship developed engine trouble on Thursday night, 11th December, she demonstrated just how bad her rolling could be:

'Everywhere throughout the ship came the sounds of falling china, bangs and bumps throughout the night. A positive inferno of noise. And over all the creak, creak, creak as the ship went 45° to this side and then 45° to that. At breakfast next morning people's chairs just shot from underneath them and breakfast things slid all over the place. It was incredible chaos.'

Fortunately it was not long before the engines were fixed, the 'Duchess' took up her place in the convoy again and the sea became calmer. Rev Godfrey remarked that apart from 'plenty of scares', the voyage 'was uneventful'. I have no doubt it was for him but others would not have shared his point of view.

The trials and tribulations of setting up a convoy were many and various.

---

[20] Jack Gunn's Army service record has no note of it either but this document has several basic errors in it, such as where he was between December 1941 and September 1945, so is not definitive.

The many files relating to convoys at the National Archives give a clear picture of the problems and agonies the organisers faced. What ships were needed, what naval escorts, what air cover? Would such-and-such a ship be ready in time to join the convoy? The minutiae of putting a convoy such as WS 14 to sea, dealing with these and many other problems, still survive in the files[21]. The Battle of the Atlantic was still raging and the U-Boat menace was not yet on the wane. The British Mercantile Marine had lost thousands of tons of shipping and, besides the immediate terrible cost in lives and the loss of the ship and its precious cargo, each sinking took that ship off the books for future convoys. At this time of the war there was a real shortage of vessels to use in convoys, especially those that could be used for carrying troops, vital at a time when aircraft carried such small numbers and had what seem today to be very restricted ranges.

But the greater part of WS 14 had put out to sea from the Clyde on 8th December as eventually planned and other vessels joined it later to make the numbers up to 27 ships with a Royal Navy escort, led for the first part of the voyage by the battleship HMS 'Ramillies'. Once at sea, the convoy cruised in eight columns of up to four ships at a nominal speed of 13 knots under the command of Commodore E N Boddam-Whetham, RNR, who sailed in the 'Duchess of Atholl' in the centre of the front row of the convoy.

It is thanks to this circumstance that we have Rev Godfrey's description of him. He liked the Commodore and considered him 'a real gentleman', describing how:

'he kept a book of quotations from the Bible which he used as messages to the skippers of the other ships. ... I can only remember one from the Song of Solomon, about "my beloved" being slow, which he said was used quite frequently on the skippers of dawdling ships.'

Pearson described him as:

'a retired admiral + such a good chap. I've played quite a lot of bridge with him + it is most amusing. He is so damned rude to everyone + we all know it's a joke so we get lots of fun.'[22]

But perhaps not for Boddam-Whetham, who had many more problems besides dawdling ships as he described in his report for the voyage from the Clyde to Durban, the port at which great changes were to happen to the convoy and the destination of its ships.[23] While he reported that the voyage was free from enemy attack, SS 'Empire Oriole' had to heave to 'to secure Tanks carried as deck cargo' when the bad weather hit on 11th December, and the 'Duchess of Atholl' broke down. 'Empire Oriole' re-joined the

[21] TNA: ADM 237/1600: Convoy WS 14 and DM 2
[22] Private papers of Lt Col Pearson, letter dated 2/2/42
[23] TNA: ADM 199/1138: WS convoys: reports: WS 7-WS 14 B, 1940-41

convoy at Freetown on 23rd as did the 'Scythia' which had hoisted the signal "Not Under Control" on the 13th and dropped out of the convoy. These were common problems for convoy commodores but there was more to be complained about.

'Snowflake Rockets' were accidentally fired by an unknown ship in the convoy on 10th and 11th December, lighting up 'the whole ocean' when 'no real attack has materialised'. A stern order to desist unnecessary firing was sent round the convoy. HMS 'Nestor' blotted its copybook on the 11th when she opened fire on an aeroplane spotted 'flying from cloud to cloud'.

'I eventually informed him that he was apparently firing at the Planet "Venus" which proved to be the case.'[24]

This was not the only time in World War II when this bright white planet was mistaken for a light on an enemy aircraft, as we shall see later!

The worst trouble came, however, when the Commodore tried to exercise his charges in Emergency Turns and the manoeuvres for scattering, vital if they were to meet with enemy shipping either under or on the waves.

'Two ships only, other than "Duchess of Atholl", were consistently correct and the majority had no idea what to do. ... It is quite impossible in my opinion to have anything clearer than Mersigs makes this very essential matter and the answer should be given by a child of 10 in about ten seconds after reading it but 98% of Masters and Officers are utterly at sea about it.'

Having got all this off his chest, he did not feel it was necessary to mention that the five of his ships that had protective balloons, including the one he himself sailed in, had lost them when they broke adrift in the bad weather from 9th-11th December.[25] There must be a limit to misery.

He was not the only unhappy commanding officer in the convoy, which was actually two combined in one: WS 14 and WS 14D. 21st LAA Regt and 77th HAA Regt were sailing with a large detachment of RAF in four ships as part of convoy WS 14D under the command of Captain H R L Shaw, captain of SS 'Warwick Castle'. The other three vessels were the 'Troilus', the 'City of Pretoria' and the 'Empress of Australia'. Lt-Col Saunders, commanding 21st Regt, had been called to the War Office on 24th November to receive a briefing on the madcap scheme, codenamed Operation 'Jagged', his regiment and 77th Regt were to carry out. This was one of those wild ideas that surfaced from time to time in the war as an effort to break the stalemate on one of the fronts and provide the vital breakthrough that would bring the war to a swift end. If Saunders' account is to be believed, it was deficient in any realism and would have ended in as catastrophic a loss

---

[24] TNA: ADM 237/1600
[25] ibidem

of the two regiments and the RAF accompanying them as eventually happened in the Far East. However, the signal for WS 14D to break off from the main convoy was never received. Saunders and all those who were slated for Operation 'Jagged' sailed on with no knowledge of their final destination or the role they were expected to play when they got there for another seven weeks and many hundreds of miles. Saunders tried at every opportunity to get information about where they were bound but without success:

'This may not be the first, but it is to be hoped that it will be the last Force of some 4,000 men that sailed with no orders to an unknown destination. ... Secrecy is important, but the complete lack of orders relative to the employment and ultimate destination of such a Force as that appeared to shew [sic] a lack of confidence in its commanders unequalled since the days of Dundas.'

Saunders must have been way down the bottom of the list of problems the British Government and the Chiefs of Staff (COS) were facing. The nightmare scenario had arrived: war with Japan while war was still raging in Europe and in North Africa. At this time there was no reason to know that the German offensive that had stalled in front of Moscow in the depths of a Russian winter was not going to be successful come the spring, and that the danger that entailed to Iraq, the Middle East and the 'backdoor to India' would not be realised. However, it was now imperative to see what could be done in the Far East to defend Singapore and Malaya without taking vital resources from the other theatres.

A fascinating file exists among the records of the Chief of the (Imperial) General Staff in the National Archives entitled 'Far East emergency: reinforcements', dated December 1941 to March 1942,[26] that gives some insights into the problems. Whatever reinforcements could be spared would take around ten weeks sailing time if they were coming from the United Kingdom, quite apart from the time it would take to assemble them in the first place and embark them and their equipment, always assuming the ships to transport them were immediately available. The right type of ships had to be available in the right ports at the right time. This was not easy even when there were weeks to organise. Now time had run out.

If forces could be spared from elsewhere, the time could be less but which commander would consider himself to be so well supplied that he would give up units without a struggle? On the contrary, requests were still coming in for more. On 8th December the Government of India forwarded urgent requirements for four modern fighter squadrons, 154 heavy and 170 light anti-aircraft guns and four RDF (Radar) sets to help defend eastern

---

[26] TNA: WO 106/2558B.

India and five major ports excluding Karachi, citing the problems that might occur in munitions production if there were air raids. As an incentive to reply favourably to these requests, it is suggested that:

'the existing shortage ... may produce most serious effects both directly and indirectly to the assistance in the war effort and the extent to which the Government of India can make available assistance for other threatened parts of the fighting front.'[27]

A barely camouflaged piece of blackmail: Indian troops were vital both in North Africa and in Malaya where they would soon be taking terrible losses as they attempted to stem the Japanese tide.

Alternatively, units already on board convoys might be diverted, such as the 21st and 77th Regts. There were several disadvantages with this, the most obvious being: would the correct resources actually be at sea now? The RAF suffered severe difficulties in Malaya, Singapore and later Java because the men who were turning up there in their hundreds were not the men they currently needed. Some - clerks, drivers, cooks and similar trades - had been sent weeks before on the assumption that expansion was coming and they would be needed to provide services to the squadrons on the new aerodromes. Other ships had arrived with ground crew but no pilots or pilots with neither ground crew nor aircraft. In Malaya (as in Sumatra and Java later) squadrons were combined and cobbled together with whatever resources were at hand and efforts were made to remove unnecessary personnel from the area. What they really needed was many more aircraft – fighters, bombers, seaplanes, transport, photo reconnaissance – and very quickly at that. And that was just what could not be either spared or supplied to them in time. Bombers could be flown in, if they were available, but fighters, with their shorter range, had to be flown off a carrier – if there was one around with them – or shipped in crates for assembly on the spot – if they were already on a ship – and this would take time.

A problem that dogged all units was the way ships had been loaded back in Britain. It was one thing to order a troopship to a different destination but their equipment might be on a ship with stores for other units already in the theatre to which the diverted troops had originally been posted. Thus complicated transhipments or even complete unloading and reloading of vessels became necessary before they could proceed on their way. On 8th December, Air Marshal Sir Wilfred Freeman, Deputy Chief of the Air Staff, stated categorically in a COS committee meeting that 'there were no Hurricanes in the Far East and it was not proposed to maintain any there'.[28] Consequently a ship that contained 50 crated Hurricanes bound

---

[27] TNA: WO 106/2258B
[28] ibidem

for Iraq would have to spend five days in Durban while the necessary trans-shipment was made. A telegram from the War Office to Durban dated 17th December gives details of the work required to re-jig the cargoes on just two ships arriving there and now going to the Far East rather than the Middle East as originally intended. The 'Sussex' will need all its cargo pulled out of it, sorted and reloaded or left for future transport to India, an exercise taking an estimated seven days, while the 'Abbekerk' must unload 'Special cold climate Lubricating Oil', mail, locomotives and tenders, and the equipment of an engineering unit and of transportation units needed in the Persian Gulf – no time estimate for the work given. Unfortunately time was just what the British government, its armed forces and its unhappy General Officer Commanding Malaya, Lt-Gen A E Percival, who had taken up his post on 16th May 1941, did not have.

Whoever decided to send Percival to defend Singapore and Malaya from the Japanese either had a cruel sense of humour or felt that only an officer who had examined the situation at first hand and already condemned it as hopeless would have any chance of producing the miracle needed to save it. Percival had been GSO1 to Major-General Sir W G S Dobbie, GOC Malaya 1936-9, who had instructed him in November 1937 to draw up a plan of attack on Singapore from the Japanese point of view. Percival's investigations led him to conclude that firstly, if the British were involved in Europe, as seemed increasingly likely they would be, the Fleet could not reach Singapore within the seventy days previously estimated. Secondly, there were clear problems of defence on the ground: the possibility that the Japanese would attack through Thailand with Thai consent giving ground and air advantages; the weakness and lack of training of the local defence forces; the possibility of a Fifth Column of local agitators and dissidents helping the invaders; the current inadequacy of air and sea defence; and the development by the Japanese of:

'new Combined Operations equipment . . in particular, the special landing craft in large numbers, the landing craft "carriers," the sea tanks, etc.'

He added:

'The effect of this is that large numbers of men could be put into landing craft out of range of our fixed defences and thrown in a short space of time on to our beaches'[29]

noting that beaches on Singapore Island itself were now vulnerable.

The Japanese attack, which had seemed to come out of the blue on 8th December, continued with lightning speed. The Japanese could not afford

---

[29] 'Operations of Malaya Command from 8th December 1941 to 15th February 1942', Appendix A: Lieut.-General A. E. Percival, C.B., D.S.O, O.B E., M.C., formerly General Officer Commanding Malaya; The London Gazette, 26th February, 1948.

to delay and they swept the badly-prepared British, Empire and Dominion forces away in front of them. The speed at which they moved meant that plans were out of date before they could be properly finalised. On 14th December, Percival had sent a telegram to the War Office. Having started by noting:

'that my estimate of minimum essential Army Forces required for the defence of Malaya submitted in August has not been approved',

he requested reconsideration of this in the 'existing circumstances' and lists his 'most immediate needs'. And it is quite a list, covering units, weapons, ammunition, MT and supplies.[30] It runs to two full foolscap pages but he might as well have asked for the moon. His telegrams as preserved in this file become increasingly desperate as the days pass. It can have been no consolation that the problems and scenarios he had highlighted earlier had surfaced with a vengeance.

An undated 'Note on the P.M's Minute' from around 16th-17th December 1941 in the same file clearly demonstrates that the situation in Malaya was well understood in the War Office, even if Churchill did keep sounding off about 'Fortress Singapore', which was clearly raising hackles there:

'The P.M's minute speaks of Singapore Island and Fortress. I suggest that Singapore is not a fortress in any accepted sense. There are no prepared defences of any great strength on the land side. Singapore is only a fortress in the sense that it has a very strong coast defence armament with which to repel an attack by Naval forces. Should it be contemplated that such Field Forces as we have available would in the end have as their task the holding of Singapore Island and Fortress, I suggest that their resistance in this position is most likely to be of very short duration.'

It gives a no-holds-barred assessment of the situation, including:

'The battle to date has been characterised by very heavy Japanese pressure in enclosed country favourable to the side with the larger number of trained troops. The attack has been pressed home relentlessly, and there is little reason to suppose that this will not continue to be the case.

'Our troops are thin on the ground; losses have been incurred; pressure has been incessant; physical fatigue in the climate of Malaya must play a great part in the duration of our effective defence.'

'There is now <u>no</u> reserve. A reinforcement of one Division would represent an increase of 37% in the Field Force.'

And there is a clear and unequivocal conclusion to this assessment:

---

[30] TNA: WO 106/2558B

'I suggest that it is essential that reinforcements of well armed trained troops should be despatched to Malaya as early as possible. A reinforcement within a month will be worth twice the reinforcement within two months.'

Moreover, the War Office had another consideration in mind besides the fate of British forces already in theatre, as the end of the memo makes clear:

'It is, however, imperative that we should clear our thoughts that we can with equanimity accept the isolation of Singapore as a beleaguered fortress. Should this eventually occur the effect on Dominion opinion and Dominion war effort and its location are incalculable. Additionally it is essential that we should remember that Malaya is the only important source of two vital war commodities – rubber and tin.'

In other words, if we fail at Singapore, the Aussies and the Kiwis might want their boys back to defend their home territory and we could end up with no rubber or tin either! There was the Empire to consider. Empire troops from India, Australia and New Zealand were essential to the Mother Country in the struggle against the Axis powers in other theatres, not to mention the invaluable contributions from their air force personnel and their navies. To retain that support it was necessary for the British government to steer a tight and dangerous course through the demands of India, which wanted forces for defence directly on her eastern frontier, and Australia and New Zealand, who saw Malaya and Singapore as their protection to the north and expected them to be adequately defended, especially when they had committed so many of their forces to other theatres.

While the COS wrestled with their problems, the men of 49th Bty and the other units sailing into the blue in Convoy WS 14 were finally getting their sea legs. The weather was improving and on 17th December they went into khaki drill. Next day wearing topees when on deck was made compulsory and sleeping on deck was now permitted, which must have been a godsend to the ORs crammed down below. Flying fish were seen for the first time and on 21st December, the convoy steamed into Freetown, Sierra Leone.

None of the troops were allowed to disembark here. In spite of this, Jack described it as the smelliest place he could ever remember as the stench hit them like a wall as they sailed into port. Neither Macartney-Filgate nor Rev Godfrey mention the smell but both comment on the oppressive heat there and were fascinated by the native boats in the harbour attempting to sell fruit and other merchandise to the ships. Boddam-Whetham had a new problem: fresh water. He had received a telegram around 16th December telling him that there was a serious water shortage at Freetown and its production of fresh water could not meet the needs of a large convoy. Ships would have to 'distil to their maximum capacity'[31] to reduce their demands on local supplies to a minimum.

But his problems were nothing compared to those facing Percival and the fighting forces in Malaya and Singapore. The initial Japanese thrust had not faltered, neither had they paused to regroup. The unrelenting momentum pushed back his troops, and the RAF they supported, from position to position, from town to town. Before the war had been going a week, Kuatan and Sungei Patani, the two northernmost RAF airfields, had to be evacuated and HMS 'Prince of Wales' and HMS 'Repulse', the only capital ships in the Royal Navy out in the Far East, had been sunk. By 23rd December, when WS 14 had been in Freetown for two days and less than two weeks after hostilities had broken out, Kuala Lumpur airfield was only 'used as an advanced landing ground for occasional flight sweeps and reconnaissance sorties'. Most of the fighters, such as remained, (and servicing problems and attrition rates were bad), were now 'restricted to the defence of Singapore Island and the protection of convoys'.[32]

If the RAF and RAAF were having a bad go of it, Percival's ground forces were having a terrible time. Besides the inexorable forward push, the Japanese had made flanking movements along the coast, taking them in the sides and rear. Inexperience was a major problem. The Indian Army units suffered from inexperienced officers and NCOs as those with experience had been posted to new units under a rapid expansion plan. There were simply not enough trained men of the right calibre to take their places at a moment's notice, while the great majority of ORs were 'young and inexperienced'. Both the British and Australian infantry regiments in Malaya lacked 'leaders with a knowledge of modern warfare'[33] and no units had been trained in bush warfare before reaching Malaya. The artillery regiments which arrived in November and December 1941 were similarly inexperienced without training in bush warfare and an Indian reconnaissance unit:

'had only recently been mechanised and arrived without its armoured vehicles. It was so untrained that drivers had to be borrowed for some of the trucks which were issued to it.'[34]

Shades of the Royal Artillery's anti-aircraft units undergoing training in Britain at the time!

Percival and his officers had done their best both to train the men under

---

[31] TNA: ADM 237/1600
[32] TNA: AIR 20/5578: Appendix 'C', Group Captain H S Darley's report
[33] Percival, op. cit., para 52
[34] Percival, op. cit., para 48

their command and to produce some defences but time was not on their side. As he admitted in his despatch, when war broke out the troops in the north were less well trained than those in the south. 'Holding Northern Malaya', explained Brooke-Popham in his despatch:

'was not an end in itself; it was with reference to the Naval Base that Northern Malaya acquired its importance. This meant that Commanders in the North had to bear in mind the possibility of withdrawal in the face of superior forces, their action - at any rate until Johore was reached - being mainly a delaying one to gain time for the arrival of reinforcements from overseas.'[35]

However there is a very real danger in implementing even a well-planned withdrawal with half-trained troops, and reinforcements would not be forthcoming, not in the numbers and the timescale that Percival needed to avert disaster. As C-in-C Far East, Brooke-Popham attempted to reinforce Percival's demands on 16th December but he had already been told that he was being replaced at the end of December ('musical chairs' amongst higher ranking officers being fairly common in this campaign) and little came of it, except a telegram from C-in-C India next day with the offer:

'We could make one or possibly two infantry brigade groups available if your need is urgent but do not wish to despatch more troops unless reinforcements required to turn scale.'[36]

On 18th December a conference took place in Singapore between representatives of the Allied nations, though China was not represented as time had not allowed. It was strangely upbeat, considering the situation. While stating that 'the importance of Singapore to the war in the Far East, and to the world war, could not be exaggerated', it:

'considered that the situation, though serious, need not give rise to undue pessimism provided the necessary reinforcements were supplied in the available time, but time was the essential feature.'

And time was one of many things that was in very short supply for the Allies. The Japanese offensive had not slackened and they were already using the airfield at Sungei Patani against its original owners.

The conference made recommendations about the level of reinforcements needed but no response was received until after Christmas, by which time the Prime Minister of Australia, John Curtin, had taken a hand in proceedings. Not surprisingly, Curtin was extremely disturbed by the turn events were taking in Malaya. Around 23rd December he sent messages to Churchill and Roosevelt on:

---

[35] Brooke-Popham, op. cit., para 138
[36] TNA: WO 106/2558B

'the far-reaching effects that would arise from the loss of Singapore and the fact that the degree of resistance to Japan in Malaya will depend directly on the amount of assistance provided by the governments of the United Kingdom and the United States'.[37]

With Australia putting pressure on the British government, there are now definite signs of an attempt to get a more substantial level of reinforcements into Singapore by diverting units already on convoys for the Middle East and from the forces in or destined for India, even if there still seems to be little appreciation of the depth of the problems there or the urgency of the time scale. One priceless entry in a telegram of 24th December from the Embarkation Commandant Bombay to GOC Malaya covering supplies being sent from India notes the despatch of 'Remington typewriter No. J273561' on the 'Medusa' with the instruction 'use and return this instantly earliest opportunity.' Missives like these must have been a sore trial for Percival, an already sorely-tried commander. On Christmas Day, Hong Kong surrendered to the Japanese and by now around half of Malaya was in enemy hands.

Meanwhile, 49th Bty and all those on Convoy WS 14 were celebrating Christmas in Freetown harbour, leaving around noon fortified by a traditional Christmas dinner of roast turkey and plum pudding. There was manic zigzagging once out of port to distract the enemy submarines believed to be lurking nearby but nothing notable seems to have occurred on the trip south down the coast of Africa, except for 'days of blazing sun and fresh cool breeze'. Pearson had been invited to dinner Christmas night by 242nd Bty which had found a bottle of dry champagne from somewhere to share with their commanding officer. As a result he was a bit the worse for wear the next day![38] The good feeling that was generally apparent in this battery led him to compare it with the other two under his command. The 95th seemed rather the opposite to him – he described their CO, Graham, as 'like a little pea in a drum on this ship', having a finger in every pie and seeming to be into everything. He would later get a 'rocket' from Pearson for handing 'his orders to a Brigadier for approval before he showed me'. In his CO's opinion he would probably benefit from going ashore and having something to do. The 49th he was not happy about:

'I feel that 49 is just a little divided in itself. I sometimes have doubts in my mind of Robert's ability to carry it off. We'll see better when we get all our equipment + guns + can really get busy.'

It seems that Major Earle may not have had an easy time with his battery when he first took over. In a letter dated 7th December 1941, just before the convoy left the Clyde, Pearson wrote to his wife:

---

[37] TNA: WO 106/2558B
[38] Pearson, as before, letter 7/1/42

'I think Robert's chaps have pretty well settled down now. Perry always smiles very sweetly. I wouldn't wonder if he felt a little bit of a B.F. now.'

What 2nd Lt J S Perry might have done or said which he might now regret is unfortunately not recorded.

From what I have been able to glean about some of them, Earle had junior officers from a variety of backgrounds. Perry had been brought up in South Africa. Pearson notes that he:

'gave us a short talk about going ashore which was quite helpful even though he hadn't been home for 8 yrs',

giving the impression of a confident young man who may have been a bit of a 'line-shooter'. 2nd Lt S E Bagnall had worked in London for the American advertising agency J Walter Thompson before he joined the Royal Artillery as a gunner early in the war. He was obviously a very competent draughtsman as his papers in the Imperial War Museum, London,[39] include some fascinating sketches. He also had what it took to be an officer as he was commissioned in February 1941. 2nd Lt R K Mounsdon had attended Wye Agricultural College and been a member of the Territorial Army before he joined 49th Bty, newly commissioned, on 8th August 1941.

The one to attract most of Pearson's attention was Lt M S Banner, a Canadian who had previously lived in Hong Kong and who had been given a commission in the British Army in February 1940. Banner, it seems, had been the boyfriend of Pearson's daughter Mary and his letters are peppered with references to the young man's promises to write to her: "I really will". Pearson wavers between hope and despair where his daughter's dilatory suitor is concerned:

'He's a wild lad. He is very fed up he is not in Hong Kong now that the trouble is on. It suddenly struck him today that he may not get any more pay from the Bank there as it must be cut off.'

'Banners has been getting himself into trouble with the ships Adjt. He had a days leave stopped at the next port. He is really rather stupid + naughty. He cannot keep his mouth shut + he gets so annoyed about things. Still he is quite a good lad.'

Pearson played golf with him in Durban, a good way to get to know the young man informally and quite an honour for Banner as the other outings he mentions are with Major Russell – again golf – and with Major Graham to the races, but still has his doubts. Nearer their journey's end he tells his wife that he had to give Banner a rocket. He:

---

[39] Private papers of S E Bagnall, IWM Documents 398

'has appeared to me rather slack + disappointing. So I hope all is now well. I hope I haven't been wrong about Banner. His knowledge is very scanty + and he has taken very little action to remedy it. He does waffle so, too. Still, I think he'll be allright in a tight corner.'[40]

But what were he and the others like for their young battery commander?

The convoy split as they rounded the Cape of Good Hope, part going into Cape Town while the major part, including the 'Duchess of Atholl' continued on to Durban, which was reached on 8th January 1942. By all accounts, whether the ships docked at Cape Town or Durban, the troops on board were given a rapturous reception by the local people. Cars were provided to take all ranks on tours of the local sights and no one could seem to do enough to make them welcome. Jack and some of his friends managed to get themselves in trouble however. Somewhat the worse for drink, they had a rickshaw ride and then in a fit of high spirits threw the rickshaw boy into the back of his own cart and took him for a spin. Apartheid was an unknown concept to them and they did not understand that it was a terrible crime for a white man to play the servant to a black man in South Africa, even if it was a drunken prank. They were arrested by the local police. But he did have better experiences. Being a keen gardener all his life, he naturally gravitated to the Botanical Gardens and described the experience briefly to his in-laws in an undated letter soon after. As they finally sailed from Durban harbour, they could see a Nazi flag flying. Many Boers had sympathy with the enemy.

When he and 49th Bty sailed on the afternoon of 13th January 1942, it was not on the 'Duchess of Atholl'. They had swapped their unloved ship on 9th January for HMT 'Dunera', a purpose-built 'British India' troopship, but all the transhipping of men and equipment between the various ships, necessary to send extra reinforcements to India and Singapore, kept the convoy in port a little longer than it would otherwise have been there. The change of ship was greatly welcomed by officers and men alike. 'Dunera' had been built with the Tropics in mind, was not overcrowded like the 'Duchess' and did not have her sickening motion. That unhappy ship was forced to turn back soon after leaving Durban to have her engines properly fixed and sailed back round the Cape on 20th January to the United States to carry American troops across the Atlantic.

Lt-Col Saunders of 21st Regt was still in the dark about exactly where he and his men were headed, though he had found out after they had docked in Cape Town that it was somewhere in the Far East. The War Office had made up its mind; they were on their way towards Singapore with 48th Regt but he still had no new orders. Unfortunately, his regiment and 77th Regt

---

[40] All quotes from Lt Col Pearson's letters as before.

had both been split in two when loading took place on the Clyde so half were embarked on the 'Empress of Australia' and half on the 'Warwick Castle'. However, he did his best to mitigate the problems of taking inexperienced officers and men into what promised to be a very active war zone with what exercises were possible and used his post-war report to make his superiors very well aware that it was 'difficult to sustain morale and interest' among your men when you are:

'embarked on a voyage of unknown length and duration with not a single clue as to the ultimate destination and employment'.

Pearson, commanding 48th Regt, had the good fortune to have all his men on one ship, the 'Dunera', and made the most of it, with lectures held for officers and intensive gun drills for 'all detachments'. At Durban, a formidable number of guns had been mounted on the ship for AA defence:

'Twelve Bofors, eight Bren guns and six Lewis were mounted in all, and these were kept manned throughout the hours of daylight. ... gun detail and mechanism instruction were carried out almost continuously'.

A canvas artillery map was rigged up for the officers to practice on:

'I think the chaps have enjoyed our battles on it. Robert rigged it up like Singapore Island as he had a map of the place.'[41]

But it was not work all the while. Jack found time to write home to his in-laws:

'As I . . . glance over the side I can see scores of flying fish they fly away from the ship as much as a hundred yards. I have also seen a school of porpoises leaping ahead of the boat.'[42]

It was an almost indescribable experience for a young man of his background at that time. For him and his fellow soldiers almost everything they experienced after sailing from Britain was totally new and unexpected: the weather, the countries, the food, the languages, the people. Little wonder that he told his in-laws that when he got back, his stories would better those told by 'Uncle Arthur'. He added:

'Tell Dad to get some pickled onions ready and also a bottle of beer, ready for when I get back.'

But that would not be for four more years and by that time 'Dad', his father-in-law, would be dead, having lost heart at the Luftwaffe's bombing of Cambridge and the disappearance of his much-loved son-in-law in the Far East.

---

[41] Pearson, letter 2/2/42
[42] Undated unpublished letter from Jack Gunn to Mr and Mrs A Hale

Pearson decided to take advantage of the voyage to learn something about the men of his new regiment, interviewing them all individually to find out something about them and their lives before they joined up. He sent a resume of the statistics he gathered from this back to his wife. The average age was 28.4 years and 60% of them were married, with an average of 1.21 children. Over three-quarters claimed allegiance to the Church of England and over a third of them hailed from London or Essex though 'almost every English county is represented', not to mention Scotland, Wales and Ireland. Their occupations were very diverse:

'labourers, miners, wood machinists, decorators, clerks, gardeners, shop assts, not to forget a couple of steeplejacks.'

He does not mention an Oil and Hardware Merchant however!

The officers meanwhile found the 'Dunera' much more comfortable than the 'Duchess of Atholl'. At least there was deck space on this ship and the lounge had not been taken over for the sergeants! Rev Godfrey described the trip as 'pleasant and uneventful'. In the new ship, where conditions were less crowded and the food much better, he had a cabin to himself. He was interested in the new passengers who had joined them, amongst them 'an entire Brigade staff complete with Brigadier, Brigade Major and two Staff Captains.' This was for 16th AA Brigade and he heard that the Brigadier, H D W Sitwell, was going to Singapore in an advisory capacity on AA measures. He describes Sitwell, who was destined to play a major part in the defence of Java, thus:

'A fat purple faced, pleasant looking individual, somewhat porcine in expression as one expects Brigadiers to be. ... though he never talked much he always used to play bridge at night with our officers.'

The Padre's memoirs are always particularly enlightening as he was not an 'Army man'. While he was an officer in 48th Regt as its chaplain, his knowledge, interests and observations are those of an intelligent bystander rather than those of a soldier. Therefore while his comments are sometimes a little wide of the mark in military terms, they present the situation as it appeared to him at the time. At this point of his story, he, like the other officers on board the 'Dunera', was very well aware of how badly things were going in the Far East. Hong Kong had fallen on Christmas Day and the 'Prince of Wales' and 'Repulse' had been sunk. The Japanese were advancing in Malaya and the Philippines. They were still heading east and the situation out that way did not look good. Pearson was concerned for friends in both Malaya and Hong Kong and was frustrated that they got 'only the sketchiest of news being on board ship' but this perception probably arose because he knew the area well.

Any misgivings they had were not helped by what the padre describes as 'a peculiar address' given by Sitwell to all the officers on the 'Dunera'. It began:

'"Since the Govt has seen fit to spend more money on my military education than on yours ....." and went on to tell us that come wind, come weather, we were going to Singapore even if we had "to get out and walk", and he urged that whatever happened, there should be no panic. He kept on saying "So you see everything's quite all right really" only somehow he failed to convince.'[43]

Boddam-Whetham, who was now flying his flag in 'Dunera', was taking no chances as the reports from Malaya worsened. The original convoy had split off Mombasa on the morning of 19th January 1942 when the seven ships[44] including 'Dunera' that were to form Convoy DM 2 turned to the east, escorted by HMS 'Royal Sovereign' as far as Addu Atoll, whilst the others continued northwards towards either Aden or Bombay. On 26th January he took the highly unusual and potentially very dangerous step of stopping the convoy at sea for sixty-seven minutes near 'Addu Attol' [sic] to transfer Bofors guns and crews from 48th Regt to other ships in the convoy for added AA protection. 2nd Lieutenants Stubbs, Wyatt and Mounsdon with 64 ORs from 49th Bty were conveyed to 'Troilus' in 'Dunera's boats while officers and other ranks from 242nd Bty and 95th Bty travelled the same way to 'City of Pretoria' and 'City of Canterbury' respectively. Stubbs and Wyatt were two of the most experienced junior officers of 49th Bty, which would explain the choice of them for deployment away from its main body. Mounsdon, who was relatively inexperienced, would have seasoned fellow officers to advise him if advice was needed. There is a pen and watercolour sketch of the Gunnery Officers' cabin, SS 'Troilus', Jan 42, amongst Lt Bagnall's papers with the note that Mounsdon shared the duties on that ship with him, and a note in one of the pamphlets he picked up at this period describes him as 'gunnery officer i/c on board "S S Troilus"', so it is possible that up to four of 49th's officers travelled on the ship.

Because the risks involved in stopping the convoy were potentially very great, Boddam-Whetham thought it necessary to justify his action in his report, complementing:

'the Masters of all ships and Lieut. Col. Pearson, Commanding the 48th Light A/A Regiment in carrying out this operation.'[45]

He was able to remark with some satisfaction that:

---

43 Rev Godfrey, op. cit., p7
44 TNA: ADM 199/1138. 'Dunera', 'Warwick Castle', 'Empress of Australia', 'City of Pretoria', City of Canterbury', 'Troilus' and 'Malancha'.
45 TNA: ADM 237/1600

'In the 7 ships of D.M.2. I eventually had mounted and manned 46 Bofors, 85 Bren and some 78 Machine Guns, not counting the ordinary ships armament.'

Just how useful the other armament the ships carried would have been if the convoy had run into trouble is luckily something that was never tested. In Jack's opinion, had 'Troilus' opened up with her 4.7" and 12-pounder she would have split herself in half!

The next day, one of the Bofors mounted on 'Dunera' was dismantled from amidships where its field of fire was restricted and reassembled on the bows. When the convoy joined up the day after that with Singapore-bound Convoy BM 12, carrying part of the British 18th Infantry Division and 3,800 men to make good the losses in the 9th and 11th Indian Divisions, it was even better protected should an air attack be launched on it. This was the second half of 18th Division; the first part had already been sent. For faced with the increasingly desperate state of the forces in Malaya, and pressure from the Australian government, the COS had been forced to divert the Division from India in an attempt to hold the Japanese. So bad was the situation on the ground that as they arrived, troops were thrown wholesale into action at the earliest possible opportunity with no chance to acclimatise to local conditions or even sort themselves out or recover properly from a long sea voyage. They sustained terrible casualties.

From Christmas onwards, whatever could be spared for Percival was sent however it could be and whatever could be promised was. He received tantalising telegrams spelling out the forces that would soon be at his disposal if only he could hold out that long. Slated for arrival on 6th February 1942 were 48th LAA Regt, 21st LAA Regt and 77th HAA Regt, plus Wing HQ and ground staff for three squadrons, with the promise of 48 Hurricanes to be flown in off HMS 'Indomitable'. What he really needed was the squadron of light tanks of the 3rd Hussars marked down for arrival some time in February – and many more to back them up. And more infantry divisions. And aircraft of all types. But this was not to be and in fact nothing destined for Singapore after 2nd February actually made it in. By the end of January British forces had been forced to retreat to Singapore Island and any reinforcements arriving after then only added to the 'Gift to Nippon', as Far East Prisoners of War sarcastically called themselves.

On 28th January DM 2, augmented by her new companions, was steaming in a south-easterly direction towards the southern end of the island of Sumatra as approaching Singapore by the usual northern route via the Straits of Malacca was now impossible because the Japanese had air supremacy in that area. The convoy was forced to go via the southern route through the Sunda Strait between Sumatra and Java. Even this had its dangers and the escort for the convoy was reinforced by a succession of Royal Navy, Royal Australian Navy and Royal Indian Navy ships. The Dutch also provided a cruiser, the 'Java', and Catalina flying boats to escort the convoy. Fortunately for Boddam-Whetham, he now had something pleasant to report back to the Admiralty, namely that Captain Caffyn, Master of HMT 'Dunera' in which he was sailing:

'had a more intimate knowledge of convoy work and books such as Mersigs, Consigs etc than any Master I have yet come across. ... He also sees to it that his Officers maintain the same standard as himself and all arrangements for Action Stations, Lookouts, Zigzags etc are entirely efficient.'[46]

Nevertheless, the news reaching the ships was far from encouraging and Rev Godfrey comments on the sense of being:

'a doomed convoy. Ships sailing into destruction. The very air was pregnant with a sense of foreboding disaster.'

The news bulletins brought them information on Japanese progress and this was marked up in red on a large map hung by the stairs in the ship. 'It made the entrance into Singapore look very tricky.' Pearson confessed to his wife in his letter of 2nd February 1942:

'I have been completely nonplussed by the course of events in Malaya', adding, 'I can see no reason why Singapore itself should not hold out indefinitely.'

Although he had served in the region, he was not aware of the true situation there.

Around 31st January, the 48th found that their destination had been changed from Singapore to Batavia (now Djakarta) on the island of Java in the Netherlands (or Dutch) East Indies (NEI). This change was caused by the difficulties of getting ships, especially large ones and large numbers of them, into Singapore. Batavia, or rather its harbour Tandjong Priok, had a good deep-water port which could take the main body of the convoy. Five ships went on to Singapore, splitting from DM 2 on the morning of 3rd February after clearing the Sunda Strait. One, 'City of Canterbury', still carried gun crews from 95th Bty, 48th Regt. Macartney-Filgate commented on passing the volcano Krakatoa and noted that the coasts of both Sumatra and Java, and their different landscapes, could be clearly seen from the ships. In the afternoon, the reduced convoy made its way into Tandjong Priok harbour.

Jack Gunn and 48th LAA Regt, RA, had reached Java – though his Army records declare he went to Malaya!

---

[46] TNA: ADM 199/1138

Four: Landfall Java

The port of Tandjong Priok was the Allied effort in the Far East in microcosm: it was in chaos. It was undoubtedly a suitable port for Convoy DM 2: just to the north of Batavia, the capital of the NEI, and close enough to Singapore to make a good staging post. Deep enough to take vessels of up to 30-foot draught alongside the quays without having to wait for a favourable tide, it had 27 feet in fairway at the lowest low water, which would give easy access at all points of the tide. There were 5- and 10-ton cranes on the quayside with a floating crane of up to 80-tons – the former two essential for offloading guns and trucks but the latter far beyond what this convoy would require.[47]

When DM 2 arrived on the afternoon of 3rd February 1942, the port was packed with vessels of all sizes, all crammed with refugees or reinforcements. By mid-February, the number there, of all types, would hit 146 but there was already a steady stream of boats and ships arriving from Singapore and Malaya carrying evacuees and excess service personnel being sent out of theatre if at all possible. Strange as it may seem to some, while Percival was so short of men to put in the line, there was no shortage of, for example, surplus RAF tradesmen or aircrew with no aircraft to fly.

At several stages in this campaign, both before this and in the days to come, people would ask (including Churchill, who should have known better) why these men could not just act as infantry. Small numbers of men who were not regular infantry did fight alongside them - as the cooks and clerks of 2nd Battalion, Cambridgeshire Regiment, did beside their mates in Malaya - but expecting, say, the survivors of the crew of a Royal Navy ship or an RAF squadron's ground crew to switch to infantry duties at the drop of a hat is impractical to say the least. The hard fact is you cannot just give a man a rifle and tell him he is now an infantryman. He has to be trained to use one and to fight as infantry and he needs officers and NCOs who know what they are doing. Training takes time, a trainer and weapons, none of which were in supply in sufficient quantities in the Far East in early 1942 - though this would not stop commanding officers attempting to do just this later on. While 'bouches inutiles' were deliberately despatched from the war zone in whatever transport was available, there was also a stream of deserters who had had enough of the conflict and decided to make an early 'home run' for friendly territory before the gates slammed shut on them.

As 'Dunera' sailed into this mêlée, the troops lining her decks could see the SS 'Duchess of Bedford' packed with women and children evacuees from Singapore, who raised a cheer for them. The 'Duchess' stayed in port for a

---

[47]TNA: WO 106/2558B: Telegram from C. in C. Eastern Fleet to C. in C. Middle East, C. in C. India, the War Office and C. in C. Far East, 10.01.42

few more days having repairs done to the damage sustained in Japanese air attacks during her trip so far before departing for Liverpool via Colombo, Durban and Cape Town. It is good to know she got back safely to the UK on 5th April 1942 – many other vessels fleeing the war zone were less fortunate. Another departure for Colombo was Boddam-Whetham who sailed on the 'Empress of Australia' on 5th February as the convoy entrusted to his care was not proceeding to Singapore, leaving his erstwhile charges to experience the fortunes of war.

48th LAA Regt had now reached port in Java in the Netherlands East Indies, where the administrative capital for this part of the Dutch overseas empire was situated. So where was the NEI, what was the NEI and did its government mind them being there? The Dutch had been building an empire overseas to sustain their trade since the seventeenth century. Always a trading nation, on winning their independence from Spain in the late sixteenth century they had turned to the sea, and the riches of the world that travelled in their ships made the Dutch Republic both prosperous and disliked in the next century. It also naturally brought them into conflict with the British, the other major maritime trading nation, and a number of trade wars followed until the two countries were temporarily united between 1688 and 1701 when they were both ruled by the Stadtholder of the Netherlands, Prince William of Orange, and his English wife, Mary, elder daughter of James II. William himself was half-English through his mother, a daughter of Charles I, a match which clearly demonstrates the importance that was attached in Britain to an alliance with the Netherlands. Mary died in 1694 and the couple were childless so the Dutch connection ceased after William's death but the two countries now kept their trade rivalry on a more civilised basis.

Nevertheless, the Far East and Australasia was where the two nations continued to come up against each other most often. Tasmania, named after Abel Tasman, the seventeenth-century Dutch explorer, bears witness to the Dutch influence in the area. If Singapore Island was British, many of the hundreds of tiny islands just off-shore were Dutch. The island of Sumatra, 1,100 miles long and 270 miles wide, laying to the south-west across the Straits of Malacca from Singapore and Malaya, was also Dutch as was the larger part of Borneo, which they shared with the British Empire. The chain of islands that runs from the southern tip of Sumatra to the west of New Guinea, the largest of which is Java, was almost entirely Dutch.

While we are looking at empires in the area, it is worth noting that two other imperial powers also had colonies in the south-west Pacific. Portugal, a neutral in World War II, held East Timor while the western part was part of the NEI. Luis de Camões, the Portuguese national poet, claimed that God had given the Portuguese a narrow strip of land as a cradle but all the world as a grave, a comment that clearly reflected the many territories world-wide both large and small that their seafaring merchant adventurers had brought under their control since the early fifteenth century. The same claim could have truly been made for the Dutch.

The other great imperial power was the United States of America. The USA had taken advantage of the weakness of the once-great Spanish Empire to take over some of its possessions at the end of the nineteenth century. The Philippines, to the east of Malaya and north of the NEI, was one of these. It was part of its great surge of interest in the eastern coast of Asia following its successful attempt to force the Japanese to open their ports to other nations back in 1853, when Admiral Perry sailed his fleet of US warships into Tokyo Bay with all guns blazing. Japan could provide useful coaling stations for American ships wishing to take a slice of the China trade that was proving so valuable to other Western nations but there was another agenda. Perry was just one of many educated Americans in the nineteenth century and into the twentieth who believed deeply in the idea of the rightful supremacy of the white race and regarded all other races as barbarians and thus without rights. In one speech Perry proclaimed:

'The people of America will, in some form or other, extend their dominion and their power, until they shall have brought within their mighty embrace the islands of the great Pacific, and placed the Saxon race upon the eastern shores of Asia.'[48]

Thus the situation in the south-west Pacific was complex and this complexity was increased by the fact that by 1942 both France, which had colonies in the area then known as 'Indo-China' on the Asian mainland, and the Netherlands had fallen to Nazi Germany. The French colonies had already been taken over by Japan to all intents and purposes. There was a Dutch government in exile in London that ran the NEI through a Governor-General based on the main island of Java and the remains of a colonial service. There were anomalies in this arrangement, for instance the Royal Dutch Navy in the NEI reported directly to the Dutch naval department in London while the army and army air force in the NEI reported to the Governor-General in Java.

Now it can clearly be seen that the western nations and the Dominions of Australia and New Zealand had good reason to make common cause against the advancing Japanese but the situation had not always been that straightforward. As we have seen, one of the two main prongs of the British

---

[48] James Bradley, op. cit., p171

strategy for the defence of Singapore was 'don't antagonise the Japanese'. Thus when the Dutch through their government in exile in London or their Governor-General in the NEI attempted to interest HM Government in an alliance against the potential aggressor in 1940-41, they were fobbed off with vague assurances of a mutual interest in the area but no clear-cut promise of help if the worst came to the worst.

The situation was complicated. Quite apart from upsetting the Japanese, who might see some sort of alliance as an aggressive step rather than a purely defensive measure intended to send out a warning, British politicians, particularly the Prime Minister, Winston Churchill, did not want to do anything in this part of the world without some sort of backing from the Americans. The pros and cons are set out clearly in documents surviving among the Prime Minister's records in the National Archives and the arguments run something like this. If we don't make formal arrangements for mutual defence with the NEI and we were attacked in the Far East, we would lose any advantage that could be gained 'from frank previous collaboration'. The Queen, government and armed forces in exile of the Netherlands were already helping in the war effort in Europe and it would be politically embarrassing if we failed to help them in the NEI. We have already been 'moving progressively towards closer co-operation' with the authorities in the NEI and it would be difficult to halt this process. On the other hand, British naval strength was insufficient to deal with the Japanese fleet and:

'our trade east of the Cape of Good Hope and our reinforcements to the Middle East from Australia would be jeopardised if we had to go to war with Japan'.

However, if the Japanese attacked in the Far East the only hope the NEI had was that we would support them. so we did not have to give any promises now. If the NEI alone were attacked:

'our very weak forces in Malaya would be dissipated in trying to defend them; and consequently we might not later be able to defend Singapore'

and the Dutch must realise that the longer we can stay at peace with Japan, the better chance we have of winning the war and thus safeguarding the long-term future of the NEI.[49]

Not stated here but certainly implied is the 'elephant in the room' when it came to the Dutch fears about the Far East. They were haunted by the terror that US policy in this area was to strip European empires of their colonies and take them over themselves, either directly or through a puppet

---

[49] TNA: PREM 3/326: Netherlands East Indies. Quotations from minutes of a meeting between the Foreign Secretary and his advisors and the Chiefs of Staff on 7th February 1941. The same arguments appear in other documents of other dates in this file.

government of some description, such as that which existed in the Philippines. This was a not-unfounded fear to which the Dutch would subsequently return in their discussions with the British but it was an issue that the British did not wish to face. The British war effort to date relied very heavily on US support and parts of the British Empire were already being let out on a 'Lease-Lend' basis to the USA to finance the war effort. There could be no question of an open-ended guarantee of Dutch colonial possessions against the policies of the USA when Britain depended almost entirely on the latter country for its survival. The fate of the British, Dutch and French empires was a matter for consideration only after the homelands themselves had been secured.

And the other problem was that without an alliance with the Americans, the British could not hope for success in any struggle in the Far East, so it was not only the Japanese that the British government did not want to upset. However, both Australia and New Zealand wanted some sort of assurances given to the Dutch, which the British government continued to refuse to do. The Australian government saw the threat to their safety from a Japanese military presence in the area as one they were not inclined to tolerate and did not see the lack of immediate US support as a problem. By July 1941 they were keen to deploy troops in Ambon and Timor in the NEI before any hostilities had a chance to break out but were told by the Dominions Office in London that although the idea made good military sense, it might well antagonise the Japanese and should not be done.[50]

There was a hope in British circles that the Japanese, should they attack, would only attack the Dutch and leave the British Empire alone. Therefore it was also important not to be bound into any agreement that set the definition of what an act of war by the Japanese might be too precisely, just in case it was possible not to be drawn into the conflict, at least not at first. Time was always of the essence although it was also appreciated that the occupation of the NEI by the Japanese would seriously damage British interests in the area. Luckily in the event, the military commanders in the Far East had been making plans together and when war broke out the Dutch in the NEI pitched in to help with commendable generosity, given the treatment they had so far received from the Allies.

In spite of the fact that the USA had not honoured contracts for new aircraft to update their obsolete war planes (with British agreement it must be said, as both major powers thought the aircraft concerned could be better used elsewhere in the world) the NEI sent both bomber and fighter units to Malaya. They also agreed to the RAF surveying their airfields with a view to using some of them for staging for flying in reinforcements or if

---

[50] TNA: CAB 121/697: Situation in the Netherlands East Indies Vol.I, Oct 1940 - Oct 1945

forced to retreat from Malaya. They had, of course, to use their own forces to resist Japanese attacks on their own territory but they did have transport and reconnaissance aircraft which proved invaluable to the British forces in the area from time to time as the RAF was chronically short of transport aircraft in this theatre. And they also provided liaison officers for the British. The unpublished typescript memoirs of one of these, Captain R A Baron Mackay, survives at the Imperial War Museum London.[51]

On 15th January 1942, ABDACOM came into being, the practical embodiment of the Western Allies in the Far East. ABDACOM was actually a telegraphic address for the headquarters but was used as shorthand for the South West Pacific Command set up by the Allied governments of Australia, Britain, the Netherlands and the United States to co-ordinate and fight the battle for this area. It covered a vast area: from Burma (Myanmar) in the north to the tip of Australia's Northern Territory in the south and from the Andaman and Nicobar Islands in the west to the Philippines in the east. In theory it would allow the area to be organised as a whole by the Allies, making the best use of whatever military resources each had locally, but by the time it became operational they were already losing the fight in Malaya, the Philippines and the outlying islands of the NEI as well as on the great island of Borneo near the centre. The British and Dutch had both been afraid of being picked off one by one by the Japanese but sadly the enemy forces in the area were quite capable of dealing with all the Allies simultaneously.

Nevertheless, it was under the ABDACOM accord that 48th LAA and the other British AA regiments arrived in Java where ABDACOM had its headquarters. Oddly enough its Supreme Commander was General Sir A P Wavell, C-in-C India until 30th December 1941. By one of those rare quirks of poetic justice which seldom strikes as swiftly as it should, he was shortly to find out the horrible truth about defending the Far East at first hand – to my mind a fairish retribution for his telegram of 17th December 1941 offering troops to Percival. What goes around comes around. Wavell was to spend the next few weeks desperately requesting reinforcements, spares and ammunition and having the frustration of seeing almost nothing arrive.

This was in the future. For now perhaps the major Allied powers felt that the Dutch in the NEI must be grateful that anything was being done to assist them but a very interesting report in the Foreign Office files[52] shows a different situation, with good cause I believe. In January 1942, just as ABDACOM was getting into gear, the Dutch government in exile in London

---

[51] IWM Documents 8148
[52] TNA: FO 371/31812. File is catalogued as 'Japanese air raids on Netherlands East Indies, 1942'

sent out a new Lieutenant Governor General to the NEI. Dr H J van Mook travelled out to take up his appointment via Washington DC, hoping by stopping off there to speak to major American politicians, including the President, and to put the Dutch point of view on the conflict in the south west Pacific to them. To his fury he was ignored, fobbed off or patronised by his hosts but he did get to talk to an official of the British Foreign Office, John de La Vallette, on 26th January. I am not sure whether La Vallette had dual Dutch nationality or was just a fluent Dutch speaker but the conversation was in that language which allowed van Mook to express himself very clearly, as is apparent in this report written less than a week later on 1st February.

Van Mook was well aware by now that he was not going to get a serious hearing in Washington and that this meeting would probably be his only opportunity to get a lot of things he felt needed saying off his chest. It must have been a great plus that he could do this to La Vallette in his native tongue. His comments on the choice of Wavell are very pertinent:

'With the choice of the Supreme Allied Commander, he said no one found fault. "Since we could not have a German General who really knows the job of modern warfare, we have probably got the best man available anywhere among the Allies" was his jocular observation. "And", he added, "since we all expected the British to do a good deal of fighting in the East, the choice of a British General seemed quite reasonable. I trust you will do such fighting as to support that ground for the choice."'

This last comment was particularly barbed given the situation in Malaya at the time. He also felt that the British and Americans had no confidence in the Dutch and that this was not a good attitude between allies, noting that the Americans underestimated the Japanese and had ignored Dutch warnings about a substantial Japanese naval force in the Caroline Islands four days before the attacks on Pearl Harbor and the Philippines. He had been amazed to find during his stay in Washington was that there was a:

'lack of collaboration between departments, deliberate lack of collaboration between fighting services inter se and between them and the State Department. Coupled with this was a "fantastic unpreparedness" for a state of war and a distrust of anyone who could teach them something.'

He believed the American army and navy forces in both Honolulu and the Philippines had displayed great incompetence and still underrated their enemy.

The British also came in for considerable criticism – and it is hard to disagree with his observations. Firstly:

'it was an unfortunate fact that Britain had an almost unbroken record of military defeats. Everyone accepted the fact that the British fighting man fought heroically, but wars were not won by heroics, but by victories. Accepting Dunkirk as a colossal feat, and the Battle of Britain as a positive victory of the first importance, what had there been since then to give the public confidence in British strategic capability?'

What indeed? It was also 'very disturbing' that Churchill had made statements promoting the war in Europe as the most important conflict and Hitler as 'the biggest of our enemies'. This gave the impression that 'the Far East was a "secondary" battle area' in which the locals were 'to fend for themselves and hope for the best.' Pretty perceptive stuff, you must agree.

All this he contrasts with Australia and her dealings with the NEI, which he characterises as 'cordial and efficient'. The 'excellent understanding' between the two countries was demonstrated to him by the great efforts they made to allow him to meet 'all the authorities, civil, army, air and naval, who he wanted to see, including the Governor General', all ready "to talk turkey" in strong contrast to the Americans. Are we beginning to see a situation among the Allies where the Dutch and Australians as the locals are on one side and distrusting the British and Americans as the more 'superior' and less focused allies on the other? That may be too strong a way of putting it, for the Australians also had leanings towards the Americans and away from the British Empire in van Mook's opinion - and there is evidence in the files to suggest that this was true, certainly at the highest levels of government. You can see their point: if the British Empire could not defend Australia, perhaps the United States of America could. Especially a United States which, in van Mook's opinion, could be out to do a spot of empire building in the area.

La Valette's report is crucial here because it shows that, even before Convoy DM 2 arrived in Tandjong Priok, some elements of the Dutch authorities in the NEI lacked confidence in their major allies - confidence in their willingness to help, in their ability to help and in their motives for helping. The Australians they trusted; they had been there giving help and talking frankly while the others were procrastinating. The NEI had resisted pressure from the Japanese to provide them with essential raw materials even though they had no backup from either London or Washington, they had provided aircraft vital to Britain after the outbreak of war in the Far East without hesitation, they had willingly allowed the RAF to make surveys of their airfields and were turning them over to them. Would the British stand firm when the time of testing came for the NEI?

At 1200 GMT on 15th January 1942, the Headquarters of South-West Pacific Command (ABDACOM) were set up at the Hotel des Indes, in the capital, Batavia, moving on 18th to the Grand Hotel, Lembang, some ten miles north of Bandoeng in central Java (around 110 miles from the capital) where the NEI military forces had their headquarters. There is a very impressive chart at Appendix B of Wavell's report on its operations (published July 1942) showing the Staff Organization at Headquarters, with a footnote that many of the appointments shown were not filled by the date of dispersal. For ABDACOM lasted a mere forty days and by the time 48th LAA Regt reached port in Java it was already half way through its brief life. The Allies needed time in this campaign - and time was something the Japanese never gave them.

The idea of a combined Allied command was good and would work well for D-Day two years later, but at the time ABDACOM was set up the British were well on their way to defeat in Malaya and Singapore and were also fighting in North Africa, while the Americans had their hands full fighting the Japanese in the Philippines. Consequently neither could devote the necessary forces or attention to the new organisation to get it properly off the ground in the short time available, as their priorities in the region lay elsewhere. The Americans especially were concentrating on the area around and nearest to their western Pacific possessions. Nevertheless, as far as the British were concerned, Far East Command, the overall umbrella command for Royal Navy, RAF and Army forces in the region, ceased at the same time ABDACOM was activated although where 'local' matters were concerned Percival was still GOC Malaya and Air Vice Marshal C W H Pulford (who had arrived on 26th April 1941) still AOC Far East Command RAF, based in Singapore. This incidentally led to some confusion of orders for RAF units in the area which also received direct and different orders from ABDACOM on occasions. There might be a mixture of nationalities appointed to the prominent roles in the new combined force but there was neither time for it to shake down and start to work nor men and materiel to work with. The Japanese had been too quick. From the very start, whatever the original intention might have been, it was a damage limitation exercise at best; a holding operation to allow the Allies a breathing space and a chance to consolidate a perimeter if this was possible. They could ill-afford the resources to do more.

What could the different Allies throw into the common pot in mid-January? The Americans were almost wholly absorbed by the Philippines, where the Japanese were pushing their troops into a corner. What aircraft and naval forces they had had there had been pulled out by now but they still had some ships in the area and a few aircraft, both B-17 and B-24 heavy bombers and fighter aircraft, based near the Dutch naval port of Sourabaya in Java. There was also 2nd Battalion, 131st Field Artillery, US Army, the only US ground forces to land in Java. The British had whatever air force was still available to them in the Far East in Singapore and some aircraft could be flown off to the NEI. The remnants of an army were there too but any hope of a 'Dunkirk' type operation to ferry this to Sumatra or Java was discounted as the Japanese had superiority in the air and on the sea, quite apart from the difficulties of providing the necessary ships for the job. Very few would be evacuated or manage to make their way to the NEI.

If we regard the Australians as part of the British forces at this juncture, the NEI Dutch would seem to have the last military force in the area which had not yet been committed wholesale to the fight. They had been both assisting the British with aircraft in Malaya and fighting the Japanese in Borneo by land, sea and air. Their military resources were few. However, the size and training of their armed forces was dictated by the same kind of imperial planning as the local British 'Singapore Strategy' – they were only required to deal with local emergencies as international threats would be countered by the imperial power, the Netherlands, using naval forces. This meant that their small but spirited navy was controlled directly by the Dutch navy in exile in Britain. Their army air force, the Militaire Luchtvaart (ML), was hampered by obsolete aircraft and inadequate airfields. Their army, the Koninklijk Nederlands-Indisch Leger (KNIL), was in essence a colonial force trained and equipped for the sort of peacekeeping or warfare that they would normally expect in a local imperial setting.

Their infantry, restricted in number, spread over a vast area and with few reserves, came from two main sources. The first was called 'the army in the Outer Possessions, i.e. the Netherlands East-Indian Territories outside Java.'[53] Its usual tasks were 'assuring internal peace, order and security', 'supporting the Civil Administration' and 'police-work such as the guarding of prisons and money offices, providing guards for transports of convicts and so on.' Extra help was given where necessary by the local militia. The other part, much closer to what the other Allies would consider to be a modern field army, was the Army in Java. However, as well as inadequacies in training and equipment, there had been severe dilution caused by many of the young white members of the corps going back to Europe when hostilities commenced there. The other Allies accepted the numbers available in the KNIL but do not seem to have realised the differences in training and capabilities between these and their own armies; it may have given rise to over-confidence where these forces were concerned. The KNIL did not have the type of troops needed to repel a Japanese invasion and it would be both highly optimistic and totally unreasonable of anyone to expect them to undertake such a task for which they had not been recruited, trained or equipped.

One thing the Dutch forces were particularly short of was anti-aircraft defences and the arrival of three complete British AA regiments, two light and one heavy, on their main island of Java must have been very encouraging for them. The said AA regiments quickly felt less than happy with their new surroundings. 48th Regt disembarked the day they arrived in port around 1730hrs and were ferried to their new barracks at Meister

---

[53] TNA: CAB 106/133: Netherlands account of the action in Sumatra, 1942 Jan.-Mar.

Cornelis, arriving late in the evening. This barracks had previously housed a Dutch infantry regiment of native troops:

'Just large long buildings with stone floors, wooden bedding (if you were lucky) and walls jutting out from the sides dividing them into partitions with a central gangway.'[54]

The worst was yet to come. There was no British base in Batavia and no proper supply system. The first consequence of this was that there was no food for 48th Regt or any other of the thousands of British military personnel now arriving. Ad hoc arrangements were made for them to receive food from the big hotels in Batavia, one being allocated to supply each barracks, but until the situation sorted itself out, the food consisted mostly of sandwiches twice a day for the first few days. The 48th did not receive their first rations until 1230hrs on the 4th and these 'consisted of loaves of bread, two slices of Dutch Sausage and a quantity of fruit'.[55]

Unfortunately all staff officers with experience of setting up supply organisations who had been sent to Java so far had moved with the main ABDACOM headquarters up to Bandoeng, leaving less experienced junior officers in Batavia and Tandjong Priok. The idea seems to have been that these would be supplemented by officers arriving with DM 2, as the report of Captain A Johnstone, commanding the RASC platoon attached to 48th Regt, makes clear. Horrified at the food debacle, he attempted to track down the senior RASC officer in the Batavia area to sort out something more suitable. When he could not locate him, he set up his own organisation, buying foodstuffs locally and distributing them from Meister Cornelis. His first contact with a senior officer was three days later on the 7th when:

'Lt Col Cope, R.I.A.S.C. came down from BANDOENG and I reported my action to him. He approved of what I had done and appointed me O.i/c Supplies, BATAVIA, under direct order of D.D.S.T., S.W.P.C., subject to confirmation by the D.D.S.T. I had by this time made the necessary arrangement for the supply of both fresh and tinned foodstuffs, and was at that moment feeding over 5,000 troops'

and at a much cheaper rate than the local hotels were charging.

Unhappily although food was a problem for all the AA regiments (and the other units) on DM 2, it was not the only one. Lt Col Saunders, commanding 21st Regt, had finally received orders at 1700hrs on 3rd February as the 'Empress of Australia' lay at anchor outside Tandjong Priok harbour. These included the instruction that part of his regiment was

---

[54] Rev. Godfrey, op. cit., p9
[55] TNA: WO 106/2539: Report of Captain A Johnstone, RASC, attached to 48th LAA Regiment

to be sent to defend the airfield and base at Koepang on the island of Timor, 1,200 miles east of the destination of the rest of his force near Malang in eastern Java. Although the need for speed in this deployment was:

'repeatedly emphasised ... The methods by which this Battery was to be disembarked, re-equipped and re-embarked was not stated. The disembarkation staff had made no plan, neither was there any information forthcoming as to the name of the ship, its berth or the date of sailing.'[56]

Saunders accordingly gave the officer commanding the battery to be deployed there *carte blanche* to take what guns, ammunition and equipment he required and sort himself out. Major J P Dempsey finally sailed with 'A' and 'C' Troops, 79th LAA Bty, 8 guns and sufficient gun tractors, plus ancillary stores on 9th February, after a ship had eventually been acquired and his men had loaded it themselves!

77th HAA Regiment was split in two, one battery (239th) being kept in the Batavia area while the other two, 240th and 241st, were sent to defend the Dutch naval port of Sourabaya in the east of Java. Disaster struck as these two batteries travelled by train to this deployment. On 5th February at 0245hrs, the brakes on their train failed and it ploughed into a goods train at Singasari near Malang. Four carriages were torn to bits and another three were thrown over an embankment resulting in the deaths of five officers and 16 ORs, with another three officers and 40 ORs injured, 241st Bty being particularly hard hit.[57] ABDACOM's reaction was to order 48th Regt to provide replacements for the dead and injured, an idea strongly resisted by Lt-Col Pearson on the grounds that his men were a LAA regiment trained on Bofors guns and thus useless to a HAA regiment.[58] There were, eventually, second thoughts at high level and the order was rescinded.

Pearson, like Saunders, had multiple problems. We know about the food. Even more pressing was the fact that 48th had no guns, ammunition or transport, which greatly limited their ability to act as an anti-aircraft regiment. These essentials of their trade were supposed to have been shipped by Ordnance direct to Singapore to await their arrival but of course 48th had never reached Singapore. Had their equipment? If not, where was it? The shipping manifests, when produced, proved to be useless. A search of the docks failed to locate any of it but in Macartney-Filgate's words:

'Some guns were located, some transport was collected (a party under the Quartermaster had some quite considerable and unprincipled success in this direction)'.

---

[56] TNA: WO 106/2563
[57] TNA:WO 106/2539: Report of Lt Col Humphries, 77th HAA
[58] Macartney-Filgate, op. cit., p19

He describes how this happened:

'large numbers of guns and vehicles were being dumped on the quayside, and there rapidly developed a game of grab in which units deliberately sent "scrounging" parties down to the quays and to the vehicle parks to lay hands on and drive away any guns and vehicles which their audacity might enable them to win. In many cases vehicles had been painted with the respective regiment's serial number and mark before shipment, and so chaotic was the situation that in several instances regimental patrols, sent out for the purpose, were able to recognise their own vehicles being driven along the road by unauthorised persons and, on recognition, were forced to eject the unrightful owners and take over the vehicles "in situ".'

It must have been like the Wild West round the dock area in the first few days after arrival!

Given that the only other LAA regiment with guns and equipment unloaded by the quayside was the 21st, it was obviously Saunders' men who were the victims of their 'scrounging'. He had already recognised the problems likely to arise from the way the ships had been loaded in the U.K. and had arranged a common vehicle park with Lt-Col Humphries of 77th Regt. There can be no question that he was proceeding in an organised and civilised military manner but, apart from his equipment being raided by parties from the 48th, he was officially required by higher authority to share as much as he could with the very reprobates who were robbing him – and this in spite of the fact that he had been forced to leave important pieces behind before he sailed on the grounds that there was no room on the ships for it. What words could be sufficient to describe his feelings on this state of affairs? He and Pearson had both been on the same staff gunnery course in the winter of 1937-8; no friendship they might have struck up then could survive the appalling behaviour of the latter's regiment.

Fortunately for Saunders and his men, 48th had another source of guns in the 'Dunera'; they unloaded those that they had mounted for her protection. And when 'City of Canterbury' sailed into Tandjong Priok later that week carrying four gun crews from 'B' Troop, 95th Bty, back from their adventures at Singapore, they were able to dismount her Bofors guns too. 'City of Canterbury' also had eighteen Bofors guns and other equipment in her hold, possibly some of 48th's missing equipment.[59] Whether it was or not, it was now possible to divide up the available guns between the two LAA regiments without a free-for-all or accusations. For gun tractors, 48th Regt found themselves a supply of 3-ton trucks, which were generally sufficient for the role though not ideal. 15-cwt trucks were also obtained, one being 'bagged' by Rev Godfrey for his own use, and of course a supply of motorcycles, an indispensable vehicle that most men could ride and

---

[59] Macartney-Filgate, op. cit., p19

which got officers around very quickly. On Sunday 8th February, Pearson and his second-in-command travelled to GHQ at Lembang to get orders for the regiment.

With AA regiments being in such short supply in the Far East, not surprisingly 48th Regt was split up with its batteries nearly as widely sited as the 21st's had been. 95th Bty was to proceed to the island of Sumatra to provide defence at an airfield near Palembang known to the RAF as P II. 49th Bty would continue to be deployed around the docks at Tandjong Priok while 242nd Bty was earmarked at this point to provide replacements for the losses to 77th Regt, an order which was later revoked. On 10th February, A Troop, 242nd Battery, was deployed to Kemajoram aerodrome and B Troop moved to Tjililitan airfield. The evening before, orders were received that 49th Bty was also to go to Sumatra to provide AA cover at Lahat aerodrome. The names are even today unusual and unfamiliar. We instinctively reach for maps to locate them yet sadly maps were in very short supply among British forces during the Far East campaign. It seems incredible that one newly-arrived RAF bomber crew trying to find its airfield in Sumatra could only be provided with a small map of the south-west Pacific cut from a newspaper article! Fortunately their navigator could find his way with this. Others had to just follow a leading aircraft, sometimes with disastrous results if the objective could not be found.

Odd names were just another element in the totally strange and foreign world 48th Regt found themselves in in Java. Their first day had been marked by torrential rain as it was the end of the wet monsoon period. This rain was going to be a constant companion to their activities. Heat, humidity and violent thunderstorms would follow them on all their travels. It was a long, long way from England! Just how well they had been instructed on the precautions to take against malaria (or how much notice they took of them!) is debateable, as large numbers were taken ill over the next three or four weeks. 2nd Lt Bagnall bought himself a copy of an English language guide book to Java, which he remarkably managed to carry with him throughout his war service and still survives among his papers in the Imperial War Museum, London,[60] but how many of his fellows thought it necessary to learn more about the area, its geography and customs? The food was strange, the language was strange and, unlike the UK, most of the people were coloured. Jack Gunn was just a country boy. At one point in his travels he called a native of wherever he was an 'ignorant savage'. The man merely replied, 'I speak four languages. How many do you?' When Jack had to reply just the one, the man asked him 'Who then is the ignorant savage?' making him truly ashamed of his insult. It is possible that it was around this time that the incident occurred.

---

[60] IWM Documents 398: Private papers of S E Bagnall

The question of race cropped up again as it did in South Africa. Rev Godfrey remarked on the differences between the 'Dutch colonial practice' and that in British colonies, deciding: 'they seem to solve their colour question much better than we do.' Although he never saw any coloured officers, he noticed that coloured men served side by side with white in the ranks of their armed forces and that:

'in ordinary life ... they intermarry, which is a thing the Britisher would never do, but they can do it without losing caste. ... they say they just can't understand our snobbish attitude over the colour bar.'

Godfrey's memoirs were written when he was a prisoner of war and it is to me a mark of his integrity as a recorder of events that, even though he lived until the 1990s and could have changed his script to reflect the different attitude to race of our modern times, he did not.

Godfrey also noted that everyone was given some Dutch money after their arrival and left the barracks to spend it. Jack got 9 guilders plus a Colonial Allowance of 88 cents for being in the NEI on 5th February and probably went to paint the town red like the others, possibly getting roaring drunk as in Durban. The padre was harassed on more than one occasion by a taxi driver wanting to take him to a brothel and remarks:

'I am afraid the British troops got a bad name for themselves over that. Their behaviour, the same as in Durban, was not calculated I feel to give the local people a high opinion of the British race.'

It would have given him some material for his sermons to the men though. He recalled that Lt Mounsdon of 49th Bty customarily hailed him with: 'Well, Padre, how about some moral rearmament?'

But now the time for merry-making was over and 49th and 95th Batteries were on the move to a proper war deployment. They had acquired twenty Bofors guns between them, four short on their establishment, but no spare parts or tools and very little ammunition. Transport was a little short as they needed a larger than usual quantity of 3-ton lorries. These were not only necessary to replace the gun-tractors that had not been found amongst the transport off-loaded from the ships at Tandjong Priok but also to carry all the men's kit as no base depot had been established. So all their European kit, including heavy greatcoats, and their spare khaki drill had to travel everywhere with them. Add to this the twenty-eight days' rations they were told to take with them and any extra ammunition and petrol they could lay their hands on (bad news for any other units around!) and it was a pretty overloaded convoy. Part of the problem was caused because 48th had lost its RASC component which was now fully occupied sorting out the mess in the Batavia and port areas.

Between 13th and 14th February, the two batteries moved by rail and sea to the Sumatran port of Oosthaven. What did the future hold for them there? Java had not been prepared for war; the first air raid on Batavia had only happened a couple of days after the 48th's arrival and the local population – even the military - seemed well set in their peace-time routines. Yet the news from Singapore was as grim as it could be. The balloon must go up in the NEI sooner rather than later. How soon would they be in the front line against an enemy who was sweeping all before him?

Five: Debacle in Sumatra

The Japanese forces had gone through Malaya like a hot knife through butter. One major reason was undoubtedly the lack of British preparation and resources in the area but there was more to it than that. The entire Japanese campaign had been meticulously planned from the very beginning. It was obvious to their military commanders that their own lack of resources would tell in a lengthy struggle so the aim was simply to take full advantage of the unpreparedness of the Allied forces in the area. It was necessary to keep pushing on and encircling the enemy, giving him no time to regroup. It was also necessary to capture as many as possible of the enemy's own resources intact and in this the Japanese succeeded extremely well.

While the successes may look like pure luck against an unprepared foe, there is no doubt that the planning was also there. The Air Ministry records in the National Archives in London have a translated copy of the plans of the Japanese air element for the capture of Sumatra and Java.[61] These clearly demonstrate careful planning involving close co-operation between all forces with starting points in Indo-China, Thailand and Malaya. So successful were these attacks that the plans were used later by the Japanese for training purposes. They cover not only the orders for the army air units but also the details of co-ordination and co-operation with the naval air forces and the naval and land forces in the area. Interestingly, the taking of Sumatra was planned as part and parcel of the action in Malaya, to be undertaken at the same time with specifically allocated forces. If the navy had been ready to go, the invasion of the island would have taken place several days earlier than it did. But this is jumping ahead of things and it is necessary to return to the Allied forces in occupation in Sumatra in January and early February 1942.

Sumatra was part of the NEI. As such, up to January 1942 the military forces there had naturally been Dutch but the formation of ABDACOM led to a rearrangement of deployment among the Allies to defend the island more comprehensively. Sumatra had little to recommend it to the casual visitor. Just over 1,100 miles long, it lies across the equator in a north-west, south-east direction like an elongated raindrop about 270 miles wide at its widest point. Near the western side of the island is the Barisan mountain range (including active volcanoes) rising to over 12,000 feet at the highest point. The eastern side of the island is low-lying and divided up by a myriad of rivers large and small that drain water and silt from the mountain range. This is mostly unsuitable for farming even today but in 1942 was largely covered with tropical rainforest.

---

[61] TNA: AIR 23/4830: Japanese air operations in Java and Sumatra, 1942

At this time communications on the island were limited. There were railway systems in the north and the south but they were not connected and all were single-track. Two different gauges were used but usually 3ft 6ins. The longest track ran around 250 miles in a curving line between Palembang and the major oil refineries round it on the estuary of the River Moesi on the eastern side of the island to the port of Oosthaven in the south. The roads were few in the huge central eastern plain and many of these were only passable in the dry season, though roads in the towns were good. All the airfields and landing grounds were served by roads of some description and one of the two major aerodromes used by the RAF, commonly known as P II, had rail connections nearby too. The sea and rivers offered transport to many areas near the coast on the eastern side, many rivers being navigable far upstream. I am greatly indebted for all this information on Sumatra and its climate, airfields and much more to a book produced by the Intelligence Branch, Air Headquarters, India, in November 1942,[62] that covers this island and many others, including Java, as well as the Malayan peninsula.

Sumatra's value lay in three main factors: its oil reserves, its tin mines and its position. The importance of the first two to the Allies generally goes without comment, except to say that the refineries also produced high-grade aviation fuel which was very necessary for the Allied aircraft based there. As for its position, it runs parallel with Malaya for about half its length and it is also an easy jumping-off point for Java, as the southern harbour of Oosthaven was only a few miles away from it across the Sunda Strait. Sea traffic for Singapore approaching from Java in the south had to pass between the main island and Banka Island near Palembang as the passage to the east was too dangerous for shipping. Above all, Sumatra provided the British with the only practicable way of sending bomber reinforcements to the Far East once the aerodromes in Malaya had fallen, so what were its airfields like?

The Dutch had built airfields and landing strips throughout the island for both military and civilian purposes and had given the other Allies permission to use these, firstly for the transit of aircraft and later for military use for the defence of the area. We actually have quite a bit of information about this, not just because British forces were stationed there in January-February 1942 so they are described in despatches, reports and memoirs, but also because the British Army and the RAF carried out surveys. The RAF surveys are incorporated in the book I have already mentioned; the Army's interest was limited to the defences already in place

---

[62] TNA: AIR 23/4959: East Indies Archipelago [Part 1]: List of aerodromes, satellites, landing grounds, emergency landing grounds, seaplane stations and alighting areas. NEI, Malaya and all of Borneo.

on the airfields as they would be providing the anti-aircraft batteries to defend them.[63]

The Dutch had very limited AA protection at their airfields[64] on the island at the beginning of January 1942, though they did have some ground forces for aerodrome protection duties. Six of their airfields, the only ones described as 'aerodromes' in the RAF book and probably the only ones the Army reconnaissance team visited[65], had two or three pillboxes, each of which had a garrison of fifteen men with two machine-guns, one light machine-gun, one twin AA light machine-gun and one sub machine-gun. One aerodrome at Palembang also had three armoured cars. These forces appear to be from the 'army in the Outer Possessions'. A number of companies and sections of infantry from the Army in Java, some 3-inch mortars and a few 75mm guns were also available for the 'general defence of the area', wherein 'the area' seems to mean the central most important part of Sumatra.

It was hoped that the Allies would eventually be able to reinforce the infantry on the island, although it was impossible to spare any from amongst those forces fighting the Japanese in Malaya immediately. The 1st Australian Corps, under General Sir John Lavarack, was on its way from the Middle East to provide infantry support in Sumatra and Java under the aegis of ABDACOM. Though this was not expected to arrive until mid-February, Lavarack and some of his staff arrived in Java by air on 26th January and commenced reconnaissances and discussions with ABDACOM headquarters. In the interim a motorised battalion of the Java Army was sent over and was split between the airfields of Palembang I (P I) and Palembang II (P II). It was also intended to serve as a general reserve.

However, the British did manage to provide some anti-aircraft cover by diverting parts of two AA regiments originally destined for the Middle East but then sent to Malaya - 12th and 15th Batteries, 6th HAA Regt, and 78th Bty and two troops of 89th Bty, 35th LAA Regt. The rest of these two regiments remained in Singapore or on the Malayan mainland. 6th HAA and 35th LAA Regts had arrived in the Far East with Convoy WS 12Z (later DM 1) which sailed from the UK on 12th November 1941 and docked in Singapore on 13th January 1942. The above-named elements were then moved on to Palembang in Sumatra where they arrived on 30th January.

In theory this deployment should have brought sixteen 3.7" HAA guns and twenty 40mm LAA Bofors guns to be divided between P I and P II aerodromes and the Pladjoe oil refineries but the stunning bad luck that

---

[63] TNA: WO 106/2527: Sumatra: aerodrome defence, Jan 1942
[64] TNA: AIR 23/4959. There were 6 'aerodromes', 10 'landing grounds', 17 'emergency landing grounds' and 17 'seaplane alighting areas' on Sumatra.
[65] Lho Nga, Medan, Pakanbaroe, P I, P II and Sabang (AIR 23/4959)

dogged the Allies in this campaign struck again. Only part of the AA force arrived with its guns. SS 'Anting', with most of the Bofors guns and all the ammunition for all the LAA guns, was sunk in a Japanese air strike. Fortunately almost all the men of 89th Bty aboard her were saved and landed at Oosthaven but without any equipment of any kind. The LAA gunners were offered Dutch ammunition of the same calibre which was rushed to them by sea and rail from Java but it seems to have taken a little getting used to. Just to compound the tragedy, SS 'Subadar', carrying the ten heavy guns that had not arrived with 6th Regt and most of the 3.7" ammunition, was badly damaged by enemy air action and had to be beached by her crew. Somehow they managed to re-float her and nurse her into Palembang on 11th February, allowing the guns and ammunition to be reunited with the Regt.[66] All this was very bad news when the airfields of Sumatra were under heavy attack from the Japanese.

And these airfields were very busy indeed. Initially, as I have said, they were going to be used by the RAF for reinforcing bomber units or bringing new bomber squadrons into the area. The range of the bombers being used in the Far East, Blenheims and Hudsons, allowed them to be flown in stages from the Middle East or from the UK to Sumatra, even after the northern Malayan airfields had fallen to the Japanese. However, the shorter-ranged fighter aircraft would have to either be flown from Australia, 'island-hopping' up the NEI island chain from Darwin in Northern Australia, or off a carrier near to a suitable Allied airfield or delivered by sea, packed in crates for assembly in theatre. Two squadrons of Blenheims were earmarked for passage in early January 1942: 84 Sqn, based at Heliopolis, which would be the RAF squadron in residence at Kalidjati when disaster struck on 1st March 1942, and 211 Sqn, based at Helwan, both in Egypt.

When squadrons were redeployed to the Far East, men who were time-expired or nearly so were usually replaced by inexperienced newcomers. In some squadrons almost every experienced pilot was replaced but 84 Sqn was lucky in that a cadre of experienced men moved with the squadron though their commanding officer was new to war flying. The plan was for the aircraft themselves to be flown by their three-man crew with two members of ground crew, tools, personal kit, some spares and an extra 55-gallon fuel tank to extend their range packed in too. The remainder of the ground crew and squadron staff would follow by sea.

The route from Heliopolis was Habbaniya (Iraq), Bahrein, Sharjah (on the Persian Gulf), Karachi, Allahabad, Calcutta, Toungoo (Burma), Rangoon,

---

[66] TNA: CAB 106/29: "ABDACOM": official account of events in the South-West Pacific Command Jan.-Feb 1942

Lho'gna, Medan and Palembang – the last three in Sumatra. The aircraft left in batches between 14th and 18th of January and 16 of the 24 arrived at P I by 26th January. If an attrition rate of 33% seems very high for the journey, it pales to insignificance beside that of 59 Sqn's Hudsons which flew out from Britain at the same time. Of the 18 that set out, only seven – just over a third - eventually reached Palembang – not much of a reinforcement in anyone's book! The surviving aircraft and crews were absorbed into 8 Sqn RAAF which also flew Hudsons. Eighteen out of 211 Sqn's 24 Blenheims arrived at Palembang between 23rd January and 14th February.

Wear and tear and the effects of forced landings claimed a number of the victims but squadrons redeploying to Sumatra also complained of faulty briefings for the final leg to the island, and within Sumatra itself, and the lack of maps, an issue that was to plague this whole campaign. Another factor that must have played a part in the problems with locating airfields in what can only be described as tropical jungle was that quite a number of them had more than one name, as the later RAF book on airfields in the area demonstrates. Thus Lho'nga was also Lhoknga or Koetaradja Aerodrome, Palembang I (P I) was also Talangbetoetoe Aerodrome and Palembang II (P II) was also Lembak Aerodrome. Given that the RAF also subtly but inexplicably changed some Dutch spellings, officers giving briefings in Burma who were not conversant with local conditions may well have been at something of a loss to find co-ordinates for the destinations.

To add to the chaos that was caused by trying to pick out a small landing strip in heavily-forested terrain, the weather in the area was just about as bad as it could be for the newcomers. From the dry Western Desert they had just pitched up into the wet monsoon of a tropical climate. Words can hardly do it justice but here is the description from AVM Maltby's despatch:

'A feature of this monsoon was the prevalence of torrential thunderstorms, both by day and night, of great local intensity which completely blacked out all visibility. Aircraft were bound to encounter one or more of them during the course of every long flight.'[67]

But of course such weather did not just affect aircraft in flight trying to find either their targets or their landing grounds. It also impacted on landing and taking off, on the conditions on airfields (most of whose runways were grass strips), on attempting to service and re-arm aircraft (as much of this had to take place in the open) and on the gunners of the Royal Artillery, of whom more later.

---

[67] TNA: AIR 23/2123, para 419

It had originally been intended to station the reinforcing bomber squadrons at P I, just north of Palembang. This had hard runways but as the former civil aerodrome for the city, it was well known to the Japanese and with no dispersal areas provided, aircraft on the ground there were an easy target. Events in Malaya and Singapore were also forcing a change of plan. By 16th January 1942, all British and Australian air force units in the area had been pushed back to Singapore Island resulting in unsustainable overcrowding of the four airfields there, especially in the face of unremitting Japanese air attacks. It was decided, therefore, to move all bomber squadrons to Sumatra to free up the airfields for the surviving fighters. I cannot, however, accept Maltby's statement in his despatch that:

'At this time, it was fairly confidently anticipated that the situation on the ground in Malaya would be stabilised and a bridgehead held of sufficient area for the deployment of reinforcements preparatory to a counter-offensive being undertaken. That it would be necessary later to transfer fighter squadrons from Singapore was not at this time "on the cards".'[68]

I simply cannot see anything promised or in transit to the area at that time in the way of reinforcements that could rationally give rise to any such optimism.

One thing not lacking at this stage was senior officers. AVM Pulford was amazed by the arrival in Singapore of Air Commodore H J F Hunter and Air Commodore S F Vincent, who had been sent to the Far East by the Air Ministry to form a Bomber Group and a Fighter Group respectively. This appears to have come completely out of the blue to Pulford, who does not seem to have been notified and really had as many senior officers as he needed. The chance to dispatch them in turn to Sumatra was a bit of luck for him, though it may well have put other officers' noses out of joint as they were superseded. Hunter arrived there on 30th January and took over from Group Captain A G Bishop, who then became SASO of 225 (B) Group as it now became.

It is difficult to overstate the terrible confusion and lack of every necessity suffered by the RAF and the RAAF in Sumatra. From the end of January they were the only air forces operating for the defence of the island as the Dutch withdrew their aircraft to Java. However, their land forces and civil authorities there seem to have done the very best within their power to help the British forces, both land and air. This could not make up for the devastation caused by the Japanese control of both the sea and air. As Maltby puts it in his despatch:

'Practically all equipment destined for Sumatra went astray. In particular no M.T. arrived except some light motor cars about the 8th February, few

---

[68] TNA: AIR 23/2123: para 417

bomb trailers, few rations, and most important of all on the domestic side, no tentage and no domestic field equipment. Aircraft spares were limited ... There were only three refuellers available.'[69]

Luckily, fuel was not a problem but the RAF had been concentrating on improving the northern Sumatran airfields that were now in range of Japanese aircraft from the former RAF fields on the Malayan mainland and therefore unusable except as refuelling stops. Bombs were in limited supply, though the Dutch tried to remedy this by providing some from their own stores for RAF use but not all bombs are the same. Not only were they different weights and sizes to the British ones (and memoirs have many stories of crew members stamping on them or kicking them over target to release them from their aircraft) but also they were not necessarily the right type for the job. General purpose is no good for armour-piercing jobs and impact fuses are not always what is required.

For pilots and ground crew alike, the living conditions were at best extremely primitive and overcrowded. There were simply not the facilities for such large numbers of servicemen around Palembang where the great majority ended up. To make matters worse, it was almost impossible to accommodate the necessary men on or around the airfields, yet perhaps that is more understandable when one reads that there were at one time more than 100 aircraft at P II. For the 1,500 personnel in the area of P II, there was accommodation for only 250, less than that necessary for the aircrew alone. Palembang, to the north, was separated from the airfield by the River Moesi, which at this point had no road bridge, only a ferry capable of carrying four to six vehicles at a time. Nevertheless, accommodation of some form for 2,500 airmen for P I and P II was found in the schools and cinemas of Palembang city. Memoirs of RAF men experiencing this billeting make it clear how primitive some of this could be – yet what else could be done? The numbers were huge, they arrived swiftly and there was no time for suitable preparation. Once again the defence of the Far East ran into chaos.

By the end of January, all surviving bomber units from Singapore had been relocated to Sumatra and were allocated P II as their airfield. 1 Sqn RAAF was the best equipped with 16 Hudson IIs, though they were in desperate need of inspection and servicing, while 8 Sqn RAAF and 62 Sqn RAF had 16 Hudson IIIs between them. 27 Sqn, 34 Sqn and 62 Sqn, all RAF, mustered a total of 14 mixed Blenheim Is and IVs. Forty-six bombers of these types, suffering considerable wear and tear, could hardly be regarded as a formidable aerial armada, even after adding the Blenheim IVs of 84 and 211 Sqns that had arrived or were arriving in Sumatra at this time (and also not in great shape after their long journey). Nevertheless, they

---

[69] TNA: AIR 23/2123: para 428

struggled manfully to undertake both unescorted bombing raids on Malaya and reconnaissance flights over the South China Sea to Borneo. Their success is difficult to establish given the conditions but the situation was not helped by receiving orders from both AHQ Singapore and Abdair, the Air Headquarters for ABDACOM, until 6th February when Abdair finally took over as communications between the two HQs had completely broken down.

The surviving fighter squadrons from Singapore quickly followed the bombers. 226 (F) Group was set up in Palembang on 1st February 1942 with the role of defending the Palembang area with its vital oil installations and airfields, protecting shipping in the Banka Straits just off the coast and, until 8th February, maintaining a token force of fighters in Singapore. By this date, the Japanese advance onto the island had got so far that it was no longer possible to base fighter aircraft there and the survivors were shepherded off by Hudsons to P I on Sumatra. There the remnant of the Brewster Buffalos that had been the mainstay of the British aerial defence of Malaya and Singapore until mid-January 1942 (though obsolescent in the western theatres of war) came to grief, strafed on the ground by marauding Japanese fighters. There is no mention of providing escorts for bombing raids in Maltby's description of 226 Group's role as there were simply not enough fighter aircraft to do this. The Fighter Group also had no administrative staff so that for the few days of its operations in Sumatra its administrative needs were met by the admin staff of 225 (B) Group.[70]

The Hurricane was now the only fighter operated by the British in the area and Maltby calculated that around fifty were available when the Group was formed. How do we, seventy years on, assess the significance of such a number? James Home, ground crew on 242 Sqn and a Battle of France and Battle of Britain veteran, summed up the forty Hurricanes which he had heard had arrived at P I on 2nd February 1942:

'If that was going to be our complement of fighters it was not going to take us very far.'[71]

Someone like Home, with his experience of serviceability and probable operational losses, was well-qualified to assess how formidable a force this was likely to be, yet even he had not factored in the climate in Sumatra or the other peculiar factors which made this such an attritional theatre of war for both machines and men. He had, incidentally, travelled to the Far East in the same convoy as 48th Regt, on the same ship as parts of 21st and 77th Regts, the 'Empress of Australia', so was doubtless originally destined for

---

[70] TNA: CAB 106/20: Report of the action at Palembang of the 6th Heavy Anti-Aircraft Regiment, Royal Artillery, and the withdrawal to Java, by Lieutenant-Colonel G.W.G. Baillie
[71] 'Their Last Tenko', James Home, Quoin Publishing Ltd, 1989, p10

North Africa. The squadron's pilots were not travelling with the ground crew.

The term 'squadron' is used loosely from now on as we are already into the period when both fighter and bomber squadrons would be combined and renumbered as aircraft became scarcer and losses of aircrew increased. For example, once in Sumatra 232, 242, 258 and 605 (F) Sqns became Nos. 232 and 258.[72] The shortage of aircraft was only one of their problems. While the survivors of the Singapore squadrons had picked up some combat experience, those pilots who had newly arrived in theatre were generally straight from OTUs with the exception of commanding officers and flight commanders, as had been the case in Malaya. In addition:

'There was a deficiency of Hurricane tool kits and few battery starters for aircraft and no battery-charging facilities were available at the aerodrome.'[73]

The radio telephone system that connected the main towns and also provided an external connection to Java was open and insecure for military purposes and at first orders from the Operations Room established at Palembang had to be relayed to aircraft via the naval transmitter some distance away. Later improvements allowed this communication to be direct rather than indirect.

'VHF was not available, nor was D/F for assisting homing aircraft. The absence of the latter was a serious handicap because of the daily intense thunderstorms. All aircraft of the Fighter Group were based on P.1. aerodrome ... [which] had a telephone from the Operations Room in Palembang but no instruments were available for dispersal points round the aerodrome.'[74]

What a way to fight a war! And this was before the Japanese took a hand in proceedings!

So the RAF was in bad straights for aircraft, for servicing, for communications, for ordnance, for billeting, in short for all necessities. Information on the British Army units in the area is a bit harder to come by, partly because of the smaller numbers involved and partly because RAF survivors are much more forthcoming when it comes to writing memoirs of what happened to them in this theatre than the Army - or could it be that interest in publishing the Army's experiences has been lacking? Whatever the reason, the Royal Artillery had to be there to defend the RAF and RAAF, even if the help it could give was limited.

---

[72] TNA: AIR 23/2123: para 465
[73] ibidem: para 466
[74] ibidem: paras 461 and 462

The RA units in Sumatra before the arrival of 48th Regt were, as we have already seen, experiencing great problems because of the disasters that had befallen their guns and ammunition. Although 89th Bty had lost every bit of kit and equipment, the RA units were probably generally better off than the RAF. The Army was used to travelling with their kit, immediate rations and basic equipment whereas the RAF squadrons in this theatre seemed less accustomed to transporting the necessities of life with them on their travels. They also suffered from simple basic kit shortages like a lack of proper boots, which made long marches virtually impossible.

The surviving RA units were put under the command of Lt-Col G W G Baillie,[75] commanding officer of 6th HAA Regt, who established his GOR 'on the verandah of the room housing the Group Operations Room'[76] for 226 Fighter Group some two miles north of Palembang and eight miles south of P I aerodrome. Here 15th HAA Bty was stationed with eight 3.7" AA guns, when all those which had survived the catastrophes at sea were finally available to the regiment. One troop of 89th LAA Bty and one section of 78th LAA Bty were also on the airfield with five Bofors guns between them, though unfortunately ammunition for all guns was severely limited. An excellent sketch map of P I survives in Maltby's report to the Air Ministry[77] which shows the guns of 15th Bty in two groups of four, one to the west of the airfield and one to the south beside the main road to Palembang. The Bofors guns of the 89th and 78th were positioned in closer proximity to the flying field near the ends of the two runways. A group of buildings marked 'A.A. HQ. MESSES ETC.' is directly across the crossroads the Palembang road makes with a 'Rough Track' just south of the aerodrome so it is likely, though not certain, that there was some provision for the gunners – or at least their officers – near the airfield.

12th Bty 6th Regt was split three ways, with four guns at P II aerodrome, 40 miles south-west of Palembang, and two each at the BPM refinery at Pladjoe, five miles from Palembang, and the NKPM refinery yards at Soengei Gerong, a mile further away but across a river from Pladjoe. The scanty LAA resources also appear to have been split up over the two sites. The problem with reconstructing the exact locations and allocations of guns arises because Lt-Col Baillie's account in the National Archives is, perhaps not surprisingly, largely concerned with what happened when the Japanese attacked but he does incidentally give some interesting information and insights.

As part of 6th Regt was, like 84 Sqn, destined to end up on Kalidjati airfield with 49th Bty, it is useful to know something about the Regiment and its

---

[75] He had changed his name from Baass a couple of years before but some sources still call him that.
[76] TNA: CAB 106/20
[77] TNA: AIR 23/2123: Appendix E

deployment in Sumatra. Baillie had started training his regiment in ground defence when they were back in England.

'The destination of the Regt. was originally IRAQ and it was appreciated that Btys. would have to be responsible for their own protection at all times. Anti paratroop and tank hunting squads were trained. In SINGAPORE the former always 'stood to' on all air raid warnings. These squads were highly mobile and trained in aggression.'[78]

Therefore while the regiment had less than its full complement of guns in Sumatra, the men were mustered as ground defence units at the sites where it was posted along with the Dutch forces also available there.

The Japanese did not discover P II until after they invaded although it could hardly have remained undiscovered if the campaign had been longer in spite of being well hidden. However, P I was known to them as the civil airport. Until 11th February, the gunners could do little to deter Japanese air attacks on the RAF on the ground there, which gathered pace from around 6th February in line with the Japanese air plan. In specific detail:

'the 3rd Air Brigade of the 3rd Air Group will begin the operation for the destruction of enemy air forces in PALEMBANG on 6th February; by 8th February three attacks will be carried out, and the greater proportion of the enemy air force in the area will be destroyed.'[79]

As in the Battle of Britain, the enemy air force started by attacking shipping and ports, but just as the Japanese would allow no Dunkirk to happen at Singapore, this was going to be no repeat of the Battle of Britain. Here there were no dispersal airfields to speak of and no RDF or experienced observer system to alert the defenders. Instead communications were poor for whatever information was available, there were few aircraft and no reserves to speak of. Should a pilot be shot down over the sea, there was no rescue organisation. If he were shot down over land, he landed in the jungle. And the monsoon was still in full swing. Yet in spite of all these factors, there was a determined attempt by the RAF and the RAAF to do everything they could to defend the island. The detail of their efforts can be found elsewhere[80] as we now have to turn our attention to the Royal Artillery.

Following standard practice on the deployment of AA Batteries, officers were sent to Sumatra to make a reconnaissance before the guns and

---

[78] TNA: CAB 106/20.
[79] TNA: AIR 23/4830
[80] There is an excellent account in *'Bloody Shambles, Volume II, The Defence of Sumatra to the Fall of Burma'*; Christopher Shores, Brian Cull and Yasuho Izawa; published Grub Street, London, 1993

gunners of 49th and 95th Batteries arrived. Major Macartney-Filgate, second-in-command of 48th Regt, and Major Graham, commanding 95th Bty, set out early on February 10th, travelling by train and boat to their destination as air attacks on Palembang had stopped the air service between that town and Batavia. Eventually arriving at Kertapati, the railhead two miles outside Palembang on the other side of the River Moesi, on the afternoon of the 11th, they were both disturbed to discover the paucity of communications on Sumatra. Though Oosthaven was a good deep-water harbour, the single-track railway and the weather-dependent road to Palembang 250 miles away did not bode well for any military operations.

'It was not evident to them how a force of any size could be sent up for the defence of Palembang within the very short time which, events suggested, remained available, and it seemed that any who did in fact get there would be, as the Americans would say "out on a limb".'

And the ferry 'of sorts' across the Moesi to Palembang 'might, perhaps, transport two guns at a time.'[81]

This particular quirk of local transport would not be a problem to 48th Regt as their batteries were to be based at P II (95th Bty) and Lahat (49th Bty). After discussions at 6th Regt HQ, they travelled to P II on the morning of the 12th from where Macartney-Filgate took a trip to Lahat 'in a small biplane of doubtful origin though apparent airworthiness' belonging to the Malayan Volunteer Air Force, which had been evacuated to Sumatra and provided a liaison service between the airfields there. He was not impressed by what he saw. Lahat was barely more than a 'flying field', mostly filled by its two grass runways 660 and 550 yards long. It was impossible to find a suitable site for anti-aircraft guns: the ground fell away steeply on three sides and the choice was between perimeter defence and being too far out to be of any use. There was also no possibility of concealing the guns. The situation was not helped by Gp Capt Noble, the RAF station commander,[82] who pointed out that there were no troops available for ground defence except untrained RAF ground crew, no material for constructing defences, no communications except the public telephone and no system to warn of approaching aircraft. There were also no aircraft yet from the two Blenheim squadrons scheduled to be based here but this was no consolation to Macartney-Filgate as he made his way back to P II, where in contrast:

'the flying field was immense, and the surroundings, flat and covered with

---

[81] Macartney-Filgate, op. cit., p22, as are the other quotes on this page relating to his time in Sumatra.
[82] Gp Capt C H Noble, previously, as Wing Commander, base commander at Kota Bahru, north Malaya

scrub and bush, gave excellent opportunities for concealment and for movement to alternative positions'

but again, no ground defence forces.

Early the next morning, after consulting with Graham on the results of his surveys, Macartney-Filgate returned to Java by air and informed GHQ in Bandoeng:

'of the problems which confronted the Sumatra batteries, and to give details of the stores and defence materials which they urgently required. These were noted, but without undue optimism as to their provision.'

When he arrived back that night at RHQ in Batavia, he found 'with some consternation' that 49th and 95th were already on the move. Most of 95th had gone by sea to Oosthaven with C Troop and 49th Bty leaving by train to catch a ship across the Sunda Strait the next morning, 14th February.

A and B Troops and BHQ 95th Bty arrived in Oosthaven at 0800hrs on 14th February and the men remained on board the SS 'Van der Hargen' on which they had travelled from Java while the guns, vehicles and stores were unloaded. Orders were received to move at dawn the next day to P II. But events up north were to change everything, for around the same time as their ship docked the Japanese started their invasion of Sumatra by dropping a force of paratroops, part at P I and part at the oil refineries at Pladjoe and Soengei Gerong. Allied accounts of numbers vary between 700 and 800 overall[83] but the original Japanese plans indicate that the number was actually 260 men for P I and 130 men for the refineries. Interestingly, these men had a few days' training for their mission in early February at Sungei Patani, the ex-RAF airfield in northern Malaya previously home to 27 Sqn RAF and 21 Sqn RAAF, before moving on to the other former RAF Malayan airfields of Kahang and Kluang for their final preparations and departure on ops.[84]

An attack had been expected. A substantial convoy of Japanese ships had been seen approaching the coast the day before and RAF bombers, with a fighter escort for once, had taken off that morning to attack it. They actually passed the Japanese raid, a mixture of fighters and bombers as well as transport aircraft, on their way out. Attempts to recall the fighters to deal with the new threat failed – not surprisingly, given the poor communications at the RAF's disposal.

---

[83]ABDACOM gives 300 at P I, 300 at Pladjoe and 100 at Soengei Gerong (CAB 106/29, p66); Baillie gives 800 between all sites (CAB 106/20); Maltby gives 350 at P I but does not mention numbers at non-airfield sites (AIR 23/2123). The Dutch report merely speaks of 'great numbers' (CAB 106/133)
[84] TNA: AIR 23/4830

Baillie's report claims the transports carrying the paratroopers were Lockheed Hudsons with RAF markings while the ABDACOM despatch describes them as Lodestars but actually they were Japanese Kawasaki Ki-56, which had a very similar configuration to the Hudson and could easily be mistaken for it. Nationality markings can be difficult to identify from a distance and it was extremely common in this theatre of war at this time to misidentify aircraft. If you can believe it, the Japanese met with Spitfires and the Allies found themselves up against Me109s at various times while the number of Navy 'O's that were encountered was phenomenal. Just as there were Tiger tanks everywhere in Normandy in 1944, so there were countless Zeros over the south-west Pacific in 1941-2.

At P I, the paratroops formed into squads to take various targets: the two HAA gun sites and the landing field itself plus a small squad (presumably an offshoot from one of these) that managed to capture one of the Dutch armoured cars on the base. This moved off to block the road to Palembang, thus preventing either an evacuation from the airfield or the arrival of any reinforcements called up by Baillie presumably when informed of the situation by Major G A Moxon, commanding 15th Bty. The Japanese were well armed: the ABDACOM account speaks of them having 'rifles and revolvers, sub machine guns, machine guns, some grenades and light mortars',[85] which made them a formidable foe from the off.

15th Bty 'concentrated on protecting itself and in attempting to withdraw its guns.'[86] The southern gun site was 'heavily sniped' by Japanese in the surrounding trees but the battery dealt with the problem by turning their guns on them. 'This rather unorthodox way of using a 3.7 was most effective.' The enemy attempted to fight back using a captured Bofors gun but this, they and the G.L. equipment was destroyed by the HAA guns. When the immediate threats had been dealt with it was decided to attempt to withdraw with the 3.7s but only one Scammel gun tractor could be found. However, this was powerful enough to pull two guns which were limbered up while the rest were disabled and the retreating battery took to the road, only to be obstructed by the road block set up by the Japanese, a problem which was not dealt with until late that afternoon. In the meantime 'small parties each under an officer and containing armed and unarmed personnel of 15 Hy Bty and 75 and 89 Lt Btys' fought their way through the jungle towards Palembang. 15th Bty lost one officer and 16 ORs killed, 36 ORs wounded and 6 missing.

At Pladjoe and Soengei Gerong the gunners of 12th Bty had also been in action. The oil refineries were a prime target for the Japanese as they were desperate to take them intact, having failed to capture those on Borneo

---

[85] TNA: CAB 106/29, p66.
[86] TNA: CAB 106/20

before they were destroyed. The Dutch had made preparations for this here but had decided they would keep them running until the last possible minute because they had a strategic value to the Allies too. They simply put plans in place to destroy them that depended on the refineries being in their hands and in working order. The gun sites here were not attacked but the gunners' anti-paratroop squads went into action alongside the Dutch troops. In a desperate attempt to clear the refineries of the enemy, Captain W L Sherrard and one of the gunners were killed. 12th Bty seemed to have held their ground but were withdrawn later. The guns at Soengei Gerong were destroyed as they could only be removed by water, which was now impossible, while those at Pladjoe were pulled back the next day to defend the railway station at Kertapati and the vital road bridge east of it.

Prior to this, the plans on the Allied side moved back and forth. Baillie himself was too junior an officer to participate in the decisions taken following the parachute attack - 'decisions' because for the next twenty-four hours the plans formulated by more senior officers seemed to be in a permanent state of flux, if his report is to be believed. Brigadier C E Steele, Chief Engineer, 1 Australian Corps, had flown in to Palembang on the morning of 14th February 'to examine the proposed demolitions of the P.1. airfield.'[87] His remit must have been wider than this as he was on his way to the refineries at 9.30am when he got news of the attack. Steele was with the Dutch Territorial Commander when Baillie visited him for the second time that day at about 1030hrs. In consultation with A/Cdre Hunter, he now issued the order for all troops to be withdrawn to P II, instructing Baillie to use his forces to cover the RAF's retreat from south of the Moesi. A rearguard position was established here and RHQ and many RAF personnel were withdrawn, only for the order to be cancelled in the early afternoon when it was decided that P I could be recaptured and all troops were returned to the north bank of the river.[88] It seems from Australian sources that by this time Steele was probably at or on his way to Oosthaven to make arrangements for the imminent arrival of the first detachments of 1 Australian Corps on the fast liner 'Orcades'.

It appears that the Dutch Territorial Commander had changed his mind in the afternoon and that this was the basis for the decision to move back across the Moesi, but he revised his decision again overnight and by 1100hrs on the 15th the main telephone exchange in Palembang and all means of communication with Java had been destroyed. Cut off from the outside world, the Allied defence of Sumatra was now run solely on the strength of rumours. From this point, plans would be made and orders

---

[87] Chapter 20: The Destination of 1 Australian Corps, p454; *'Australia in the War of 1939–1945; Series 1 – Army; Volume IV – The Japanese Thrust'*, (1st edition, 1957), by Lionel Wigmore
[88] TNA: CAB 106/20

issued purely on the basis of guesswork or a visceral reaction to whatever tale was circulating at the time. It was not intelligence-led and there was no photo reconnaissance to guide decisions as all flyable aircraft were leaving for Java from late 14th February. It was no way to run a war.

The RAF were retreating. Their aircraft had gone to Java or would shortly be on their way and they had no reason to stay on Sumatra. Trains were requisitioned to move men and whatever equipment could be salvaged south to Oosthaven to embark on any shipping that could be found. Although Baillie's men had been defending RAF airfields and he himself had been reporting to their senior officers, it appears that no one thought it necessary to inform him of the retreat:

'The regiment had not been included in the R.A.F. scheme for withdrawal nor were any orders received. It was thought that the dismounted personnel would have to march to P2 (72 kms) but good initiative on the part of all officers made it possible to transport them to the railway and to find a place for them on the R.A.F. train. ... All personnel had been accounted for by 1300 hrs. Two 3.7 guns 12 Hy. Bty. were withdrawn to P2. One 3.7 gun 15 Hy. Bty. had to be abandoned N. of R. Moesi, there being no way of getting it across the river.'[89]

Baillie left P II with the surviving heavy guns of 12th Bty at 1530hrs. Sadly, after all their struggles, these did not make it to Oosthaven as the road south had a number of substantial roofed road bridges that were too low for a Scammel and 3.7" gun to pass. The first bridge had its roof cut away but the process could not be repeated indefinitely and there was no option but to destroy the guns. At Oosthaven at 0800hrs on 16th February, Steele showed Baillie his operation order for the evacuation of Sumatra. Personnel were to be concentrated for this and guns destroyed. Steele had been given information of an enemy landing on his flank which was forcing him to advance times for evacuation. Like much of the other information circulating, this was nothing more than an unsubstantiated rumour.

The first two troops of 95th Bty, 48th Regt, already at Oosthaven received orders at 1930hrs on the 14th to the effect that in view of the Japanese paratroop attacks their destination was now changed to Lahat, previously allocated to 49th Bty. They had not yet moved when this order was also countermanded. In the meantime, 49th Bty and the rest of 95th Bty arrived on Sumatra.

'Orders and counter orders now circulated in a bewildering manner, as people at G.H.Q. and others on the spot began to take a hand in the game. The complete absence of any information as to what was happening further north in the island, coupled with the most wild rumours regarding the

---

[89] TNA: CAB 106/20

movement of Japanese troops and their proximity to Oosthaven added, of course, to the general confusion. In Sumatra, as in Java, the outstanding feature of the campaign all through was the complete lack of information given to unit commanders by higher formations.'[90]

However, Steele now took charge of proceedings on behalf of the Australian and British troops in the area or arriving in port, calling a conference of senior officers for both forces on the morning of 15th February. Discovering that there were no Dutch troops south of P II aerodrome, he decided to defend Oosthaven using whatever forces he had. That afternoon A and B Troops, 95th Bty, were deployed thirty-six miles away at Branti flying field; B Troop were to defend it while A Troop were to guard the road leading to it in case the Japanese were really in the neighbourhood as no infantry were available for such tasks. While Macartney-Filgate gives the airstrip's name as Branti, no flying ground of that name – even an emergency strip – appears in the RAF's list of Sumatran landing grounds but an internet search suggests it was possibly an alternative name for Teloekbeteong Emergency Landing Ground. Meanwhile C Troop and 49th Bty, which had arrived that morning, were deployed around Oosthaven itself along with the light tanks of B squadron, the 3rd Hussars, and about 500 RAF personnel armed with rifles.

That afternoon 'Orcades' arrived with the 7th Division, AIF. Steele determined to use these troops to strike north to P II and Palembang, an odd decision given that he had been up-country and must have been aware of the limited road and rail system to deliver them there, especially as it was now swamped by both retreating military forces and civilian refugees and he had no reliable intelligence from the area of the enemy's forces and positions. However, before they could be disembarked he received a signal from Wavell's headquarters via the destroyer 'Encounter' not to land any troops but to re-embark the 3rd Hussars on the 'Orcades' for immediate departure. ABDACOM believed that the Japanese had at least a division now landing at Palembang, with a huge air support element, against which they could do nothing with the troops and aircraft available and at some time on the 15th ordered a withdrawal from Sumatra.[91] This order apparently did not reach Steele until well into the 16th but after discussions with the Dutch and aware by then of the hopelessness of attempting even a defensive action with very limited forces, he gave orders for evacuation, to be completed by the 17th. [92]

This was by no means easy. Quite apart from the large numbers of military personnel, both army and air force and from three Allied nations, the place

---

[90] Macartney-Filgate, op. cit., p23
[91] TNA: CAB 106/29: ABDACOM despatch, p67
[92] *'Australia in the War of 1939–1945; Series 1, Vol IV,'* Chapter 20, p455.

was being flooded with civilian refugees whose cars blocked the road not just for the Army and RAF convoys but also for the RA's guns. 6th Regt had already lost its guns but 78th Bty, 35th Regt, which had borrowed RAF tractors to tow two of their guns from P II, were forced to abandon them only three-quarters of a mile from the port because of the congestion. 95th Bty lost one gun on the retreat from Branti for the same reason. Their problems did not end when they reached the harbour.

Chaos reigned in Oosthaven although the Japanese were nowhere near (and in fact did not reach the port for another four or five days). Baillie reported:

'Ships seemed to leave the port at the discretion of their Masters. In this way valuable equipment was left behind. A ship had been detailed for the regiment but while the Quartermaster was abroad [sic] supervising the stowage of equipment it suddenly put to sea leaving a lorry-load of predictors and height-finders behind.'[93]

48th Regt suffered even more:

'The guns, vehicles and stores of 49 and 95 Batteries were on the quay, as well as a large quantity of stores marked "O.O. Singapore" and others intended for the force which was to have landed in Sumatra. There was no sign of any enemy activity whatsoever, but the masters of the ships sent to evacuate the batteries refused to wait while vehicles, etc. were loaded on board, and insisted on sailing as soon as the guns and ammunition had been embarked.'[94]

This meant losing the vehicles they had so painstakingly acquired in Java besides one gun that dropped between the ship and the quay when the ship's tackle broke, not to mention a load of kitbags and a quantity of stores. These were all losses which were hard, if not impossible, to replace.

So between 17th and 18th February, 48th LAA Regt bade farewell to Sumatra and Oosthaven, having seen no action there. It had merely moved around the landscape, lost guns and equipment, and stored up trouble for the future. Oosthaven was notorious for its malaria-ridden climate and over the coming days as the Japanese air raids intensified on Java, men would be going sick just when they were needed to defend the island.

I have a strong suspicion that Jack Gunn's passage back to Java was interrupted. He claimed that a ship he was on in the war was sunk, either by torpedo or by a mine, and gave a graphic account of the affair but without exact information about where or when it happened. It was obviously not on the journey out, as the convoy records do not report any

93 TNA: CAB 106/20
94 Macartney-Filgate, op. cit., p24

sinkings, and it was not when he was a prisoner of war, therefore it must have happened at this point, his only other sea voyage before captivity. Japanese submarines were certainly active in the area and some vessels leaving Sumatra were sunk. Jack's wife told me that he had been posted missing at one point but she had received a telegram from him very soon after asking her to wire him cash from The Business as he was short of funds. She contacted the War Office to tell them she had heard from her husband and knew where he was. Would they like to know too? Yes, they would. Whatever happened, Jack had made it back to Java.

Six: Java – command and control

While it is clear that information, instructions and assistance from a higher command were in very short supply for the Royal Artillery units in the NEI, it is gratifying to report that at regimental level and below the officers and men seemed to show remarkable initiative in dealing with the situations they found themselves in. 49th and 95th LAA Batteries had lost their transport in Sumatra. Very well, new transport would just have to be found and found it was. A convoy of lorries was sent from RHQ in Batavia to Merak on the west coast of Java where most of the men, their surviving guns and equipment had been landed. Here C Troop 95th Bty had set up six guns as temporary AA defence for the port while equipment was loaded and guns were hitched up to the newly-acquired trucks. Perhaps one reason why a number of 48th Regt's personnel went on to Batavia by train was because there were large quantities of stores simply jettisoned on the quayside with little or no indication of ownership. By now the regiment had experience of kitting itself out in the absence of any organised RASC operation and it seems to have done well out of the situation. Macartney-Filgate speaks only of 'at least' thirty Tommy guns being brought safely back to Batavia but it is difficult to believe that the refit stopped there!

Jack Gunn felt all his life that he and his comrades had been betrayed by Churchill. He complained bitterly of being landed in the Far East with no weapons or equipment but plenty of silk dressing gowns. However, it was not only the British AA units that suffered these sorts of problems as Chapter IV of the History of the 2/2 Australian Pioneer Battalion makes clear. A draft of this survives in the National Archives in London.[95] Arriving in Sumatra on 'Orcades' on 15th February and ordered to disembark to form part of 'Boost Force' which Steele intended to use against the Japanese, the writer comments that the battalion:

'was in no condition to fight. Some units possessed no arms at all as transport and stores had not accompanied the troops ... but the most serious problem was the shortage of ammunition. Owing to the foresight and insistence of the C.O. Lt Col J M Williams men of the battalion carried 50 rounds, but some units could manage only five rounds – the equivalent of 20 seconds rapid fire.'

It was with some relief that they heard when they reached shore that the situation:

'had deteriorated rapidly during the afternoon and that the Japanese were then only 20 miles away'

so they were to re-embark. Eventually 'Orcades' made her way into Tandjong Priok harbour, Java, at midday on 17th February.

---

[95] TNA: CAB 106/140

Here they received 'a somewhat boisterous greeting' from Australians troops already there. Some were reinforcements from Fremantle destined for Singapore but unloaded in Java as Singapore was effectively lost while others were deserters from the stricken island who were now engaged in looting on the quayside 'and behaving rather badly'. These were promptly seen off by a patrol from the ship and later rounded up with the reinforcements and taken into the Australian force or deported back to Australia. The new arrivals were disembarked the next day then made to wait around the docks for two hours while rumour and counter-rumour did the rounds. The battalion historian comments:

'In a less disciplined unit the speedy Japanese advance, lack of information, rapid readjustments to plans, orders and counter-orders, rain and uncertainty must have affected morale, but the men had been battle-tested and accepted the general confusion philosophically.'

That was fortunate for them but wherever you look, the situation appears to be chaotic. So what exactly was going on in Java? The fall of Singapore on 15th February only just preceded the fall of Sumatra. It was inevitable from the start and confused and bloody in its conclusion. Many books have been written covering the whole Malayan campaign in great detail and explaining how it unfolded and why, so little more needs to be said here. Perhaps the saddest thing I have read summing up the whole fiasco is a comment attributed to AVM Pulford to General Percival, just before the former left on his abortive attempt to reach the NEI:

'I suppose you and I will be held responsible for this, but God knows we did our best with what little we had been given.'

Years of neglect - no money, no men, no new equipment, no defences and no sensible plans - could not be made good overnight but scapegoats could be found and an army abandoned to its fate.

To understand the situation in Java in all its confusion we must ask where and what command structures were there for the British Army and the RAF. I am not going to deal with the Royal Navy as they play no major part in the story in this book. In Singapore there was a clearly-defined Army HQ headed up by GOC Malaya Command (Percival) and for the RAF (and RAAF) there was Far East Command under Pulford. Each had its staff organisation dealing with all aspects of the forces at each CO's disposal. The NEI (and Java) was a very different matter as we shall see.

First the RAF, as this has rather more material available to throw light on what they actually thought was or should be happening. As Singapore became untenable, personnel were evacuated, mainly by sea, either to Sumatra or Java, or even if possible back to India or Australia. All evacuations became more difficult as January turned into February as the Japanese command of the Malay Peninsula not only gave them airfields for their air forces but also allowed them to control traffic by sea around the area, particularly through the Straits of Malacca. This cut off a vital direct route to India, not just for Allied reinforcements but also for any vessels carrying refugees from the conflict. By early February, the Japanese had superiority by air and sea for miles around Singapore. This not only made reinforcement virtually impossible but also meant that there was no hope of evacuating forces in any structured way. Who survived the trip to freedom and who did not was a lottery.

AVM P C Maltby had arrived in Singapore on 4th January 1942 as Chief of Staff designate to Lt-Gen Sir H R Pownall, who had been appointed C-in-C Far East in succession to ACM Brooke-Popham w.e.f. 27th December 1941. Pownall's appointment must break some records for shortness of tenure as his position was rendered obsolete by Wavell's assumption of command of ABDACOM on 15th January 1942, at which point Pownall became his Chief of Staff. Maltby meanwhile, with Wavell's agreement, had made himself Pulford's deputy in Singapore on 12th January. Undoubtedly Pulford was worn out by his struggles to run his command but his determination not to leave until as many as possible of his men were evacuated meant that he did not leave until 13th February. The boat he was travelling in was attacked by Japanese aircraft and forced to beach on an island off the coast of Sumatra with little food and no medical stores in an inhospitable and unhealthy climate. Pulford sadly did not survive this.

Meanwhile on 10th February Wavell had ordered the evacuation of all remaining RAF personnel to the NEI and Maltby was appointed AOC WESGROUP there (effectively the RAF and the RAAF in the area[96]) under the aegis of Abdair, the air division of ABDACOM, w.e.f. the next day. Maltby accordingly flew to Sumatra, where he made no friends amongst squadron personnel slogging it out flying and maintaining aircraft in the jungle in appalling monsoon conditions by suggesting they could take more care of their appearance, before departing in his pristine uniform to Java two days later.

His comfortable journey was not one shared by many of his officers or men. The lucky ones were the pilots and aircrew who could fly aircraft off from Singapore to Sumatra or those senior officers who could get a seat on the few Dutch transport aircraft operating in the region. For the rest, evacuation was a hairy ordeal as it was for Pulford. Maltby admits in his published despatch that there was a lack of suitable shipping for both men and equipment at Singapore and that Japanese air raids on the docks lead to great problems with loading ships:

---

[96] TNA: AIR 23/2123: para 450

'Conditions at the docks became confused as the scale and intensity of air attack increased. Plans made for the embarkation of personnel and stores were disorganised. Units became split up and personnel became separated from their equipment.'[97]

And once out on the open seas, they were at the mercy of Japanese air and sea attacks. Pulford was not the only senior officer lost; others included A/Cdre C O F Modin, AO i/c Administration, Air HQ, Far East Command, and Gp Capt E B Rice, former AOC 224 Group. They were taken prisoner along with Sqn Ldrs Clouston and Howell, ex-488 and 243 Sqns respectively, when the ASR launch they were escaping from Singapore on was captured by the Japanese. W/Cdr R A Chignall, formerly CO RAF Kallang, had been killed earlier when the boat suffered an air attack. All this impacted negatively on the speed with which an organisation could be set up in Java and also on the personnel available to staff it.

The other problem was that there was no effective RAF organisation there until mid-February yet men were flooding into the ports. Maltby estimated that between 12th and 18th February approximately 10,000 RAF of all ranks evacuated from Singapore and Sumatra 'arrived in considerable confusion in Western Java'. This was in addition to RAF personnel who had arrived directly in Java, such as the force that sailed in with Convoy DM 2 and that had already been in the country for a week by the time the main influx arrived. Maltby comments on the chaotic scenes on the quaysides at Tandjong Priok as refugees coming into Java mixed with refugees trying to leave the island and:

'the quays, warehouses and the roads leading from them rapidly became congested with an inextricable confusion of merchandise, equipment, M.T., abandoned cars and goods of every description.'

Unfortunately, owing to the problems both in Singapore and in Oosthaven, little of this equipment and MT belonged to the RAF but what aircraft they still had after the evacuations from both places were arriving at Javanese airfields from 15th February.

'It was from personnel and equipment so placed that a maximum air fighting strength with ancillary services had to be evolved, and surpluses evacuated from Java, during the twelve days before the Japanese landed.'

Maltby arrived with a small staff at Soekaboemi west of Bandoeng on 14th February to set up his WESGROUP HQ. This assumed administrative command of the RAF and RAAF units in Java two days later, operational control remaining with Abdair for the time being. Squadrons were allocated airfields, with RAF Station Commanders alongside the Dutch ones where ML units shared the aerodrome with them. No 225 (B) Group

---

[97] TNA: CAB 106/86: Maltby's despatch

and No 226 (F) Group from Sumatra were reformed, at least for the present, and a Fighter Ops room, a local warning system and RDF (Radar) stations were constructed. Maltby exaggerates a little here as to how much was achieved before the Japanese struck as the RDF stations were not in fact operational until around 27th February, while the Fighter Ops organisation had considerable problems with directing fighters onto incoming raids. Unfortunately the radios used by the Dutch and British fighter aircraft used different crystals so the British fighter ops organisation could only talk to the British aircraft. Other networks had to be built up for the Dutch.

Assessments were also made of what units and manpower would be required so that surplus personnel could be evacuated to other theatres where they would be of some use. RAF Base, Batavia, under the command of A/Cdre B J Silly from 18th February, had theoretically been established since 24th January:

'to organise the reception, sorting and despatch of personnel arriving by sea from Singapore and Sumatra and of air reinforcements from the Middle East and the United Kingdom.' Presumably it had not been informed of the imminent arrival of Convoy DM 2 as the commander of the RAF detachment on that convoy received no orders when it reached Java. By the time Silly took over, it administered five transit camps in Batavia and another one in Buitenzorg further south. In all, 12,000 men went through these camps according to Maltby's despatch. How accurate this was I cannot say but just compare the numbers to the British and Australian Army personnel on the island on 23rd February: 4,992 and 2,920 of all ranks respectively, a total of 7,912.[98] Most were at least in theory likely to have been of some use in defending Java while the RAF men were largely unarmed and usually without any kind of ground fighting training. If they had only been trained infantry then Java might have had some hope of being held and history would have been very different. As it was, they were a total liability but one which it was almost impossible to shift. Getting them away from the island became more difficult as every day passed and shipping became scarcer and Japanese control of air and sea became more complete. In theory, though, the RAF had a HQ on Java to run its operations and to organise its manpower, whether it was with the squadrons or in transit, but what about the Army?

No attempt was made to set up a British GHQ for the British Army or Commonwealth detachments fighting with it on Java and there was no GOC British troops on the island until around 23rd February 1942, when Sitwell was promoted to Major-General and took on the role as ABDACOM was leaving. This was abandonment on an epic scale and the buck must stop with the War Office. There can be no excuses for it. The War Office

---

[98] WO 106/3302: Defence of Java. 'GHQ' has been deducted: ABDACOM staff.

knew that units were due to land on the island even if it had not been their original destination – it had diverted them there as part of the British commitment to ABDACOM. The British Army had a structure within which all the pieces knew their place. It operated as a machine. How were the units on the island to be directed, equipped, provisioned or used in any meaningful fashion without the organisation provided by a local garrison HQ there? Proper provision should have been made for them.

In practice, the gap was filled in some fashion by branches or officers of ABDACOM, which was not, of course, a British Army HQ. It was the beginnings of a Command structure aimed at co-ordinating the strategic operations of the forces of the four Allied nations in the south-west Pacific area. It was not intended to have any responsibility for the 'internal administration' of the forces under its command but, as the report on its activities after its demise explains:

'In practise, however, it became necessary for the Intendant General's Branch of ABDACOM staff to make all administrative arrangements in respect of many units and details which arrived in the Netherlands East Indies during the later stages of the existence of ABDACOM.'[99]

This is a good attempt to put a positive gloss on an appalling situation. Most of the 'units and details' that it had to make arrangements for had been sent there specifically to defend the NEI and should have had their own organisation to support them, however rudimentary at first.

Before the departure of ABDACOM, it is clear that officers commanding British AA units approached ABDACOM or Sitwell's Brigade HQ with their problems and trusted to them to fulfil the roles of a GHQ. Operational orders came down via Brig Sitwell's brigade staff as Lt-Col Humphries, commanding 77th Regt, relates in his post-war report.[100] According to his own post-war report to the War Office,[101] Sitwell was then Anti-Aircraft Advisor to Wavell, Commander-in-Chief, South West Pacific Command, a post he had been co-opted to on his arrival on Java to fill a gap in the ABDACOM staff, as so many officers were. Presumably, though I have no direct information on this, his brigade staff went with him and when officers like Saunders, Humphries and Macartney-Filgate speak of GHQ, this is what they mean.

But the situation was far from satisfactory. Saunders once again provides a vivid insight of the problems commanding officers faced on a daily basis. One reason for his visit to 'G.H.Q.' between 17th-19th February was that:

---

[99] TNA: CAB 106/29, para 10
[100] TNA: WO 106/2539: Lt Col H R Humphries' report
[101] TNA: WO 106/5983 and others

'Since arrival on the island, and the interview I had on board ship with the G.S.O.1., no orders of any kind whatever appertaining to 'G', 'A', or 'Q' matters had been received.

No information had been forthcoming on ammunition supply, rations or pay.'[102]

He was able to add with satisfaction:

'Twelve hours at G.H.Q. enabled all necessary details on these subjects to be settled.'

Macartney-Filgate's trips to Sitwell and ABDACOM on behalf of 48th Regt appear to have been less fruitful!

What was left of ABDACOM HQ after British, Australian and American staff officers were generally evacuated from Java was turned over to the Dutch and absorbed into the AHK, their GHQ. Wavell promoted Sitwell to Major-General on 23rd February in command of the British, Australian and Indian troops in Java in readiness for his own departure from the island, ordering him 'to continue the fight for the defence of Java with the utmost determination.'[103] It is probable that Sitwell constructed such a staff as he needed in his new role as GOC from his former 16th AA Brigade staff but his appointment did not make things any easier for the British and Commonwealth troops. He was in fact a powerless figurehead and had been selected as the most senior dispensable Army officer on the spot. He was under the operational control of Lt-Gen Ter Poorten, commander of the KNIL, while orders for the RA regiments would come to him from van Oyen. In all matters relating to the Australians he had to consult with Brigadier A S Blackburn, VC, AIF, and he had to use AVM Maltby, who would be Senior British Officer on the island, as his 'channel of communication' with 'higher military authorities' – which were of course far away from Java. Apparently Sitwell's reaction was that 'big game shooting in Java has always been one of his ambitions in life.'[104] That, ironically, was probably all he would have been allowed to do.

The RA regiments were fortunate in that they did have some sort of command structure, even if it did often fall short of providing them with the instructions, intelligence, help and support they needed. The other British army units in Java were not so lucky. I have no definite information to suggest what the chain of command might have been for the seventeen-hundred-odd other British troops of all other Corps and Regiments on the island, but the AIF forces on Java were in a much better position altogether in this respect. They were all part of the first detachment of Lavarack's 1

[102] TNA: WO 106/2563
[103] TNA: WO 106/3302: Telegram, Wavell to the War Office, 24.02.42
[104] ibidem: Telegram, Wavell to British Joint Staff Mission, Washington, and the War Office, 25.02.42

Australian Corps that had arrived on the 'Orcades' on 17th February after a confusing time in Sumatra and had now been formed into a brigade under the newly-promoted Brigadier Blackburn.

Arthur Blackburn was a force to be reckoned with. Having qualified as a lawyer, he enlisted as a private in the 10th Battalion, AIF, in October 1914, and served all through the Gallipoli campaign. He was commissioned second lieutenant in August 1915 and later served on the Western Front. On 23 July 1916 at Pozières, he commanded a party of fifty men which, in the face of fierce opposition, destroyed an enemy strongpoint and captured nearly 400 yards of trench. He personally led four successive bombing parties, many members of which were killed. He was awarded the Victoria Cross 'for most conspicuous bravery' for this exploit. Shortly afterwards he was evacuated sick, invalided back to Australia and discharged on medical grounds. Between the wars he returned to the law but also served in the militia, being promoted lieutenant-colonel in 1939 and taking command of a motorised cavalry regiment. He ceased legal practice in 1940 and was appointed to command the 2nd/3rd Australian Machine-Gun Battalion, AIF, which fought under his command in Syria in 1941. Blackburn, as the senior Allied officer present, accepted the surrender of Damascus on 21st June that year, and was a member of the Allied Control Commission for Syria after the campaign finished. Now he was in the NEI with the advantage of experienced troops under his command. What he lacked in years of training and experience was compensated for to a great degree by his personal qualities. He was brave, intelligent and level-headed and knew how to deal with people. While the senior officers of 1 Australian Corps remained on Java he reported to them.

Lavarack had arrived on the island with some of his Corps HQ staff on 26th January and was under no illusions whatsoever about the situation in the Far East. He had made many enemies as an officer in the tiny Australian regular army during the interwar years with his outspoken views on the failings of the 'Singapore Strategy'. While he was not an easy man to get along with, and was probably even less so when his doubts about the Singapore Strategy were proved to be well-founded, he seems to have formed a very positive relationship with Wavell when he served under him in the Western Desert in 1941. However, he was not at all impressed by the suggestion that once his Corps arrived in theatre it should be split in two, half in Sumatra and half in central Java, with the Dutch KNIL forces in between in Western Java.

Quite apart from the obvious difficulties facing any commander of a force divided in this way, his reconnaissances in southern Sumatra and central Java in late January and early February convinced him that the troops under his command could not be deployed in time to defend the NEI.

Besides unrealistic estimates of what the combined Allied forces in the area could achieve in the present situation, the major problem facing his force, as we have seen from the report of 2/2 Pioneer Battalion, was the same old problem that had hampered the RA regiments on their deployment: his ships had not been loaded in a way that allowed instant action. It would require up to three weeks both to sort out equipment, weapons, ammunition and supplies after it was unloaded from the ships and to allow the units themselves to be sorted out after disembarkation.

On 13th February he sent an appreciation of the situation to the Chief of the Australian General Staff, General Sturdee, for the information of Prime Minister Curtin. Recognising that the imminent fall of Singapore would release large Japanese forces for further action, he did not believe that the one Australian division that would shortly arrive in the NEI could do anything, along with the scanty Dutch forces available, to save Sumatra, while the arrival of another division would not be enough to save Java. Neither could be ready to fight in time to make any difference. Wavell sent a similar report to the Combined Chiefs of Staff (CCOS) and the War Office in London and suggested Burma or Australia as a more suitable destination for the Corps. Sturdee saw things somewhat differently and, seeing little possibility of holding Java, considered the only suitable destination for 1 Corps was Australia. This would form a good strategic base for offensive action against Japan for the future while safeguarding Australia in the immediate term.

Sadly what seemed eminent good sense to the Australians did not appear in the same light to either the British, particularly Prime Minister Winston Churchill, and the Americans, who from a distance of thousands of miles saw 1 Australian Corps as the saviours of Burma and the back road to China. Oblivious to the difficulties of deployment, which would be just the same in Burma as in the NEI, both Churchill and the USA put pressure on Curtin and his CGS to back down – luckily without success. Had they succeeded, the Australians would have become just another few thousand miserable prisoners of war as Burma collapsed before the Japanese onslaught as rapidly as Malaya had done.

Basically there was fundamental difference in viewpoints between the USA and Britain on one side and the Australians and NEI Dutch on the other. The two great powers were leaders of empires and the imperial necessity was at all times the priority: defend the heart of the British Empire; preserve India, the Imperial jewel with all its resources and manpower; keep open the road link to China. Wavell's assessment:

'Burma and Australia are absolutely vital for the war against Japan. Loss of Java, though severe blow from every point of view, would not be fatal' was fine from their point of view but could not be expected to strike the same chord with the NEI Dutch and the Australians who were thinking of their own homes.

They were effectively fighting in their own backyards; it affected how they understand the situation and where they thought they should fight. In addition, as offshoots of great maritime empires, they had each looked to their mother country to defend them and both expected Singapore to give them protection against Japanese expansion. The fall of Singapore was a mighty psychological blow to both, quite apart from the actual physical danger that this left them in. They had already drawn closer together to face the common enemy, both in pre-war discussions and in early military action in Timor, and as van Mook's conversation with La Vallette makes clear, the NEI Dutch felt they had much more in common with the Australians than with their other two major allies in the area.

So where did all this leave Blackburn's force? Originally disembarked from 'Orcades' on 19th February 1942, it was to prove politically impossible to remove them once the situation in the area deteriorated even further a few days later. Blackburn, however, was not a man to sit back and allow things to happen to him and his force without doing his best to ensure that if they were going down, they would not go down without the chance of putting up a good fight. At first he received his orders from the officers of 1 Australian Corps, starting with Major-General A S Allen, commanding 7th Division, AIF, who had arrived in Java a few days before him. These directed him to split up his force to provide airfield defence for five airfields in Western Java.[105] Thus it was that a detachment of 2/2 Pioneer Battalion was alarmed by automatic weapons fire nearby when they were guarding Tjililitan aerodrome, only to find out that it was not a Japanese raiding party but a British LAA battery testing its Bren guns. Could it be that some of the arms 49th and 95th Batteries had picked up a few days before at Merak had been shared with their sister battery, 242nd, which was providing the AA defence for Tjililitan?

In these first few days, Blackburn (and his men) dealt with their problems of shortages of equipment and supplies in the same way as the RA units had done before them: setting up their own supply train and scrounging and scavenging. This initial period was a chance for him to size up the military situation in Java. Thus when Allen and other 1 Australian Corps staff officers sailed away in 'Orcades' on 21st February and Blackburn was promoted to GOC AIF forces in Java, he was ready to reorganise the forces at his command into a fighting brigade and had his own ideas as to the best

---

[105] TNA: CAB 106/139: Report of Brigadier A S Blackburn, GOC AIF Java. The airfields were Kemajoram, Tjisaork, Tjililitan, Semplak and Tjileungsir, but not Kalidjati as some accounts state.

use for them. He had now been put under the control of General Ter Poorten, C-in-C of the NEI forces in Java, with orders:

'to assist the NEI forces to the utmost of my ability in resisting the Japanese and in the defence of JAVA and to do all in my power to delay the Japanese forces in their advance towards Australia.'[106]

On 23rd February he had 'a long conference' with Maj-Gen W Schilling, GOC KNIL, Western Java, and pointed out to him that his forces, mostly battle-hardened infantrymen, were wasted scattered in penny-packets defending Javanese airfields, a task that could fall equally well to less-experienced troops, leaving Blackburn's men free for the serious fighting that would undoubtedly come sooner rather than later. The Australians were under no illusions about the training and composition of the KNIL: Sturdee had described them as 'well-equipped Home Guards rather than an army capable of undertaking active operations in the field'.[107] This contrasts sadly with the impression found in British reports, like Maltby's and the ABDACOM despatch, where the emphasis seems to be more on the number of troops the KNIL could muster rather than their composition and training. In the kind of war that was to come, composition, training and experience would make a great deal of difference. Incidentally, Blackburn and his forces had an asset that the British forces on Java did not have – a booklet on Japanese tactics. This was probably a draft version of the one that became compulsory reading for all Australian Army officers and NCOs in this theatre, having been drawn up by two of Lavarack's senior staff officers following an interview with Lt-Col Stewart of the Argyll and Sutherland Highlanders after his evacuation on Wavell's orders from Singapore.[108] Such a booklet could have been extremely useful for the British in the days to come, especially 49th LAA and 12th HAA Batteries.

Whether it was a feeling of 'being in the same boat' existing between the two junior partners of the ABDACOM alliance or whether it was simply based on personalities, it appears that Brig Blackburn got on well with the NEI Dutch. The next day, the 24th, he was not amused to discover that his orders had been changed again. He was now under the command of Brig Sitwell, 16th AA Brigade, newly promoted to Maj-Gen Sitwell, GOC British Forces Java, as ABDACOM was leaving the island. He drove from Batavia to Bandoeng where he 'interviewed' Maj-Gen C E M Lloyd, Deputy Intendant General of ABDACOM and the highest-ranking Australian staff officer still in Java.[109] Wavell saw Blackburn the next day and personally repeated to him the orders he had already received from Lavarack, adding:

---

[106] TNA: CAB 106/139
[107] 'Australia in the War of 1939–1945; Series 1; Vol IV', Chap 20: p445
[108] ibidem, note 6, p443
[109] TNA: CAB 106/139.

'that the troops under my [*Blackburn's*] command were practically the only British troops remaining in JAVA who were equipped and trained to fight as the English troops in JAVA were mainly RA without guns and ground personnel of the RAF and for this reason I was to use my troops in offensive operations against the Japanese wherever possible.'

Blackburn did not need any further prompting. He visited Sitwell and 'discussed very fully with him the tactical situation', outlining the plans he had made with Schilling and pointing out the deficiencies of his own force in artillery, armour and signalling. Sitwell appears to have supported him without interference and provided him with whatever he could, going so far as to strip 48th Regt of their signal section to make good his deficiencies in this department – Blackburn had been without any signals or wireless equipment in Java up to this point. It seems that the determined Australian Brigadier was more than a match for Sitwell and plans went ahead for 'Blackforce', as it was known, to form a striking force alongside the KNIL under Schilling in Western Java to counter any Japanese attack in the area.

Nevertheless, however effective or ineffective the commanding officer of a force was, several thousand British and Commonwealth soldiers were abandoned in a military limbo, with no effective GOC or GHQ and, after the departure of ABDACOM, no real interest from the War Office or COS in London. Java was a lost cause and there were other battles to fight that might be won. The British units left behind were a symbol of the British determination to fight alongside their allies in the Pacific region in spite of the loss of Singapore. They were there to show that Britain would still try to defend its Empire and Commonwealth and that Dutch sacrifices were acknowledged and truly appreciated, even though the units concerned to could do nothing to stop the inevitable catastrophe.

And to make matters worse for these forces, if worse they could be, Java was part of the NEI. It was effectively a foreign country with a different language and one that few British would have known. They had only just arrived there, some after traumatic evacuation from elsewhere, some after diversion from a previous destination. While the armed forces in residence there were allies, and co-operative and helpful from all accounts, they had their own organisation and systems. Communications and any air control systems were largely in the hands of their hosts. 'Knowing the country' was an ideal they had little time to achieve. Medical provision, intelligence, supply of food, equipment, weapons, ammunition and reinforcements, all things that they would have looked to a local GHQ to co-ordinate, were in chaos or non-existent. How was it that the British Army left its officers and men there with only ABDACOM to provide a fall-back?

It also raises a question about the figures given for British and Australian troops on Java in the Order of Battle that Wavell submitted to the War Office[110] on 23rd February 1942. How could anyone be sure just how many British troops were on the island without a British GHQ? How many British soldiers were there unaccounted for if they had not been absorbed into formations recognised by ABDACOM? We know there were a couple of hundred Australian refugees from Singapore who were taken under Blackburn's wing but British unattached infantry (for example) number only thirty-two ORs from four named regiments. It is possible that the lack of a GHQ meant more than the difficulties listed above for the established units: it could have meant a total failure to provide for those who had managed to escape thus far. It also explains why the War Office did not know where Jack Gunn was for a while, even though he had clearly got back to Allied territory as he could send a telegram asking for money. Without a GHQ and proper Army organisation at the docks, he would not be picked up on the radar until he got back to his own unit, which could take several days.

Another consequence of the lack of a GHQ and the structure it would produce was that each unit that landed had to reinvent the wheel and establish its own supply train. This would, of course, have been a lot easier if ABDACOM had ever reached its full establishment but it attempted to make good the deficiencies in its staffing and equipment by absorbing into itself units and elements of units arriving in Java. Thus there was a shortage of experienced supply officers at Tandjong Priok when Convoy DM 2 arrived because these had been diverted up to ABDACOM in Bandoeng and Blackburn lost his CCS on disembarking in Java as it was whisked away to form the basis of an Allied General Hospital, also in Bandoeng. However necessary this latter was, it meant that 'Blackforce' was without a field ambulance section when it went into action a few days later. Administratively ABDACOM had neither the personnel nor the time to organise Java properly but it wasn't in its remit to do so anyway!

Consequently a great deal fell to the NEI Dutch and, while it has become common practice in some later British accounts to blame them for lack of co-operation and failure to deliver, there is no reason to believe from reading the original sources that the Dutch were less than helpful in any possible way. Deficiencies arose because the resources were not readily available to them any more than to the allies who had suddenly descended upon them in large numbers. You cannot magically conjure up unlimited numbers of armoured cars or produce extensive and sophisticated communications or air-raid warning systems any more than you can produce at will an endless supply of rations or ammunition. They seem to have done their best with what was available, produced liaison officers to

---

[110] TNA: WO 106/3302

smooth the way and accepted being a junior partner within their own country with commendable goodwill. The fault lines would show when the situation worsened and a sense of betrayal would sour the Dutch mood.

This would not be very long coming. Wavell was in complete agreement with Lavarack regarding the possibilities of a long-term defence of the NEI. His report to the War Office on his time as Supreme Commander ABDACOM makes interesting reading.[111] I do not believe he had relished leaving India on this assignment and was probably not encouraged by being told by the COS in London in early January that:

'they themselves did not know what Allied resources would be at my disposal and that they assumed that this information would be supplied by the Allied representatives attached to my staff.'

Quite apart from not knowing what he had to do the job with, he saw from very early on that the NEI were indefensible for important geographical reasons if for no other. Once Sumatra to the west and the chain of islands to the east of Java have fallen – and the Japanese pincer movement achieved that by 20th February – Java could no longer be reinforced by air. Bomber aircraft could not use the route via India and Sumatra and fighter aircraft from Australia required the adjacent islands as staging posts. The Japanese command of the sea was becoming more overwhelming with every day that passed, so surface transport was finding it harder to reinforce, to resupply and to evacuate key or unnecessary personnel.

Wavell did not wait nearly this long before making warning noises to the CCOS in Washington and the COS and Prime Minister in London. Telegrams winged their way back emphasising the difficulties he faced. Thus one on 13th February includes the information:

'If Southern SUMATRA is lost prolonged defence of Java becomes unlikely. ... Garrison is weak for size of island. ... From air aspect defence of Java is a hard matter without Southern SUMATRA it is formidable. ... Naval view is that loss of South SUMATRA would render reinforcement and maintenance of JAVA almost impossible. ... It is clear that retention of South SUMATRA essential for successful defence of Java.'[112]

On 16th February when Sumatra was falling he spelled out the situation to the War Office and the British Joint Staff Mission in Washington in a 'Most Immediate' and 'Most Secret' cipher telegram:

'With shipping and escorts available enemy can probably engage four divisions against Java within next 10 to 14 days and reinforce with two or

---

[111] TNA: WO 106/2556: Despatch on operations in South West Pacific, January 15th – February 25th 1942 by General Sir Archibald Wavell, GCB, CMG, MC, A-D-C
[112] ibidem

more divisions within month. Maximum scale of air attack possibly 400 to 500 fighters (including Carrier-borne) and 300 to 400 bombers.'[113]

His slim resources to counter this were clearly delineated:

'Maximum of 3 to 4 cruisers and about 10 destroyers . . . three weak Dutch divisions of only seventeen battalions . . . with little artillery and few light tanks . . . One squadron 3 Hussars and complete with light tanks and about 3000 Australians . . . These have rifles only and no transport. . . . several thousand R.A.F. ground personnel available but proportion unarmed. American. One field artillery regt. but without full equipment. Combined Dutch American British A/A 56 Heavy and 44 Light guns 12 more tomorrow. . . . about 50 fighters possibly rising to 75, 65 medium or dive bombers 20 heavy bombers additional 50 fighters may be received before end of month . . . Lack of adequate warning system increases difficulties defence.'

He continues that only local naval and air superiority, which he does not have and cannot achieve with the forces at his command, will stop an invasion. Once landed, there is nothing to prevent the enemy 'rapidly occupying the main naval and air bases' on Java and even if they were landed, 1 Australian Corps cannot be operational before the attack begins. It is improbable that naval and air reinforcements could also reach the island in time to be usefully deployed. The long and short of it is that resources could be used better elsewhere, preferably Burma.

Wavell had to wait four days for his reply as the various Allies were consulted and the US President and Churchill mulled over the wording. He received a telegram on 20th February from the CCOS, Washington, setting out the situation in an uncompromising manner:

'Java should be defended with the utmost resolution by all combatant troops at present in the island for whom arms are available. Every day gained is of importance. There should be no withdrawal of troops or air forces of any nationality and no surrender.'[114]

However, he must have been considerably relieved to receive the offer of the post of C-in-C India once again from Churchill in a personal telegram sent the same day. This also set out the major powers' attitude to the Far East situation quite clearly:

'The President's mind is turning to United States looking after the Australian flank and we concentrating everything on defending or regaining Burma and Burma Road' ... 'of course after everything possible has been done to prolong the resistance of Java.'[115]

[113] TNA: WO 106/3302
[114] ibidem
[115] TNA: CAB 120/805: telegram from Churchill to Wavell, 20.02.1942.

'Everything possible' was defined in a telegram from the CCOS, Joint Staff Mission, Washington:

'All men of fighting units for whom there are arms must continue to fight without thought of evacuation but air forces which can more usefully operate in battle from bases outside Java and all air personnel for who there are aircraft and such troops as cannot contribute to the defence of Java should be withdrawn.'[116]

Thus came the green light to evacuate ABDACOM staff and as many RAF as could no longer play a useful role in theatre for whom transport could be found but this decision also sealed the fate of 49th Bty and a number of other Allied units.

To assist him in carrying out these orders, he could 'augment' the defence of Java with whatever naval forces he could acquire and 'with U.S. aircraft now at your disposal assembling in Australia.' Reinforcements to land forces were not coming his way (they were off to Burma or Australia) and the US were carrying out combined naval and air operations to the east of New Guinea (implying that these might help relieve the pressure). In short, do the impossible with the inadequate. Not surprisingly, the COS received a telegram from Wavell with a thinly-veiled hint that it might be a good idea to withdraw his headquarters.

To be fair to him, there was little he could do in the situation. He and his command structure were effectively trapped in Java and unable to fulfil their primary function of co-ordinating Allied forces over the whole south-west Pacific area. Instead, they were becoming involved in the minutiae of defending one small part that could not be reinforced or re-supplied sufficiently to save itself. There was no logical reason why they should not be withdrawn in the very near future, even though such an act would have a very detrimental effect on confidence among the NEI Dutch.

It would also cause considerable problems to British Army units on an island where they had no proper GHQ. Even now, the Royal Artillery anti-aircraft batteries were moving around Java from airfield to airfield as priorities changed. Both Saunders' 21st Regt and Humphries' 77th HAA wandered a thousand miles around eastern and central Java between 12th February and 8th March. They could have been forgiven for feeling there was no consistent overall plan. 48th Regt did not move so much. 242nd Bty, 'after numerous moves to and fro between Kemajoram and Tjililitan',[117] was deployed at Tjililitan, ten miles south-east of Batavia, with two guns at Tandjong Priok seaplane base. 95th Bty, after its excursion to Sumatra, was

---

[116] TNA: WO 106/3302: telegram 21.02.42
[117] Macartney-Filgate, op cit, p25

now off to Andir aerodrome, a major Dutch military base two miles south-west of Bandoeng. For 49th LAA Bty, however, its fate was already sealed. On 19th February 1942, the order came to move to Kalidjati.

Seven: Anatomy of an airfield: Kalidjati

To understand some of the problems the British AA Regiments faced defending airfields in Java, it seems a good idea to look at one and see what happened in one particular case. Kalidjati is an excellent choice as it was the key to the defence of the island and more is known about it and the personnel involved there, the national forces both air and land, the problems they faced, etc. We can draw general conclusions of the sort of things that might occur anywhere as well as seeing the development of situations unique to Kalidjati that would be vital in the future.

Kalidjati was a major air force base for the ML, the Army Aviation Corps of the KNIL. When Rev Godfrey describes the airfield in his memoirs as 'a lonely aerodrome in the jungle north of the road from Batavia to Bandoeng', we must not confuse seclusion with insignificance. It lay about eighty miles east of Batavia on the vast alluvial plain that stretches across the north-west side of Java, an area of rubber plantations and general agriculture mixed with swamp and jungle. Kalidjati itself was 330 feet above sea level and there were ravines in the nearby countryside. The nearest town was Soebang, some seven miles ESE, while the village of Kalidjati itself was about three-quarters of a mile away on the road to Soebang. The RAF book on airfields in the NEI[118] remarks that 'The whole of Java has been well developed and communications are good' adding that the airfields and landing grounds were served by 'good metalled roads'. Kalidjati, like most of the other Java airfields, also had a railway station nearby: Pasir Boengoer, five miles due north of the aerodrome and accessed by a good road. This was on the main Batavia-Cheribon line, one of the major east-west arteries.

It was a large and important aerodrome. There were three grass runways, 'All-weather except after heavy rain': 'N.-S. 1,200 x 330 yards, E.-W. 1,000 x 400 yards, S.E.-N.W. 1,500 x 200 yards'. Naturally this does not coincide with the two plans of the airfield I have found but as these were sketch maps drawn after the events, one by Rev Godfrey and both described as not to scale, it merely serves to demonstrate some of the problems faced in dealing with the information available. Whatever the detail, its runways were much bigger than the metalled strips of P I, longer than those of the other main ML base at Andir aerodrome near Bandoeng, though a bit shorter than the three grass runways of P II. There was, however, no runway lighting for night operations. It also had wooded dispersal areas, unlike so many of the airfields in this theatre, though these were clearings in the surrounding bush and jungle rather than European-style concrete dispersals. Airfield defence was provided by a detachment of IIIrd Battalion

---

[118] TNA: AIR 23/4959

Anti-Aircraft Artillery (A III Ld), 'elderly KNIL personnel', with two 4cm Bofors guns and six 12.7mm machine-guns.[119]

The airfield was well supplied with hangars, workshops and other facilities, with a medley of permanent airfield offices, as this was the major flying training base for ML pilots while the ML Technical Services had workshops here and, besides some civil flying, it was both a fighter and bomber base for the Dutch military. The ML organisation was very different from the RAF. As I understand it from Boer, an afdeling of fighters on Java was around 16-18 aircraft, depending on date. ML afdelingen were grouped in Aircraft Groups – Vliegtuiggroep, abbreviated to Vl.G. – which were administrative units. Thus 2-Vl.G.IV would be the 2nd Afdeling of the IVth Vliegtuiggroep. 2-Vl.G.IV moved to Kalidjati on 15th February with their twelve Hurricane IIBs, reduced to ten by the 19th as two were lost in training accidents. Unfortunately, given that the Allies were so short of aircraft of all types, these Hurricanes never became fully operational in the campaign to defend Java as it was not possible to locate the correct crystals for their radio sets to link them up to Dutch air control systems. The RAF asked for them back on 24th February, or at least for their ML pilots to fly from RAF airfields under RAF radio control, but this was unacceptable to the Dutch so they stayed where they were. While they did fly defence sorties against the Japanese later, these were undertaken without any kind of control from the ground.

Three Dutch bomber squadrons were also there – 1-Vl.G.I, 2-Vl.G.I and 1-Vl.G.II flying Glenn Martin medium bombers, mostly WH-3As – but these were combined for operational deployment as an extended squadron from 17th February. Numbers available for operations were very low; on 18th February there were only seven operational Glenn Martins at Kalidjati out of the thirteen available that day to the ML. Like the RAF and RAAF, it had suffered a heavy rate of attrition during the earlier part of the campaign in the south west Pacific.

The base commander was a ML officer, Lt Col J J Zomer, whose official title was Commandant Luchtstrijdkrachten, local AOC NEI forces at Kalidjati. He had previously been an NEI liaison officer at Singapore and formed his staff at Kalidjati on 16th February. As the RAF insisted on an RAF commander for the 'British' operations and personnel on any joint airbase, RAF Station Kalidjati was also formed over the next few days. Nevertheless, Zomer still remained responsible for managing the base as a whole and arranged accommodation, food and fuel for the British. Communications followed two separate tracks: the established lines of communication remained under the control of the ML's Radio Service

---

[119] *'The Loss of Java'*, by P C Boer, published in English by NUS Press, Singapore, 2011, for the information here and for much else relating to the establishment of Kalidjati

while the RAF used a radio truck to communicate with HQ WESGROUP when atmospheric conditions allowed. Given this was the wet monsoon season with regular downpours and many thunderstorms, it was not a very reliable service. And of course, while the RAF reported to WESGROUP, the Dutch reported to ML HQ.

It seems very possible that Zomer had already met Gp Capt G F Whistondale, the officer appointed Station Commander RAF Kalidjati. Whistondale was a regular RAF officer who joined the RAF in the mid-1920s. His career followed an average sort of progression for an officer of his time and he was promoted to Squadron Leader in August 1938, by which time he was with 215 Sqn based at RAF Grantham.[120] By midsummer 1941, still a Squadron Leader, he was at Sungei Patani airfield in northern Malaya when he was called down to Singapore on the orders of A/Cdre C O F Modin, AO i/c Administration, and promoted to Wing Commander i/c Organisation. In this capacity he met F A Briggs[121], another locally-appointed man but one who came from the professional class in the region not from the RAF. Briggs served under him during Whistondale's time as W/Cdr Organisation when the latter might also have met Zomer. In November that year G O Hamilton-Ross[122] turned up in Singapore, having been appointed to the post by the Air Ministry in London, and he and Whistondale shared the work between them for the next few weeks until late January. Ross later went on to head the Organisation branch in Java.

When Gp Capt McCauley, commanding the RAAF squadrons in Malaya, moved to Sumatra to establish the RAF/RAAF bomber air base at P II, Whistondale took over as Station Commander, RAF Sembawang, Singapore. He does not seem to have been cut out to run an airfield if the reports of officers who met him are to be believed. Sqn Ldr Harper, OC 453 (F) Sqn, describes him thus:

'This officer was eccentric and often spent time discussing his hobby of stamp collecting with the airmen, when the Station Organisation was in urgent need of assistance.'[123]

The anonymous historian of 84 Sqn[124] took a dim view of conditions on the airfield when his squadron's Blenheims staged there on their way from P II to raids in Malaya at this time. Commenting on how there seemed to be no effort made to make repairs after Japanese bombing raids he adds:

---

[120] IWM London: IWM Catalogue No: 2008.1108: Collection: Group Captain G F Whistondale
[121] Later Wing Commander
[122] Later Wing Commander. From his report in AIR 20/5585.
[123] TNA: AIR 20/5578: Sqn Ldr Harper's report. This sentence has a line through it – presumably because he is making a disrespectful comment about a senior officer. It is still, however, clearly legible and I quote it as it is very significant later on.
[124] TNA: AIR 20/5573: Bomber Ops NEI

'in fact the most remarkable thing about the station was the absence of personnel during daylight hours. ... At about 09.30 hours, the yellow warning [air raid imminent] would be broadcast round the camp, whereupon the great majority of the personnel, officers included, left the camp and hid in the rubber most of them remaining there all day.'

It was not a situation that the crisp McCauley would have tolerated. As W/Cdr Jeudwine, commanding 84 Sqn and soon to be based at Kalidjati, flew in there at that time, it is more than probable that he also met Whistondale while he was commanding Sembawang.

Why then, in view of his apparent shortcomings, was Whistondale appointed to command RAF Kalidjati only a couple of weeks later? It seems to have come about through a curious chain of circumstances. As Singapore approached its inevitable fall, the RAF evacuated as many of its personnel as possible to Sumatra or Java. Those who survived the evacuation eventually ended up in one of the RAF transit camps in Java from where they would be posted to squadrons in Java as the need arose or moved to Australia or India as transport became available. On 16th February, A/Cdre H J F Hunter, now AOC 225 (B) Group in Java,[125] was given an airfield each for his Blenheim squadrons (Kalidjati) and his Hudson squadrons (Semplak) and flew to each to look them over and make some preliminary arrangements with the local Dutch forces. The next day he visited the transit camps in Batavia:

'in order to find Station Commanders and Station Headquarters personnel for the two stations'.

Two days later he sent Gp Capt Bishop and Sqn Ldr Furse to Semplak and Sqn Ldr Briggs to Kalidjati:

'to discuss establishments, to get what personnel they could from the Transit Camp on the spot, and to ask Batavia to make up what they could not find'.

According to his report, Briggs found a frustrating situation at Kalidjati.[126] He met W/Cdr Jeudwine, commanding 84 Sqn, and W/Cdr Bateson, commanding 211 Sqn, but neither of them was willing to take command of the station and 'even declined to tell me which of them was the senior'. To be frank, this was hardly surprising. By now both men will have been well aware that squadrons were being merged almost daily and their excess personnel evacuated as numbers of serviceable aircraft steadily dropped. Whoever got stuck with the job would be likely to still be on Java when the balloon went up - as it obviously would very shortly. Any sensible man

---

[125] Until 19th Feb pm when he became AOA Abdair. His report appears in AIR 20/5573
[126] TNA: AIR 20/5585

would wish to get off the island permanently as soon as possible and the fact that Briggs was not a regular RAF officer but a civilian commissioned in emergency and a junior rank to both probably did not make them feel any urgent need to co-operate with him. The upshot was, in Briggs' words:

'I ordered Wing Commander Jeudwine to take command and on returning to A.H.Q. recommended that an officer senior to both be sent to supercede him. Group Captain Whistondale was sent there and was later killed in the Japanese attack'.

His bald final statement makes me wonder if he considered it an unfortunate choice, knowing Whistondale as he did from previous experience.

This is backed in my opinion by the fact that Maltby claims both in his post-war report to the Air Ministry and in his despatch published in the London Gazette that the appointment of Whistondale was 'pending availability of Group Captain Nicholetts'.[127] Nicholetts was a bold and decisive officer who took a party of fifty volunteers from 605 (F) Sqn back to Oosthaven on 18th February on board HMS 'Ballarat'. For twelve hours they loaded as much abandoned RAF equipment and Bofors ammunition as they could onto their ship and undertook such destruction as possible to other stores and facilities around the harbour before making their way back to Java with their haul. He was appointed to head the Plans Branch at Maltby's HQ and it seems counter-intuitive to suggest that he seriously considered making him station commander at Kalidjati. It is much more probable that after the events of 1st March 1942, Maltby felt it looked better to suggest the unfortunate and less-able Whistondale was simply there as a very temporary measure.

The Blenheim squadrons were quick to arrive at Kalidjati. The first were on 17th February: a total of seven aircraft from 27, 34 and 84 Sqns RAF with some air and ground crew. Stores and spares were thin on the ground but it is good to report that the RAF ground crew resorted to that traditional standby of British forces bereft of equipment in Java: they raided the storehouses on the dockside at Tandjong Priok! The ML Technical Services also did what they could to assist with spares and servicing facilities. In the meantime, the Blenheims began undertaking operations as soon as (and whenever) they became serviceable against targets in Sumatra, particularly the oil plants their compatriots in the RA had just been defending. With insufficient fighter aircraft available in Java to provide escorts for them, the bombers of the RAF, RAAF and ML were forced to organise their raids to take advantage of the cloud cover provided by the tropical storms of the monsoon. Raids had to be aborted on occasions when the skies were clear over their targets.

---

[127] TNA: AIR 23/2123, para 510, and CAB 106/86, para 497

Very few Japanese aircraft were seen on the few days immediately after the evacuation of Sumatra and it was hoped that the bad weather was slowing them down. However, the sad fact was that they were just reorganising themselves on their new airfields ready to undertake the next step in their carefully-structured plans. Not for them the insecurity of unescorted raids. When their attacks started in earnest around 20th February, bombing raids were led in by reconnaissance aircraft and escorted by fighters. Contrary to the reports often found in near-contemporary Allied accounts, these fighters were rarely Zeros (or 'Navy Os') as they were generally from the Japanese army air force. Clever use was made of the different types of fighters at their disposal: short-range fighters were used to fly standing patrols over airfields or to escort bombers on short-hop raids on the Batavia area while the longer-range fighters were used for more distant targets. While the RAF might sneer at the presence of the older short-range aircraft, the fact is that they could still give the less-than-modern Allied bombers a tough time when they flew over to raid.

By Friday 20th February Java was surrounded. The Japanese had now taken the islands round it, robbing the Allies of their vital airfields that had 'staged' both fighter and bomber aircraft through to the NEI. There had still been an outside possibility that some Hurricanes could be flown off the aircraft carrier HMS 'Indomitable' to reinforce the squadrons on Java but now Wavell heard that the earliest this could happen off was 8th March.[128] He knew that was far too late to prevent disaster. No salvation could be expected by sea. The Japanese were rapidly gaining supremacy there and any reinforcements or re-supply within striking distance of the island would be running a grave risk should it attempt to approach. Java was doomed to fall to the enemy – only the exact timing was in doubt.

It was round this time (dates are often difficult to pin down in this campaign) that 29 and 34 Sqns were disbanded, with all their aircraft and some of their aircrew being divided up between 84 Sqn and 211 Sqn while the rest of their personnel were evacuated from the island. 84 Sqn had been given a new commanding officer for its Far East adventure, W/Cdr J R Jeudwine, who we have already met having a discussion with Sqn Ldr Briggs. Jeudwine, newly promoted to Wing Commander, had not flown operationally in the war until this time, indeed his last flying posting had been with HMS 'Glorious' in August 1938. A qualified interpreter, he had spent the earlier part of the war in signals intelligence in the Middle East. His experience of flying Blenheims was limited but undoubtedly helped by the long flight eastwards. However, this did not include night-flying, as his crew found out on their first night raid when they realised he had never landed a Blenheim in the dark. It appears to have been a hairy experience for all concerned!

---

[128] TNA: WO 106/3320

Whistondale's Station HQ was near the north-east entrance of the ML airbase at Kalidjati close to Zomer's HQ, while 84 Sqn HQ and the flight offices were 'off the edge of the airfield' in the immediate vicinity of Kalidjati village and relied on despatch riders to keep in touch with Station HQ as no telephone service was available. Mr Jackson 'of the Palmenlanden & Tjiassendlanden Company, Soebang' provided accommodation for all the officer aircrew in his house at Soebang while the aircrew sergeants were billeted in 'Mr Fletcher's house' in the town. Jackson also arranged for his company to carry out 'the almost phenomenally rapid building of a hutted camp' for the ground crew close to Squadron HQ.[129]

General facilities were a bit primitive for the squadrons compared to what they had been used to in other theatres. Bombing up and making ammunition belts had to be done manually and, for the non-commissioned aircrew at least, messing with the Dutch lacked refinements. Sgt Eric Oliver described lining up with a plate by:

'a big tub of bubble and squeak (mashed potatoes and green-leaf vegetables); we were supposed to dip our plate into the mashed mess and pull out a dollop!'[130]

But whatever was lost in sophistication should have been amply replaced by the goodwill their hosts seemed to show whenever possible, even if the bombs they supplied to the Blenheim crews were the wrong shape to allow the bomb doors to close properly and the American .30 rounds at their disposal almost fell out of the muzzles of the .303 guns of the British bombers![131]

The Japanese made their first air raid on Kalidjati with ten Ki-48 bombers escorted by 24 Ki-43 fighters on 20th February at 1300hrs local Dutch time[132]. No fighter defence was possible because of expected raids on Batavia and Bandoeng: there were just too few fighters for all contingencies. The Dutch Hurricanes at the airfield were about to become operational, now that problems with the supply of 100-octane fuel, hydraulic oil, Glycol and .303 ammunition had all been resolved and oxygen supply and masks from ML Buffalos fitted by the ML Technical Service. The radios were still not working but their pilots had almost completed their type conversion training and would be able to fly operationally in a day or two without them. Sadly, however, not that day.

---

[129] TNA: AIR 20/5573 and AIR 20/5585 are the sources for all information and quotes here.
[130] 'Bloody Shambles', vol 2, p193
[131] ibidem, p246
[132] The Dutch at Kalidjati used Central Java Time (CJT) and I am using this mainly for consistency.

The alarm came only seconds before the raid started and while most aircraft were fortunately hidden in the dispersal areas, the Glenn Martins that had been on ops that morning and were now being serviced in the pens on the south side of the airfield were in full view. Two were complete losses while another was badly damaged but repairable; one more sustained light damage. A Lockheed trainer from the ML's flying school was also destroyed and damage to the airfield itself, though not severe, closed it to flying for the rest of the day. The wet and stormy weather would have stopped operations anyway.

The weak anti-aircraft units resident on the airfield had scored no hits but help was on its way. 49th Bty arrived at Kalidjati that afternoon with ten Bofors guns and was operational by 1645hrs. The airfield had been visited by Macartney-Filgate and Lt Stubbs on the 19th when they undertook a reconnaissance of the site. While the former left the same day, Stubbs stayed on to finalise preparations for the battery's arrival. Meanwhile back at Batavia, Major Earle was busy preparing his battery for its new deployment, filling gaps in its vehicles, stores and equipment by the familiar expedient of scavenging in Tandjong Priok docks along with Major Graham of 95th Bty, which was off to Andir aerodrome near Bandoeng as soon as possible. Fortunately there had been a new consignment of vehicles landed there, obviously destined for Libya or India from their paintwork and clearly without their proper owners. In Macartney-Filgate's words: 'these, and other vehicles were distributed to the batteries' and this time Lt-Col Humphreys, 77th Regt, was not around to complain some units were making efforts to obtain 'more than their own share'![133]

Earle was briefed on Kalidjati aerodrome and conditions there by Macartney-Filgate at dawn the next morning, the battery was on the road by 0845hrs and at Kalidjati with its guns deployed and operational by 1645hrs. In Macartney-Filgate's words it was:

'a very creditable performance taking into account the weariness of the men, the strange vehicles, the eighty mile march, and the disorganisation which the batteries had suffered forty-eight hours previously'.

For 49th Bty had of course only just arrived back from their trip to Sumatra and over the next few days a number of its officers and men would have unpleasant reminders of this as malaria took hold. In spite of all this, and the appalling monsoon weather, there must have been many new sights and sounds for the lads out from England with no previous experience of the tropics. Jack Gunn told me how as they travelled through the countryside someone remarked they were passing a field of peanuts. He called him an idiot as there were no trees to be seen there - only to be told

---

[133] WO 106/2539: Humphrey's report on 77th HAA, Appendix B

of course that peanuts grow in the ground rather like potatoes. It was a totally different world from the one he knew.

We know something of how 49th Bty was deployed at Kalidjati as the Rev Godfrey included a rough sketch map in his memoirs as well as leaving some descriptions of the battery facilities.

'Their B.H.Q. was a modern well equipped and furnished bungalow, one of a row of bungalows in a little road leading off the main road to the aerodrome. The neighbouring bungalows (all evacuated by their owners) were being utilised as billets and offices by the battery Headquarters and one of the troops.'

They also had telephone communications which went through the exchange in Soebang and for at least some of the time a radio truck, courtesy of the 48th Regt's Signals Section. This had established short wave communications with RHQ immediately on arrival at Kalidjati[134] and seems to have maintained them in spite of the monsoon thunderstorms. We are so used to excellent and simple communications nowadays that it is easy to forget that radio communications in World War II were very susceptible to many factors. Distance was one – the 48th's wireless trucks were operating at the very edge of their range – and weather was another. Bad weather played a disastrous role in radio communications at this time, not only in the Far East but all over the globe, including notoriously at Arnhem in 1944.

Supplying the 49th with the necessities of life, particularly food and petrol, was a problem that was never properly solved in the nine days the battery was at Kalidjati, in spite of the strenuous efforts of Macartney-Filgate. Apparently they relied on the civilian shops and petrol pumps in the nearest town, Soebang, for these and paid with chits. This was both extravagant and rather hit and miss:

'and often resulted in quite unsuitable rations. ... Every help was given them but shops ran out of supplies and pumps dried up and the position at times was most serious.'

As Macartney-Filgate pointed out, if there was an invasion this system would immediately collapse anyway as civilians shut up shop and fled. The supply situation was even worse for ammunition: the Battery had to send trucks to Malang, a two-day expedition away. We have already seen the chaos at the docks caused by no proper supply system being in place but according to Macartney-Filgate the situation was no better at Bandoeng, where most senior supply officers had been collected and where he tried to get a unified response for the whole regiment:

---

[134] Macartney-Filgate, op. cit, p26

'the officers responsible for supply matters at G.H.Q. changed with bewildering rapidity and seldom was it possible to get hold of any officer who would admit responsibility or who was capable of inaugurating a proper system.'

But of course they were ABDACOM staff officers, not a British GHQ.

Back to the airfield itself and the gun positions. As can be seen from the map, the ten Bofors guns of the 49th were spread around the perimeter. The three guns of A Troop were ranged along the southern end of the flying field near the aircraft 'pens'. C Troop's No 3 Gun was alongside them and to the rear of the hangar used by the ML's bomber squadrons in the south-east corner of the main flying field near a road that ran in a northerly direction beside the site and through the major hangar, workshop and office areas. Just before it reached these it made two right-angled bends, first left, then right, and No 2 Gun C Troop was sited in the crook of the first of these. Continuing northwards up this road to the aerodrome's main gate and then turning left to move westward on the road to Poerwakarta, the usual way to Batavia, No 1 Gun C Troop was sited on the north side at the extreme northerly edge of the airfield on the side of the minor road that led north to the railway at Pasir Boengoer. Battery HQ was situated around where this road met the airfield road to Batavia. Passing westward along this and then turning south along a track, B Troop's No 1 Gun was sited towards the south side of a hangar known to the Dutch as the Ryan Hangar. B Troop's other three guns were sited to the south of this on the other side of the track, with the Dispersal Area West, an area of grass and low shrubs, in front of them. Thus 49th Bty's guns surrounded the whole flying field. The two Bofors guns of the KNIL AA detachment were actually on the airfield itself, north of the main runway and east of the Ryan Hangar.

Of course all this came as something as a shock to the Japanese when they raided Kalidjati around 1100hrs the next day. The weather was extremely bad over Batavia that morning but was good enough elsewhere to make Kalidjati and Andir possible targets. 95th Bty did not arrive at Andir until that evening but the nine ML Buffalos despatched from there ensured that it was not attacked. There was no air defence for Kalidjati as the Allies had only twenty-seven serviceable fighters that day and the thirteen RAF Hurricanes available at Tjililitan near Batavia were grounded by the weather. In addition, before radar became available at the end of the month, ground observers were the only way of spotting a raid was in the offing and bad weather with heavy clouds made this very difficult.

The raid on Saturday 21st February opened with a strafing run by 17 Ki-43 fighters of 59th and 64th Sentai. Whereas the day before there had been negligible anti-aircraft fire, they now ran into a withering barrage. It must have been very satisfying for the gunners of 49th Bty to be able to open fire at long last after two months cooped up on ships at sea and another two weeks being shunted around the NEI in a disorganised manner. However, the shock the enemy felt would not have been long-lasting; they were experienced units and the fighters were joined by fifteen Ki-48 bombers of 90th Sentai, also flying at low level. Even the most experienced men of the AA battery would not have been used to an attack of this intensity as most of their previous experience was around the docks and coastline of Essex. A few guns had been dispersed for airfield defence at that time but would never have experienced such an onslaught as this.

The Japanese strategy in attacking the airfield was to destroy the Allied air force on the ground and they were bombing and strafing from around two hundred feet to achieve this.[135] The southern dispersal pens at Kalidjati were within a few yards of A Troop's guns and at the time of the raid, three Glenn Martins of 1/2-Vl.G.I were there undergoing final preparation for an armed reconnaissance flight[136] – just the sort of target the attackers were looking for. The fighters succeeded in destroying all three, explosions from the bombs on board ripping them apart and flinging the engines up to fifty yards away, making craters ten yards across and four deep.

It was hardly surprising that with all the action – Bofors guns chewed up shells at an alarming rate - and the supply problems affecting the battery, one of A Troop's guns ran out of ammunition. Jack Gunn noticed that it had fallen silent and, for some reason that he could never account for afterwards, leapt into an ammo truck and drove it across the airfield to the gun, only to be greeted (not surprisingly) by a barrage of curses for his trouble! A truck driven at high speed across an aerodrome was a prime target for any fighter pilot. It would seem quite insane to unload Bofors ammo right under the very noses of the Japanese air force in these circumstances and hardly surprising that the gun crew refused to leave their trench to do it! When he got back, an officer greeted him with: 'Gunn, that is the bravest thing I have ever seen. I am going to put you forward for a medal.' He recalled years later that the officer was killed only a few days later and the recommendation was never made – and that he himself never did anything 'brave' again!

The story has a very sad conclusion. Macartney-Filgate tells us that the Japanese bombers were dropping anti-personnel bombs on the airfield and one landed five yards from a gun, killing two of its crew and injuring five others. Lance Bombadier W G Gafney and Gunner A Bown were killed outright. Among the injured were: Gunner B D Mayhew, who died later of his wounds, Bombadier E J Iron and Gunner C Gissing. The last two were evacuated to hospital in Bandoeng on 28th February and became separated

---

[135] Macartney-Filgate, op. cit., p26
[136] P C Boer, op cit., p119

from their unit from then on. Iron died in a PoW camp in Burma while Gissing survived to be liberated. By incredibly bad luck the gun that was hit was the very one that Jack had tried to take the ammunition to.

The Dutch also lost two Lodestar transport aircraft in the raid in addition to their bombers but the enemy did not get away scot-free. 49th shot down two attackers, 'confirmed' as wreckage was found, with two more 'possibles'. That evening they received a message from Maj-Gen L H van Oyen, commander of the ML, congratulating them on their shooting. The next day they would bury their dead in Soebang, just the first of their terrible losses in the Far East. Men were posted in from other batteries in the regiment as replacements.[137]

The next day, 22nd February, was a Sunday. Rev Godfrey was at Tjililitan airfield with 242nd Bty attempting to 'take short prayers round the gun sites' but being cut short each time by air raid warnings. These never materialised into full-scale attacks but did disrupt his efforts. He remarked that each of the airfields where 48th Regt had a battery had 'a very bad pasting' at some time in this period, adding:

'the men stood up to it very well. 49 Battery had it at Kalidjati the day after they got there, but their unexpected presence there so surprised the enemy that they soon left'

but of course not without loss to the battery. Lt-Col Pearson and his adjutant, Capt Williams, visited Kalidjati that day as part of a two-day trip covering the 49th and 95th to check how the men were taking things and seem to have been satisfied that they had stood up to the challenge.[138]

There were no air raids on Kalidjati on the 22nd and 23rd. On 23rd February, the surviving Hudsons of the RAF and RAAF moved to Kalidjati. They had been based at Semplak, which had no AA defence, and had suffered terrible losses on the ground. Three days earlier, 8 RAAF and 62 RAF Sqns had been disbanded and their aircraft and some of their crews transferred to 1 RAAF. This now had thirty crews in all, far beyond their operational needs as by the 23rd only thirteen Hudsons remained on charge of which just two were classified operational. Surplus aircrew were ordered to Darwin and left Java on the 22nd.[139]

As the result of combining both air and ground personnel there were by now just two Blenheim squadrons operating, 84 and 211, both at Kalidjati. 84 Sqn sent a patrol of three aircraft to investigate reports of enemy submarines in the Sunda Strait between Java and Sumatra and claimed to

---

[137] TNA: WO 361/342
[138] Rev Godfrey, op. cit., p14
[139] Shores and others, op. cit., p212

have bombed four, sinking one.[140] Sadly JAC later decided that their targets had probably been 'sea mammals'.[141] 84 Sqn had spoilt the day for a pod of whales! The weather was bad in the afternoon and no ops were flown. Perhaps it was this which also kept the Japanese from attacking Kalidjati that day.

The aerodrome was not so lucky the next morning, Tuesday 24th February, when sixteen Ki-48 bombers (Macartney-Filgate says twenty Ju-88s) escorted by 13 Ki-43 fighters attacked at around 0920hrs. It was a low-level raid that hit the airfield hard, initially denying the nine surviving AA guns of 49th Bty any targets. Unfortunately the weather that morning had been bad so bombing raids by the Blenheims and Hudsons stationed there had been delayed to allow it to clear and these, and Glenn Martins from the Dutch squadrons, were caught in the open. Two Hudsons and two Blenheims were destroyed with another Blenheim, three Glenn Martins and other Hudsons suffering lesser damage as the Japanese used both heavy and anti-personnel bombs and strafed the airfield. The 49th suffered no casualties this time, though one previous gun position, now abandoned, received a direct hit, but claimed three enemy aircraft destroyed with one more 'possible'. The Kalidjati Hurricanes were scrambled but without result. The aerodrome had been badly damaged: the main runway had been put out of action and the taxiways and short emergency runway had bomb craters in them. There was no option but to close the airfield until the next day to allow it to be repaired.

---

[140] TNA: AIR 23/2123, para 520
[141] Boer, op. cit., p130

Eight: Java at bay

Meanwhile, there were developments further afield on the ground in Java that would affect the fate of 49th Bty, as preparations were made both for a final stand on the island and for the departure and dissolution of ABDACOM. We have already seen Blackburn working with the local KNIL commander on defence plans and organisation of forces but what is of crucial importance to Kalidjati is the way Java was divided up into military areas by the Dutch. Western Java Command was divided into two: 'Blackforce' and Schilling's force covered the 'residencies' of Bantam, Batavia and Buitenzorg while the adjacent area, the 'residencies' of Priangan and Cheribon, fell to another Dutch officer, Maj-Gen Pesman.[142] The dividing line between these two commands was only about fifteen miles east of Kalidjati, meaning that the aerodrome fell into the area of the best professional force on the island but based over 150 miles away – too far to come swiftly to its aid if a crisis arose.

Sitwell had been visiting his two AA regiments in the east of Java in his role of Brigadier, 16th AA Brigade, from 19th to 22nd February until he was called back to be promoted as ABDACOM withdrew. Neither 21st LAA Regt nor 77th HAA Regt had had good experiences on Java so far, though both had been spared the Sumatra debacle. Both had lost their experienced RAOC officers to ABDACOM in Bandoeng on arrival in Tandjong Priok and both had suffered in the free-for-all in the docks there. 21st LAA had been billeted in two very different places miles apart. One was in a camp half a mile from the docks.

'It was infested with mosquitoes, had a sparse water supply and had no sanitary arrangements of any kind. The other camp was a well equipped modern Dutch army camp, six miles from the docks, in the centre of Batavia.'[143]

And of course, rations had not been organised.

Both regiments had had batteries split off. 'A' and 'C' Troops of 79th LAA Bty had been sent to Timor while the rest of 21st Regiment was centred round Malang, while 239th HAA Bty stayed round Batavia while the rest of 77th Regt travelled to Sourabaya. An advance party of 48th LAA Bty also travelling there were involved in the same railway accident that caused so many casualties to 240th and 241st HAA Btys but apparently without any losses. Nevertheless, there were plenty of other problems. For a start, the new Bedford QL gun tractors were useless, according to Lt-Col Saunders. The gears were difficult, they overheated too quickly if driven for distances in low gear and they bogged down easily.

---

[142] TNA: CAB 106/134
[143] TNA: WO 106/2563

Getting the LAA batteries and their equipment across Java took four days and it was not until 15th and 16th February that they reached their final destinations. 48th Bty at Sourabaya were perfectly prepared to defend the airfield with assistance from 77th HAA Regt but unfortunately the American fighters that had been stationed there had already left, never to return. The nearby seaplane base had 5 Catalinas, of which three were dummies. The remaining batteries of 21st LAA also defended airfields used by the USAAF: Singosari (Malang) with B-17s and Madioen, which had both fighters and bombers but never more than 5 fighters and 4 B-17s on the airfield together. From an anti-aircraft perspective, both sites posed problems due to the nature of the surrounding countryside. And it could be difficult to contact the American CO.

Saunders travelled to Bandoeng on the night of 18th/19th February with his adjutant to sort out a number of problems that could not be done over the telephone as contact was by civil line only and took up to 24 hours to organise. It made communications with HQ in Bandoeng 'practically impossible'. He quickly got answers to all his queries about 'G', 'A' and 'Q' matters, plus questions on pay, rations and ammunition supply. At the same time 'various 'G' officers on the Staff' (of ABDACOM) told Saunders that:

'H.Q., S.W. Pacific Command was probably evacuating the island in the course of the next few days. My Regiment and 77 H.A.A. were to remain on the island to aid the Dutch.'

Needless to say, he was less than impressed by this. As he pointed out post-war, in the end four RA regiments (21st, 77th, 48th and 6th) were left on Java to face what was even then known to be inevitable captivity or death when at that juncture there was sufficient shipping to evacuate them to places where they might have made a real difference. But of course this was a necessary political decision and one that also affected Blackburn's men.

Whether Sitwell travelled back with him to finally visit 21st LAA Regt at their new aerodromes on 19th-21st February entirely of his own volition no-one can say, but it gave him an opportunity to see conditions in the field at this end of the island. It also gave Saunders the opportunity to repeat his request for 48th Bty to be moved away from the empty aerodromes of Sourabaya to somewhere they could be of use. They duly received orders to deploy to the port of Tjilatjap three days later.

On the 22nd Sitwell moved on to visit 77th Regt at Sourabaya. Here Lt-Col Humphreys also had his problems. He was still short of men after the railway disaster earlier in the month. Many of the gun spares the regiment had brought out from Britain were faulty and it took massive amounts of work to get twelve of fourteen damaged guns operational. Then there were all the problems arising from deploying half a battery to the island of Madoera, just off Sourabaya . . . Sitwell was probably quite relieved to return to HQ in Bandoeng, after witnessing 'A' Troop, 240th Bty, shoot down a Japanese aircraft in their first encounter with the enemy.

Before Sitwell left 21st LAA, Lt-Col Saunders had extracted written standing orders from him on the steps to be taken by the regiment should the Japanese invade. Saunders, who likened the Java campaign to the shambles of the Walcheren Campaign of 1809 in his post-war report to the War Office, was no fool. He could smell a fiasco in the making and was determined not to be the scapegoat![144] Reproduced in his report they read:

'unless orders to the contrary were received, ... to remain in position until a direct threat of capture was made.' If his batteries were threatened and 'if the aerodromes they were protecting were evacuated by our own or Allied aircraft, then I was to withdraw ... In no circumstances, if Allied Air Forces had withdrawn, were the batteries to be left to carry out an unsupported resistance.'

When he departed for a visit to Bandoeng a day or two later, he left them with his second-in-command, Major Steele, and on his way there he told Humphreys at Sourabaya about them. These were crucial to understanding when the batteries should stand and when they should retreat but apparently did not reach 48th Regt.[145]

Meanwhile, Tandjong Priok harbour had been crammed with over a hundred ships, including those of 48th Regt's convoy from 3rd February which still had not left, but now around 22nd-23rd February a concerted effort was made to empty it of as much shipping as possible. It was an opportunity to get rid of refugees and odds and ends of units that had ended up in Java. The harbour was now closed to civilian shipping and evacuations of as many surplus RAF and RAAF personnel as possible began in earnest.

This latter evacuation was not favourably received by van Oyen, who had just experienced a rapid promotion. Up to the evening of 22nd February, command of the Allied air forces under the ABDACOM umbrella had fallen to Abdair, commanded by AM Sir Richard Peirse, RAF. But now Abdair was disbanded as part of the general dissolution of ABDACOM and van Oyen was appointed to command Java Air Command (JAC), effectively all Allied air forces left on Java. Col E T Kengen became acting commander ML in his place. Van Oyen would have liked the airmen to stay on in Java, yet the Allies had few aircraft left by this stage and fewer still were operationally serviceable: only 35 fighters and 25 bombers on 22nd

---

[144] TNA: WO 106/2563
[145] Macartney-Filgate, op. cit., Appendix A

February, pathetic when you consider that the Japanese had sent over half this number to attack Kalidjati alone the previous day. Churchill had demanded why the cooks and clerks and other services of the Army in Singapore could not fight to defend it and van Oyen was now asking why the RAF and the RAAF could not fight as infantry to defend Java rather than leaving. But it would take time to organise, arm and train them and time was running out for Java while they might make a difference in some other theatre.

JAC had three subsidiary HQs: BRITAIR (previously WESGROUP) for the British and Australian squadrons and ML Command (Central Group) for the Dutch squadrons, which together covered western Java, and East Group (also EASGROUP) for the American squadrons based in central and eastern Java. The reconnaissance group (RECGROUP) and the Combined Operations and Intelligence Centre (COIC) also fell to van Oyen. The plan for the limited air forces available had contradictory tendencies. The overall military strategy called for reconnaissance aircraft to locate and identify Japanese invasion fleets and all available bombers to attack these as soon as they came in range, with the fighters defending the Allied fleet. JAC's strategy envisaged a campaign aimed at destroying stocks of aircraft fuel captured by the Japanese and reducing the numbers of operational Japanese aircraft both by bombing raids on their airfields and by shooting them down when they appeared over Java, with the objective of attaining and maintaining air superiority and forcing the enemy to delay his invasion (hopefully giving time for reinforcements to arrive).[146] Another role was providing some aerial defence for Allied shipping around Java, using both fighters and bombers besides the small reconnaissance group. Unfortunately the Allies had insufficient aircraft for even one of these plans and certainly could not afford to do what they tried to do - carry all out simultaneously.

Wednesday 25th February was the official day for handing over command in Java from ABDACOM to the Dutch. It had been shutting down for the last couple of days but finally departed in a rush of wholesale appointments and promotions and a rather undignified dash for the coast. Maltby was down for evacuation but declined to leave, considering the recently-promoted A/Cdre Staton, his projected substitute in command of RAF and RAAF forces, insufficiently experienced for the role. It is possible that his decision was in some way influenced by the fact that his brother, Maj-Gen C M Maltby, Commander of British Troops in China, had been taken prisoner at the fall of Hong Kong. Sitwell was of course another promotion but it went way down the scale as staff officers tried to get a passage off the island. Capt Johnstone, i/c 48th's RASC detachment, who we have previously seen trying to make order out of chaos in Tandjong Priok, had a

---

[146] Boer, op. cit., ppxxiii-xxv

very strange experience. Originally due to be evacuated, he was told to go to Bandoeng, where he arrived midday on 24th February. That afternoon the entire S.T. staff left with the exception of Lt-Col Rush, RIASC, who was due to go early the next morning. Johnstone's superior officer, Lt-Col Petrie, was long overdue at Bandoeng and was feared to have been a casualty of Japanese air attacks on the road from Batavia, so Rush told him that if Petrie had been a casualty:

'I was to get myself appointed Lieut. Colonel and take over command of the R.A.S.C. in Java.'[147]

Saunders described the departure of the Allied staff, witnessed by his RHQ and two Troops from 69th and 79th Batteries, as a 'stampede'. They were forced to the side of the road by:

'a long stream of cars bearing high military and naval officers, who rushed by at top speed to the southern port.'[148]

Unfortunately the ships at Tjilatjap would not wait for any staff officer who was late!

The British Consul-General on the island reported back to the Foreign Office that:

'Feeling is gaining ground among the Dutch, with demoralising results, that the Allies are going to leave them in the lurch.'[149]

While the Governor-General of the NEI received Wavell and his departure plans with the *politesse* of a born diplomat, van Mook, his deputy, did not disguise his displeasure. Much to the credit of the Dutch, they agreed to keep the news of the departure of ABDACOM secret until 27th February to allow Wavell and his staff to get clear from the area.[150]

The Dutch had felt that there was still an outside chance that fierce and stubborn resistance to the enemy would buy more time for reinforcements to reach the island but those hopes were dashed by the 25th when a potential Japanese invasion fleet was sighted off the east coast of Borneo. Another invasion fleet was expected to the west to perform a pincer move but this had not yet been located. This was also the day when the Japanese ended their air superiority offensive prior to invasion, which had now been put back to 28th February as their navy felt the army's analysis of probable Allied air losses was too optimistic. With that in mind they also called in a light aircraft carrier and its supporting units from Indo-China but overall the focus of both army and navy air forces switched to defending the

---

[147] TNA: WO 106/2539: Johnstone's report
[148] TNA: WO 106/2563
[149] TNA: WO 208/1611: 'Most Secret' telegram dated 23.02.42
[150] TNA: WO 106/2572: telegram dated 25.02.42

invasion fleets and their airfields in Sumatra.[151] Meanwhile the Allies had lost one-third of their fighter strength in a week and were losing bombers at a steady rate both on the ground and in the air. Macartney-Filgate summed up the situation very well:

'Day by day the number of aircraft steadily diminished as the workshops and riggers found themselves without the tools and spare parts necessary to make good the wear and tear and the damage resulting from encounters with the enemy, and almost from the outset the Japanese had supremacy in the air which, by mid-February was virtually complete.'

Kalidjati was not much affected by the generally bad weather over Batavia and the Bandoeng plateau on the morning of the 25th and was hit by two Japanese air raids. The first was a high-level attack by sixteen aircraft at around 1200hrs and resulted in one man from 49th Bty being injured. Three more were injured about an hour later in the other raid,[152] a low-level attack by sixteen bombers and twelve fighters of which two were shot down and five others hit by the intense barrage put up by both British and Dutch Bofors guns and the 12.7mm machine-guns round the perimeter. The Hurricanes at Kalidjati, still without radios, had started flying standing patrols that morning and, though low on fuel, intercepted the fighter escort for the first raid. Four Hurricanes were lost either in the ensuing fight or in the raid later that day while several bombers standing in the open were damaged to some degree and a hangar and some small fuel dumps were set ablaze. The airfield's water supply was also destroyed.

In the very early hours of Thursday 26th, Capt Newman arrived at RHQ in Batavia with Lt Perry to pick up a Bofors gun that had been repaired and was able to give very positive accounts of the battery's morale in the face of the 'determined enemy attacks'. However morale was suffering among the squadrons as more and more ML, RAF and RAAF personnel were evacuated from the island and those left behind felt they were fighting a losing battle. 211 Sqn was the latest to pack up and head for the port of Tjilatjap with 84 Sqn staying on at Kalidjati with whatever Blenheims were left and odds and ends of personnel from other squadrons to make up their numbers.

There were no air raids in western Java that day - just as the transportable radar units meant for Malaya had finally become operational.[153] Allied bombers concentrated their efforts on attempting to locate and track the expected two invasion fleets but still failed to find any trace of one to the west. In the meantime, 49th Bty at Kalidjati received a number of visits

---

[151] Boer, op. cit., p66
[152] Wounded included Sgt A G Hoye, Gnr L H Farrant and Gnr E F C Parsons. Parsons died next day.
[153] Boer, op. cit., p70

from senior officers. While Pearson was there during the morning, Maj-Gen Sitwell arrived to discuss 'the ground defence of the aerodrome'. The conference they held also included Gp Capt Whistondale, Major Earle and 'a major of the 6th H.A.A. Regiment' whose men would be providing an infantry force to defend the aerodrome as they had lost their guns in Sumatra. Unfortunately Macartney-Filgate, simply records that the conference was about 'ground defence problems' and does not say specifically what they were considered to be.

The major from 6th Regt was Maj N Coulson, commanding 12th Bty. He had been stationed at P II in Sumatra while his men had been divided between there and the oil refineries near Palembang, where his second-in-command, Capt Sherrard, had been killed. The regiment itself had just lost its Colonel, Baillie, who Sitwell had dismissed on the grounds that he found him 'unsatisfactory'. 'Unsatisfactory' was a favourite word of Sitwell's to describe something he didn't like without being specific about why, and that is the case here, but there were potentially several bones of contention between the two. A Regular soldier and a World War I veteran like Sitwell, Baillie had been visited by Sitwell's Brigade Major while he was in Sumatra. The young officer had attempted to instruct him on how to site his guns and was probably given a flea in his ear for his pains.[154] Baillie had also been appointed AADC in South Sumatra and claimed he had:

'had no instructions from the General Staff to inform me that Brigadier Sitwell had any executive command.'

After their evacuation to Java without their guns, some fifty of Baillie's men had been taken from him to make up the numbers for 77th Regt who were lacking personnel as a result of their train accident. Baillie may well have objected to his command being split up and Humphreys at 77th was certainly unhappy with the standard of training and discipline of the men he received.[155] Baillie prided himself on the training in airfield defence he had made his men undertake even before their deployment out east and it is just possible that he wanted to organise his men in this in Java and it proved a bit too much for Sitwell. Whatever the point of friction was, Baillie was 'evacuated' to India on 26th February and command of the remains of his regiment was given to Lt-Col E H Hazell. This remnant and 35th LAA Regt, both now without guns, were sent to Tjimahi Barracks about three miles west of Bandoeng to be formed into and trained as infantry units.[156] 12th Bty would follow Coulson to Kalidjati on 28th February.

Macartney-Filgate also visited Kalidjati on the 26th to discuss petrol, rations and ammunition supplies, all still major problems. It was probably about then that four lorries left the base to get more ammunition from

---

'somewhere near Malang',[157] resulting in them and the personnel with them being away when the Japanese attacked a couple of days later. That evening the Allied intelligence departments in Bandoeng warned of a possible Japanese invasion from an Eastern invasion fleet the next morning and the Allied naval squadron in Sourabaya sailed in search of it. The anticipated western invasion fleet had not yet been definitely sighted and would not be until around midday on the 28th. In the meantime, bombing raids on Sumatra, reconnaissances out to sea and fighter defence of the Allied naval force were the order of the day for the Allied air forces.

On land, such ground forces as were available were moved around to prepare for the defence of Java itself. The overall plan was based on the assumption that the Japanese would make a two-pronged attack, landing simultaneously in the east and west of the island. There were patently not enough Allied troops to defend the whole so it was decided to have the main defensive thrust in the west where it seemed probable that the enemy main attack would come. Batavia, Tandjong Priok and Bandoeng, the capital, the military HQs and one of the two major ports on the north side of the island, were all situated there. This larger defence force comprised two regiments of the KNIL under Maj-Gen Schilling and 'Blackforce', now augmented by two batteries of 2nd Battalion, 131st Field Artillery, US Army, and the light tanks of 'B' Squadron, 3rd Hussars, and under the command of Brig Blackburn. These two forces would hold the roads and railway leading from the anticipated western landing sites and Batavia to the military citadel of Bandoeng and its nearby towns. It was decided that Blackburn's more mobile, better trained force would do some manoeuvring to cut off parts of the invading force at which point Schilling's men would attack it from the front and flanks. They would then fight a series of rear-guard actions culminating in a retreat to the Bandoeng plateau, which would act as a kind of fortress or redoubt for a final stand, assuming no Allied aid came in time.

The Allied planners assumed that attacks in the east would be lesser ones aimed at taking the naval port of Sourabaya. Here Maj-Gen G A Ilgen, KNIL, had a 'reinforced regiment' of infantry and territorial units that was intended to hold on to this. Unfortunately, the small Allied naval force that used it had been wiped out in its valiant but futile attack on the Eastern Invasion Force on the night of 27th February. When the invasion came a few hours later, Java no longer had a fleet and her Admiral, Helfrich, had departed to somewhere outside the immediate war zone where he thought he could be more useful. Even if time had been available, there were neither the communications nor the transport to move Ilgen's forces to where they might be of more use. That leaves only the central zone of the island where the bits and pieces of what was left over, odd units, local

---

[157] TNA: WO 361/342: Information from BQMS F H Webster

Home Guard and so on, were swept up as a last line of defence for Bandoeng under the command of Maj-Gen J J Pesman.

It wasn't much of a defence or a defence plan but then resources were so few. It was already clear that the Japanese had air and sea supremacy and without doubt would have more properly trained and well-led troop to put ashore for the invasion. HQ at Bandoeng had to make military decisions based on what they expected the enemy to do to attempt to limit the damage. There were simply no reserves to deal with the enemy doing anything that differed from this. Unfortunately, as with so many Allied predictions of Japanese actions, this latest one was also wrong, with disastrous results not just for Kalidjati but for the whole of Java.

Interestingly, while the KNIL units and 'Blackforce' were settling down into their defensive positions, all three remaining RA AA Regiments on Java were on the move at this period to some extent. RHQ and 240th Bty, 77th HAA, had been ordered to Tjilatjap on 26th February to defend the port there – the only major harbour on the south side of the island. It was not a straightforward move and these batteries were still in transit when the invasion came. 241st Bty remained in Sourabaya and 239th stayed on in Batavia for now. The RHQ of 21st LAA moved to Bandoeng on 28th February, while 48th LAA Bty had moved from Sourabaya to Tjilatjap, arriving on the 27th and was in position to defend the expected arrival of the ill-fated 'Langley'. The other two sections of the regiment still on mainland Java, 69th Bty less 'B' Troop and 'B' Troop, 69th Bty plus 'B' Troop, 79th Bty, had moved to Jogjakarta and Tasikmalaja by 28th February.

The batteries of 48th LAA Regt stayed where they were but its Signals Section packed up and moved to Buitenzorg on Friday 27th to provide 'Blackforce' with some signals capacity. Its RASC platoon had become absorbed into the general supply system on the island but while its RAOC workshop was staying for the moment in Batavia, RHQ was preparing to move to Tjimahi Barracks near Bandoeng, which would place it nearer its batteries at Andir and Kalidjati. It was at these barracks that Macartney-Filgate was now trying unsuccessfully to sort out fuel and rations for 49th and 95th Batteries. The latter was only a mile or two away from the proposed new location of RHQ. The move itself did not actually commence until 0800hrs on 1st March,[158] after the Japanese invasion had happened, so RHQ would have no contact with any of its batteries at this vital time.

Meanwhile it was the calm before the storm for 49th Bty at Kalidjati. There had been no air raids since 25th February, though their sleep may have been disturbed on the night of the 27th when the first night raids by

---

[158] Rev Godfrey, op. cit., p15

bombers from the airfield took place in an attempt to destroy some of the large number of Japanese aircraft on P I aerodrome in Sumatra. The last chance of fighter aircraft reinforcements carried in the elderly US aircraft carrier 'Langley' had sunk with it during the day as it approached Tjilatjap. Java was surrounded and awaiting its fate, its pitiful defence forces at the ready. On the afternoon of Saturday 28th February, Rev Godfrey left Batavia to spend the weekend at Kalidjati with 49th Bty, arriving 'a few hours before dusk'.

Nine: Kalidjati, 1st March 1942 - Prelude

In his despatch dated 26th July 1947, published in the London Gazette 26th February 1948, Air Vice-Marshal Maltby claimed that 'It has been impracticable as yet to obtain a clear picture of what exactly happened at Kalidjati.' This was not actually true. Almost all the information I am using here would have been available to him when he drew up his despatch if he had asked for it. The only major exception is the Dutch accounts based on contemporary Dutch reports from military personnel on the airfield at the time. Maltby admitted in his report to the Air Ministry that 'Dutch views have not been sought' but what follows here clearly demonstrates that very few other ones were either. And he would have had the advantage of being able to ask men to clarify obscurities or apparent contradictions in their accounts, while seventy years later, I have to make my best guess on these. I have generally followed the Dutch times for events except where these appear to be contradictory or problematical.

Everything was 'perfectly normal and quiet' at BHQ when Rev Godfrey arrived late on Saturday afternoon, 28th February. He was allocated a bed in the Battery Captain's room in the BHQ bungalow and after dusk wandered round to one of the nearby bungalows used as billets and talked to some of the men out on the veranda about the heavy raids the airfield had suffered. Though it had been 'bloody hell', they declared they would 'continue to stick it'. Later he wandered back to the officers' mess in time to meet the first of a number of visitors on what was to prove a most memorable night.

Now RAF sources for the next twenty-four hours rarely mention the Army while Army accounts for the same period hardly ever mention the RAF. The result is that there are hours at a time when it would be easy to believe that they did not share the same aerodrome. Just now is one clear example of this. The Padre's account has an aura of calm while out on the airfield itself all the operationally-serviceable RAF, RAAF and ML aircraft were taking off in relays from around 1800hrs. Sometime during that afternoon the Allies had finally definitely identified the western Japanese invasion force and were tracking its progress, noting with alarm late in the afternoon that it had divided into two. The larger part was heading towards land west of Batavia as expected but a smaller convoy of seven transports plus escort vessels was approaching Eretan Wetan on the coast of Java just north-east of Kalidjati.

At a stroke the enemy had neutralised the entire Dutch plan of defence. Units landed here would not just threaten the major air base at Kalidjati but also would be on a shorter - if less easy - route to Bandoeng (via the Tjiater Pass) than the force landing near Merak. The two western Japanese battle groups could perform a pincer movement on the city too swiftly to allow the planned fighting withdrawal. There were no substantial Allied forces to face the enemy moving south from Eretan Wetan; Schilling's men and 'Blackforce' were 150 miles to the west preparing to take on the main western battle group. If Kalidjati was taken, the Japanese could move in their own aircraft and destroy with impunity whatever Allied forces were left. What could be done to salvage things at this very late stage?

The answer was, of course, the classic air power response that the RAF had intended to use to defend Malaya: bomb the approaching convoy out of the water. To achieve this, the Blenheims, Hudsons and Glenn Martins of Kalidjati spent most of the night taking off and landing by oil lamps, trying to locate the convoy approaching Eretan Wetan and destroy it. Dutch General Headquarters (AHK), which had taken over from ABDACOM after the latter's hasty departure, had decided that fighting off this convoy was a major priority and JAC formulated plans for the attacks that were issued to the squadrons at around 1730hrs. In a post-war report, Flt Lt Campbell Hill, 59 Sqn, who had arrived at Kalidjati two days before and was observer on one of the two remaining operational Hudsons that made the first bombing raid, recalled:

'Briefing was haphazard and available information as to the 'night flying' facilities of Java dromes indefinite. We were airborne however, just before dark, still with no precise information of the night flying facilities of Kalidjati itself even.'[159]

A very important consideration as sunset was at around 1825hrs Central Java Time!

The weather was clear for the first part of the night but mist formed later as usual in the area during the monsoon, which made finding the convoy impossible at times. Six Blenheims took off by the light of storm lanterns at 1830hrs followed by six Glenn Martins an hour later but these latter landed back at Andir to reduce the numbers landing in the dark at Kalidjati. A Hudson and four Blenheims left the airfield at 2100hrs but by the time of the next raid at 2330hrs, the convoy could not be found through the mist. The Japanese invasion force had actually landed when the final raid by RAF and RAAF bombers took place shortly after 0300hrs and they attacked the anchored transport ships in poor visibility, returning to the aerodrome around 0500hrs.[160]

There was one exception to this. Sgt G W Sayer's Blenheim crew, on their first op, believed they were being hunted by a Japanese night-fighter with a searchlight in the nose. Their subsequent evasive manoeuvres continued

---

[159] TNA: AIR 20/5573. Flt Lt Campbell Hill's report
[160] Boer, op cit.

until the aircraft ran out of fuel and had to make an emergency landing.[161] However, the Japanese did not use night-fighters in this campaign. What they had seen – as the ML knew, for at least one of their own pilots had been tricked by this in the past – was the planet Venus!

Naturally there is a fair difference between the hits claimed by the Allies and the losses admitted by the Japanese. It is pointless to debate the discrepancies and irrelevant to this story anyway as the important fact is the enemy's invasion fleet had reached land at around 0100hrs and was busily organising its beachhead before despatching the various components of its forces over the next three hours. Suffice it to say that bombing a convoy of moving ships, defended by anti-aircraft guns, from between 4,000 and 5,000 feet (the height ordered by JAC) with four 250lb bombs, in the dark, is not likely to produce any notable success![162]

Meanwhile, 49th Bty went about its duties in happy ignorance of the peril at sea directly north of them. At around 2000hrs, 12th Bty 6th HAA Regt arrived to take over from 3-Inf. II, a small Dutch force of about 180 men commanded by Captain L J Prummel, KNIL, which had been guarding the aerodrome. Major Coulson, commanding 12th Bty, had of course been at Kalidjati for a couple of days, making a reconnaissance of the terrain and meeting the other officers on the base but his battery arrived at this totally new location in the dark. It also appears to have been considerably reduced in numbers from its war establishment, consisting of only around 140 men armed with rifles, Bren guns and Tommy guns. These were deployed on and around the airfield in consultation with Major Earle but would inevitably have had minimal knowledge of their immediate surroundings.[163]

The officers of 12th HAA made their way to 49th Bty officers' mess and a convivial evening followed. While Earle and Coulson discussed how they would deal with any emergency, the junior officers chatted and drank beer before those from 12th Bty wandered off to their new billets. Rev Godfrey now got the opportunity to start 'an improvised meal of toast and fried egg' as the next visitor, Group Captain Whistondale, arrived at around 10pm.

The Padre describes him as being 'in a clear state of nerves', perhaps not surprising considering he was about to tell them of the approaching enemy convoy. 'His face was expressive of sheer harassing bewilderment.' Godfrey recalls his opening words as "There's a party on tonight" before he

---

[161] Shores and others, p.150. Parts of the account there are contradicted by the 'Statement of W/O Wm Procter R.A.F.,' TNA: WO 361/1589
[162] Particularly when the GP bombs they use have impact fuses. The bomb load given is for the RAF/RAAF bombers. ML Glenn Martins had a bomb load of three 300kg bombs apiece.
[163] Boer, op. cit., p265

explained that the bombers would be attacking the enemy all night but that a landing would probably be effected just the same and the Major should be prepared for this. This must have been a considerable shock to Earle as I believe both he and Coulson had expected that any assault on the airfield would be by paratroops and the tactics they had agreed for defence and the positions 12th Bty had taken up or would take up in the morning had been decided on that basis. They both probably assumed, like all the various Allied HQs on the island, that the Japanese invasion would be a two-pronged attack in the extreme east and the extreme west of Java. Not surprisingly Earle now departed swiftly to find Coulson and apprise him of the situation, pausing only to order the BSM to warn BHQ and 'make arrangements to put the place in a state of defence'. The other officers dispersed and the Padre retired to bed, intending to rise early to await developments. He was preceded by Captain Newman, the Battery Captain, who had unfortunately picked up a dose of malaria.

The only other significant movement amongst the ground forces on the aerodrome over the next few hours seems to have been just after midnight when Prummel transferred command of the airfield defences to Earle. The telephone lines to Bandoeng were not working so he had no orders on where to proceed with his men and decided to stay around Kalidjati for the present until the situation clarified. JAC had realised as soon as the Japanese convoy heading for Eretan Wetan had been spotted that Kalidjati was not only a prime target but also undefendable. Even combined, Prummel's tiny force and Coulson's even smaller band of barely-trained gunners would be no match for the invaders, and there were no sizeable Allied ground forces near enough to reinforce them at this juncture. Preparations were started for the aerodrome's evacuation and destruction and in the meantime it was hoped that the bombing raids would at least slow the enemy down, even if he could not be stopped. However, no-one at JAC seemed to think it necessary to tell the units supposedly defending the airfield what was going on although the RA received its orders from that source.

There was also some indecision which fatally handicapped things. Part of this was later on the airfield itself but crucially in the early hours, AHK decided not to order any major troop movements yet on the grounds that it could not assess the size of the Japanese forces in the several landing areas.[164] This is strange, as the ABDACOM despatch published later in 1942 clearly states that they had drawn up a formula to calculate the size of Japanese forces from the number and types of ships in the convoy and by the evening of 28th February AHK would have had a fair idea of these.[165]

---

[164] Boer, op. cit., p251
[165] TNA: CAB 106/29, para 35

The same passage sets out the observed pattern of Japanese operations for taking islands in the area:

'secure an undefended airfield, put in anti-aircraft defences, develop the airfield and stock it with fuel and ammunition then bring in aircraft; working from this new airbase, to attack the air forces at the next objective'.

AHK had been working with ABDACOM. It was ABDACOM's successor and had inherited its intelligence units (albeit in a reduced form). Surely someone there must have been aware of the enemy's tactics and realised the very real danger to Kalidjati in its exposed position near the north coast and away from any substantial ground forces. Between 0200 and 0300hrs, as reports of the landings at Eretan Wetan began to filter in, there was some softening of this line as 2nd Cavalry Sqn, KNIL, was ordered to advance to Djatibarang to reconnoitre the invading forces. This move would still leave them nearly sixteen miles to the east of Eretan Wetan, while Kalidjati lay many miles further to the south-west. An infantry battalion at Cheribon (again to the east) was ordered to counter-attack: they would have to cover around thirty miles to do this.

These were, however, the nearest regular KNIL units. The other troops deployed that night and early the next day on the roads away from the beachhead were Landstorm or country guards, a kind of local Home Guard. Their numbers were small and, quite apart from differences and deficiencies in training and equipment compared to the KNIL, they crucially lacked communications. The only way they had of warning other units that the Japanese were on their way was to send some of their number to the nearest town or telephone – if any survived the encounter and assuming that the telephone would work when they reached it. And no-one could warn them of the enemy's approach.

Sadly, the Dutch ground defences were doomed from the start. Just as the Japanese had a plan for taking islands, so they had units specially tasked to take particular objectives including airfields. The Shoji detachment that landed 'in the vicinity of Patrol', seven miles west of Eretan Wetan, at 0400hrs Japanese time (0300 CJT) was not large but was perfectly formed for the purpose. Named after its commander, Colonel Shoji, it comprised two battalions of 230 Infantry Regiment, a tank company, a machine-gun battalion (less two companies), a mountain gun battalion (less one company), an engineer company (less two platoons) and an anti-aircraft company. In addition there were air force units whose job it was to repair and organise airfields, guarding the aircraft when they were flown in, with its own radio unit. The whole force was mechanised. It had light tanks and its own field telephone system that kept it constantly in touch with HQ.[166]

---

[166] TNA: AIR 23/4830: JAF book

On the good roads of Java it could make excellent progress and sweep through the feeble forces intended to halt its passage. The orders contained in the Japanese Air Force book state that only 'a section' (unspecified) of the Shoji detachment was 'to occupy the KALIDJATI airfield' after which it was to be used by the army's air force. The overall impression is of a carefully planned operation in stark contrast to what was happening amongst the Allies on Java.

At around 0200hrs on the morning of 1st March, the duty NCO at Zomer's command post took a telephone call from the assistant village chief at Eretan Wetan who told him that the Japanese were even then making a landing in front of his house and that their force included tanks.[167] Zomer himself was not present as he had been on a routine trip to Bandoeng but by the time he returned an hour later an alert had been put round the ML, RAF and RA units on the base. Faced with the news, Zomer did not hesitate. He would have learnt at HQ before he left Bandoeng that the Japanese were approaching as the Eretan Wetan convoy had already been identified and, as JAC were making plans even then to demolish and evacuate Kalidjati,[168] he would have been briefed on the actions to take should the need occur. He immediately despatched the only air-worthy Glenn Martin on the air base to Andir and tried to contact ML HQ in Bandoeng, which proved impossible because both the landline and radio had been put out of action by tropical storms. Meanwhile, Whistondale was also failing to make contact with BRITAIR for the same reason.

At around 0500hrs, having heard from an officer of the rural police at Soekamandi that the Japanese had not only landed but were advancing on Soebang, Zomer decided to act on his own initiative and start the airfield demolition process and evacuate his men.[169] He probably misheard the caller as the Japanese force heading for Soebang did not go via Soekamandi. If they had, they would have been at the airfield within the hour - and they were not. He probably said Sadang, a village or small town at the end of the road west from Kalidjati to Poerwakata. Zomer would have been just as concerned about the enemy being there, as it would cut his best road connections to the west and south, that is, to Batavia and Bandoeng. It could mean he would be surrounded and would certainly mean the vital rail line was cut. Whatever was said to Zomer, like the other officers commanding units at the base, he could only work on the

---

[167] Boer, op. cit., p262. There are discrepancies in the times given for various events. I can only suggest: firstly, that the various forces worked on different time systems, secondly, that some times may be start or finish times for the same lengthy event and thirdly, that men had other priorities besides double-checking the time. A fourth reason could be that the time given is the one they wanted to be taken as correct for any of a number of reasons.

[168] Boer, op. cit., p261

[169] ibidem

information he had and either option was very bad. He told Whistondale the news but the latter refused to act without orders from HQ so Zomer informed the other British and Australian unit commanders on the base to allow them to make unilaterally whatever decisions they felt to be appropriate.

While trying to locate Earle, he rushed into the bedroom in Battery HQ where the Padre was sleeping.

'The Colonel incidentally seemed in one hell of a flap, like the Group Captain.'

Macartney-Filgate's account reads:

'At dawn on March 1st a Dutch colonel visited 49 Battery H.Q. but left again almost immediately, having no information to give; nor did he make it clear what the Dutch plan was.'

It is reasonable to assume that Macartney-Filgate's version of events that day is based on Earle's own report to him later as he took command of 48th Regt the next day so from now on I will refer to his account as Earle's. I believe that Zomer tried to contact Earle at his HQ but the major was not there and he left to find him rather than leaving a message with the BHQ staff. It is possible that at this stage he did not find Earle, who could have been anywhere on the airfield.

As his crews returned from their last bombing ops around 0530hrs, Zomer ordered them to depart for Andir after debriefing and refuelling of the aircraft. Two British sources state that only one runway was still operational following bombing[170] so I believe that they would have been parked up in Dispersal Area West ready to take advantage of proximity to the useable runway. Meanwhile the training aircraft from the flying school and unflyable ML machines were parked up in Dispersal Area East. Zomer also started to make arrangements for the evacuation of aircrew while organising preparations for the demolition of the airfield and its stores, using personnel of 1-Vl.G.II Afdeling. He had already given orders for all afdelingen personnel to assemble at the base.

Prummel, still unable to make contact with HQ in Bandoeng to determine where he should take his men, had handed over his HQ at the southern edge of the airfield to Coulson and retired to Zomer's HQ to await instructions. In the light of the information of enemy movements now coming in, he despatched a section of about forty-five men under Sgt-Maj H J Heijligers towards Soebang to man a road block and a similar number under 1st Lt J van den Berkhof to do the same at Pasir Boengoer, thus covering the road from Soekamandi. For some unexplained reason, van

---

[170] Flt Lt Campbell Hill's report and 84 Sqn report, both in AIR 20/5573

den Berkhof's men simply built an obstruction on that road and moved off to take up positions on the Soebang-Poerwakarta road west of the airfield.[171] Prummel did not, however, tell Earle what he was doing: he was under no obligation to do so having handed over his local responsibilities. The major did not know where he had gone and what he was doing after he and his men moved off at 0600hrs from the pillboxes they had been manning.[172]

It was unlikely that Prummel had told Coulson of his movements either. The two men appear to have fundamentally disagreed on tactics the day before when the airfield defence was handed over to the British. Coulson rejected the 'strongpoints' which Prummel's men had constructed and proposed to 'divide his men over the four corners' of the airfield, a policy that was obviously at odds with the Dutchman's views[173] though the British did in fact use some of his ground works in what seems to be a revised scheme.

Coulson had had his meagre force reinforced by 84 Sqn's defence section of thirty men. It had become common practice at this stage of the war to allocate ground crew for airfield defence as the RAF Regiment had not yet been formed. There was no formal training for this and weapons were of no standard type – merely what was available – so the capability of individual forces would vary widely. That of the projected RAF Lahat on Sumatra had been basic to the point of being non-existent. I have no information on 84 Sqn's force. Around a hundred men of the resulting joint unit were divided between the pill box and barbed wire defences to the north-west and the south-east of the flying field. The usefulness of the fortifications was limited by their line of fire. This was solely across the airfield, fine if the enemy is landing paratroops on the runways but useless if he comes from the surrounding terrain. The rest were given patrolling duties, using some jeeps and semi-armoured lorries gifted to them by Prummel.[174]

Communications with both ML HQ and BRITAIR were finally re-established at around 0700hrs using what was known as the 'Abdair line', a military telephone link. Both HQs tried to assure the Station Commanders that Kalidjati was not under threat and that a counter-attack against the invaders was on its way. Zomer was not convinced. He was well aware of the distances involved for any force from the Cheribon region and of the

---

[171] Boer, op. cit., p264-5

[172] Macartney-Filgate, op. cit., p30

[173] Memoirs of Captain R A Baron Mackay (Dutch Liaison Officer), IWM Documents 8148: p68

[174] Boer, op. cit., p265-6. The lorries had armoured sides but open platforms which gave their occupants limited protection. 12th Bty had no armoured cars of its own. The only ones available to 6th HAA Regt when they were converted to infantry stayed with 15th Bty at Tjimahi.

calibre of any defensive forces otherwise in front of him. To his mind the only sensible option was to get out as soon as possible after destroying as much as possible. He failed to convince Whistondale that now was the time to act on one's own initiative and sent his remaining Glenn Martins off to Andir, much to the RAF officer's amazement. The ML Hurricane squadron that had been based at the airfield had been sent further east to Ngoro to provide air cover for the Allied fleet a couple of days before and had not returned, so that was one less unit for him to evacuate.

The Group Captain was clearly out of his depth – to be honest, it was a pretty alarming situation for any officer to be in - but what follows seems to demonstrate that he was struck with a fatal attack of indecisiveness at this critical moment. All his years of training and experience as a peacetime RAF officer must have been in revolt at the thought of taking the huge step of ordering his squadrons and the defending ground units to abandon the airfield without receiving specific orders to do so from HQ. Whether it ever crossed his mind that RAF HQ, indeed all Allied HQs on Java, did not have a clue where the Japanese who had landed north of his airfield actually were at this moment it is impossible to tell. He told Jeudwine:

'that the Dutch were evacuating all their serviceable aircraft to Bandoeng and destroying the petrol dump, but R.A.F. Headquarters at Bandoeng had ordered maximum dispersal and concealment of 84 Squadron's aircraft as usual.'

This would mean that the eight serviceable Blenheims left would finish up in Dispersal Area East, five minutes taxying from the only remaining useable runway at Kalidjati[175].

Jeudwine obviously thought the orders were a recipe for disaster as he apparently took the precaution of ringing AHQ himself to get them confirmed. He then visited Soebang where the off-duty aircrew were trying to sleep after their busy night, woke them up and organised them for evacuation back to the airfield. While in Soebang he was told by a Dutch Volunteer Force officer that they had been ordered to abandon the town and withdraw to the hills, news that must have given a new impetus to his efforts. He returned to the airfield to apprise Whistondale of the current state of affairs in Soebang.

In the interim, the Group Captain had visited Earle. He had obviously changed his mind about following RAF HQ's orders by now for he told him that he had no details of the enemy landing that he thought had happened on the coast but that his aircraft were in the process of evacuating the airfield and he himself was leaving almost immediately for Bandoeng. This

---

[175] TNA: AIR 20/5573: 84 Sqn report. The time given there is 0600hrs but the RAF were working one hour behind CJT which is used in the Dutch reports.

was the last Earle saw of him, giving the time of his departure for the capital, via Soebang, as 0800hrs. However, it was undoubtedly later, between 0930 and 1000hrs, but Earle's HQ were well away to the west from Station HQ so he would not have known when Whistondale, who was travelling via Soebang, actually left the airfield.[176]

Once back at his HQ after speaking with Earle, he was again visited by Zomer and by then had changed his mind yet again, according to the Dutchman's account. Zomer took a firm line. He told Whistondale that the Dutch squadrons were evacuating the airfield, the petrol dumps were being destroyed and the Dutch defence troops were also withdrawing. Destroying an airfield is not a simple matter, as the British had already discovered in Malaya, but even with a restricted amount of time it would be possible to make away with stores, fuel, ammunition and surplus airframes, thus denying their use to the enemy. Zomer alone could command a force that could do this as he had the knowledge within his HQ of where everything was and the personnel to do it. Everything at this point would seem to hinge on who was the senior Allied officer on the airbase. Maltby claimed later it was Whistondale and certainly now the Group Captain stopped the demolitions and rang Maltby for instructions. He was told that while the reasons for the Dutch withdrawal were not known, he should carry out his previous 'dispersal' orders. Nevertheless, he should make preparations for evacuation 'quietly so as not to cause alarm' and:

'in the event of his being unable to communicate with Bandoeng he was to use his discretion and evacuate the aerodrome if things became critical.'[177]

Before he could put any of his plans into action, he met Jeudwine who had just returned from Soebang with news of the projected Dutch retreat. According to the history of 84 Sqn in the National Archives, Whistondale:

'decided to go to Soebang himself. He was never seen again.'[178]

This is a drastic contraction of events as other accounts show and, if they are to be believed, also possibly a diplomatic version of the truth.

It took Zomer until around 0930hrs to persuade Whistondale to act on his own initiative, trusting in the better information of the local officers on hand rather than sticking rigidly to the letter of HQ's orders when HQ was clearly wildly out of touch with the situation on the ground. Until then he fended off all requests to despatch his squadrons, which meant that 49th and 12th Batteries could not leave either. Until the Allied air forces had quitted the aerodrome, they had to stay to defend them. Finally, he announced that he was going to Soebang to investigate the situation,

---

[176] Macartney-Filgate, op. cit., p30
[177] TNA: AIR 23/2123, Appendix H, Capture of Kalidjati Aerodrome
[178] TNA: AIR 20/5573

adding that it would give him the opportunity to pick up his luggage. A number of bystanders apparently felt what he really wanted to retrieve was his all-important stamp collection.[179] He took with him a passenger, Flt Lt R Richards of 59 Sqn, who had only arrived at Kalidjati overnight. Neither of them were ever seen again. Crucially, he does not seem to have given orders for evacuation before his departure, leaving both squadrons and RA units in a state of limbo. If he had taken on himself the command of Kalidjati as a whole, he did the same to the Dutch. It was a totally unacceptable action for a senior officer to take and foolhardy to the ultimate degree.

So what was the situation in Soebang? It seems that, after leaving the beachhead at around 0445hrs, the vanguard of the 1,200 strong Wakamatsu unit tasked with taking Kalidjati had travelled down the road from Pamanoekan, the first forty-odd infantry reaching the northern outskirts of Soebang in two trucks around 0800hrs. The local troops were no match for even this small number, whose reinforcements, lorry-mounted cannon and six tanks were still a distance behind. The Dutch could not call Bandoeng for reinforcements as the civilian telephone lines were still out of action and fell back to the western part of the town. Messengers were sent to Kalidjati to warn the airfield of the invaders' progress and the local troops retreated in this direction. By 0915hrs the Japanese vanguard, nearly two hundred strong and complete with tanks, was in possession of Soebang and their forward unit had passed through and come up against Sgt-Maj H J Heijligers' force at their roadblock on the road to Kalidjati. A fire-fight ensued but Heijligers' men were outflanked by the enemy and retreated to the south, being strafed by their own ML Brewster Buffalos, apparently leaving the road open to the Japanese. By the time Whistondale left Kalidjati, the Japanese were already only a few miles away travelling up the same road towards him.

There may have been a lack of intelligence at HQ and a shortage of orders for the evolving situation but the officers commanding the forces at Kalidjati were not all paralysed in those early hours like the Group Captain. The most decisive of these was Flt Lt C C Verco (commanding 1 RAAF Squadron in the absence of W/Cdr Davis). After the early morning warning from the Dutch, preparations were started for a speedy departure. The two airworthy but not operational Hudsons were flown off to Andir while the rest of the squadron got ready to move, with transport lined up on the west side of the airfield.[180] The two operational Hudsons waited only for their crews and orders to go.

Zomer had also been busy, evacuating his squadrons both by air and by bus

[179] Shores and others, op. cit., p297
[180] Australian Air War History, Chapter 22, Loss of Timor and Java, p441

and car on the roads to Andir. Around 0930hrs he warned the KNIL anti-aircraft detachment on the airfield to make ready to go. But at this point he seemed to stop like Whistondale. Why did he not warn the personnel at the ML Technical Services workshops? In fact, why did he not evacuate all Dutch forces on the aerodrome and go himself? Was it because he had to accept the British officer's superiority and this was as far as he felt he could go? Or was it because he had not received orders from HQ to evacuate, in fact had been encouraged to stay? If he could persuade Whistondale that the only sensible option was to go and they both left, he would not appear to be deserting his post. Whatever the reason, he did not complete his preparations and in fact failed to notify all ML units on the base of the approaching danger. Some ML ground crew were still continuing their repair activities when the Japanese struck. However, he did make substantial efforts to change the Group Captain's mind, although unfortunately this came too late to materially affect the outcome.

Jeudwine meanwhile had alerted his aircrews and made the arrangements that got them to the airfield before Soebang was taken. The squadron was warned to be ready to move out, transport for this was collected at the western end of the airfield and, after Whistondale's departure, a demolition party was organised to destroy the unserviceable aircraft in Dispersal Area North to the north-west of the flying field. It was hoped that it would be possible to fly off the airworthy Blenheims in Dispersal Area East if they got enough warning for the crews. While all this was going on, some of the aircrew who had been at Kalidjati overnight took advantage of the lorries going back to Soebang to go themselves to 'fetch their kit'. P/O Macnally made the trip and reported on return that the village was deserted. This was probably around 0815-0830hrs at a guess as the Dutch would have broken off contact with the Japanese to the north and be retreating to the west of Soebang. P/O D W Kewish and F/O J E W Bott[181], both 84 Sqn, F/Sgt McBride and four other airmen then took another truck to collect kit, probably soon after 0900hrs, and did not return. They paid the highest possible price for their curiosity.

Earle meanwhile was having a very bad morning that would shortly become much, much worse. He could get no instructions from RHQ which had started its move from Batavia to Tjimahi at 0800hrs that day. Lt Col Pearson and Capt Williams had started earlier and were intending to go there via Kalidjati but were turned back by the Dutch (possibly van den Berkhof's patrol?) some ten miles away. They attempted to reach the airfield by using roads sweeping round to the south but this too proved impossible and they were forced to go on to Tjimahi. Thus Earle had lost

---

[181] CWGC gives his date of death as 05.03.42, a mistake which was made in the original reports of his death and never corrected. They do report that he died at a 'gun post' at 'Kalidjata', Java

his best chance of advice. He decided to try GHQ Bandoeng and the impotent Sitwell. Rev Godfrey tells us:

'Earle had got through to Sitwell at G.H.Q. on the phone to ask for instructions. But nothing was forthcoming and I think they told him to ring again later.'

As the telephone line went via Soebang, the exchange there was no longer working when the Major rang later – it was in the hands of the Japanese.

Unfortunately the Padre rarely gives any timings for events but he does give a very vivid picture of what was going on. He describes events after Whistondale's departure from BHQ around 0730hrs that morning:

'From then on uncertainty reigned in B.H.Q. There was a complete lack of intelligence. No wireless reports came in, no despatch riders arrived with messages. No one knew where the Japanese forces were, how many they were in number, which direction they were taking, or whether the Dutch were at any point offering resistance. All was surmise.'

Little did he know it but this ignorance was spread through all HQs on the aerodrome and indeed probably in at least some of the HQs in Bandoeng! Unfortunately, as Earle's HQ were some distance from those of the air force commanders on the airfield, what little information they had of whatever accuracy never reached him – yet he and Coulson were responsible for the defence of the place.

Coulson spent most of the next hour or two with Earle looking at maps, talking over the possibilities and probabilities and trying to make what plans they could with the limited intelligence to hand. They had a very basic difference of opinion about tactics: Earle was in favour of a strategic withdrawal as soon as the RAF left and allowed him that option while Coulson appears to have favoured 'stand and fight'. There was a lot of sense in what Earle was suggesting. They had no knowledge of the strength of the approaching enemy force or its whereabouts and very few resources in men or machinery at their disposal. The airfield was a vast area to defend especially when you didn't know exactly where the attack or attacks might come from. Coulson's men had little infantry training, only a couple of lightly armoured vehicles, few defensive positions and did not know the ground they would be fighting over. Earle's instinct as an artillery officer would be to save his guns if at all possible and the Allies could not afford to lose any AA guns on Java.

Looking at the situation seventy-five years later it is easy to misunderstand how ill-prepared the RA units were and here Macartney-Filgate's contemporary appreciation of the situation is vital to put things in context. In an appendix to his report entitled 'Additional Comments Concerning Events at Kalidjati Aerodrome' he writes:

'However it may have looked on paper, the futility in practice of leaving to R.A.F. ground staff and anti-aircraft gunners, untrained even in musketry, much less in infantry tactics, the task of opposing a ground attack by troops of a type which had overwhelmed fully trained infantry in Malaya need no emphasis. Yet, time and again in Sumatra and in Java, the only ground defence on aerodromes and elsewhere had to be provided by men such as these who, one assumes, were supposed to gain from supernatural sources some hitherto unacquired knowledge by the mere fact of having a firearm thrust into their hands at the last minute, whereas in the majority of cases the men to whom Tommy guns for example were issued had to have explained to them the method of firing this weapon which they were then seeing for the first time.'

In short, Earle was right in his opinion.

Why did Coulson favour a defence in these circumstances? Without more information, and this we are now unlikely to get, it is only possible to speculate. One possibility is that 6th HAA Regt felt that when they came up against Japanese paratroops in Sumatra at P I and the oil refineries, the regiment had come off best and retreated too early, as Lt-Col Baillie stated in his report.[182] I believe that Coulson himself had not taken part in the fighting, as the HQ of 12th Bty was at P II, but Sherrard, his captain, had been killed in the action at Pladjoe oil refinery. Did he overestimate his men's ability or underestimate the calibre of the troops they would be up against or did he hope for some form of revenge for their earlier losses? Perhaps like the Rev Godfrey he just felt 'strategic retreats' were getting a bit too common in the British Army. We will never know.

At around 0830hrs, Earle issued a warning order to 'Prepare to move' to 'a previously selected rendezvous on the Kalidjati-Sadang-Poerwakarta road'. Rev Godfrey records that the result of this order was that:

'everyone was standing by at B.H.Q. with transport under cover along the road and everything loaded up. But no guns had been drawn out from their positions or altered from their A.A. role though there was evidently no aerial activity that morning.'

The Padre does not seem to realise that Earle was in a very difficult position. Just because there had been no air raid that morning did not mean there would not be one at any moment – after all, during the Battery's deployment at Kalidjati no air raid had yet come before 0920hrs so there was still plenty of time for an attack to develop. Also, the fact that there had been a landing on the coast did not inevitably rule out the possibility of a paratroop attack on the airfield. Earle did not know either

---

[182] TNA: CAB 106/20: 'The Regiment were bitterly disappointed . . . they were confident that they could give a good account of themselves if only they had been allowed to stop and fight.'

the size or the position of the Japanese force that had landed north of him. If he withdrew his guns it would take several minutes to unhitch them from their tow trucks and ready them for either anti-aircraft duties or to combat a land assault. If he did not and there was a surprise attack and he had to retreat, he could lose his guns and much of his battery. He was damned if he did and damned if he didn't. To make matters worse Newman, his WWI-veteran battery captain, had malaria and may not have been able to give him much cogent advice. He seems to have decided on a policy of 'half-way house', hoping that he would get more information which would allow him to make a reasonable decision and that the RAF would get a move on and evacuate, allowing 49th Bty to do so too.

A little later, probably around 0915hrs, a 15-cwt truck left BHQ to go on its daily routine trip to Soebang to collect rations, carrying Bdr R R Pennell and Gunners W B Garrett and A Staplehurst.[183] Rev Godfrey had doubts later, and possibly at the time, about whether this was a good idea:

'No one suggested it might be inadvisable and at any rate they said the driver could bring back information if he could not get through. So off the ration truck went. And it did not return.'

Both the men who reported the circumstances of their loss in detail post-war commented that the road they were on was the one the Japanese used to attack the aerodrome, BQMS Webster adding: 'There was no side road or way by which they could take evasive action.' All three men now lie in one of the mass graves at Djakarta Ancol War Cemetery.

Around 0930hrs another member of the Battery was sent down the road to Soebang, this time an officer, 2nd Lt R Mounsdon, of 'A' Troop. Earle's account states that he:

'set off on a motor cycle for Soebang on purely administrative matters, having no knowledge of the proximity of the enemy.'

Once again the Padre puts a bit more flesh on the bones with his account:

'with no information yet coming young Mounsdon was sent off on a recce to try and find out the enemies' whereabouts. I remember him still, sitting on his motor-bike outside B.H.Q. with his Tommy gun on his back and two revolvers in his belt, waiting for his orders. He was not worried or concerned about anything but was his normal cheerful self. "Well Padre, what about a bit of moral re-armament?" for that was his customary greeting. I wished him luck as he set off on the Soebang road.'

Dick Mounsdon, 'one of the best that I have met in this war', was never seen by his battery again.

---

[183] TNA: WO 361/342: 25A - BQMS Webster's list of missing, 11A - Gnr C Lilley's letter

Quarter of an hour later, something made Earle decide to deploy two of his guns and some of Coulson's men in defensive roadblocks on the Kalidjati-Soebang and Kalidjati-Poerwadadi roads. This latter was the road directlynorth from the aerodrome to the railway line. Perhaps Earle had had a message from Zomer, who had been visited by retreating country guards from Soebang at around 0930hrs[184] telling him that the Japanese had taken the town and their tanks were approaching the airfield. The guns allocated for the action were pulled out and while the platoons from 12th Bty were being organised, Earle and Lt Bagnall, who was to command the roadblock on the road to Soebang, moved out on motorcycles to recce suitable positions for the guns.

They had not got far when, according to Earle's account, they saw a Japanese AFV coming down the road towards the aerodrome. To cover the gap of time there undoubtedly was between this sighting and the armoured force arriving on the airfield, not long but longer than simply driving down the road would take, I wonder if at that point what they actually saw was the Japanese dealing with a patrol of about ten men in an armoured car under the command of Vdg J R J Rugebregt that Prummel had sent up the road at around 1015hrs according to the Dutch account,[185] a time that must almost certainly be wrong. Prummel's squad must have left earlier than the RA officers as Earle does not mention seeing them at all and would certainly have warned them of the danger on his way back if he had passed them on the way out. Also Zomer speaks of hearing gunfire up the road slightly before this and it would be extremely unlikely that a small patrol would have been dispatched if the enemy were known to be in the offing. Nothing that travelled up the road to Soebang from about 0900hrs onwards returned to the airfield and therefore must have been intercepted by the Japanese. As the Japanese took the men from this patrol prisoner and did not take the RA officers, I think it is reasonable to suppose that the British officers may actually have seen the end of an episode that would not only have held up the enemy but would also explain other events reported by eye witnesses.

Earle and Bagnall turned their bikes and dashed back to the airfield. Here in Station HQ Jeudwine, now in charge of RAF Kalidjati in the absence of his superior, had just found a copy of the signal allowing OC RAF Kalidjati to 'evacuate at his discretion' if circumstances warranted it. Any decision he was about to take on this was rudely speeded up by the arrival of 'an R.A. officer' who explained that 'the Japanese had been sighted three miles up the road towards Soebang'.[186] I would like to believe, like the Padre, that this was Mounsdon but I fear that he was probably already dead far up the

---

[184] Boer, op. cit., p268
[185] ibidem, p269
[186] TNA: AIR 23/2123: Appendix H, para 10

road and that this was Bagnall on his way to warn Coulson and to reach C Troop HQ to evacuate his men while Earle rushed back to Battery HQ to move all the RA units out.

Ten: Kalidjati, 1st March 1942 – The Storm

Kalidjati now awaited its fate, its senior officers hoping in vain for some kind of guidance from HQ in Bandoeng. They did not know the enemy's strength, armament or whereabouts. They were in no position to make sensible plans or to draw up any meaningful plan of defence and when the blow struck, it would be sudden, ferocious and overwhelming, like a flash flood. So far, the story of what happened there on 1st March 1942 has been taken from several interlocking and fairly coherent accounts furnished later by officers who were on the aerodrome that day. It has been a reasonably straightforward case of combining them into one narrative stream but from this point on, the eyewitness statements tend to give fragmentary evidence for events.

There are good reasons for this. Any military airfield is a huge expanse and this one was a major base with three runways, four dispersal areas, multiple workshops and offices and several hangars, a couple of which were quite substantial structures. It was an area of land over a mile across in any direction with some sightlines obscured by buildings or bush. Therefore even at the best of times you could not hope to see what was going on at the far side of the field with any accuracy. The communications between units based there were either poor or non-existent. As we have seen, Zomer personally did the rounds of units to inform them of the Japanese advance and 84 Sqn HQ relied on despatch riders to keep in touch with RAF Kalidjati HQ. It seems likely that communications between Earle and Coulson were equally bad.

Now add the 'complication' of enemy action, a traumatic experience. If a man believes he will be shot in the next two minutes, he is unlikely to be staring at events in the middle distance with any particular interest. Everyone from the Allied units involved would be focussed on what was going on directly around them, who was firing at them and how they could retaliate or get away - not on what was happening almost a mile away on the far side of the airfield. It is therefore reasonable to suppose that any comments they make or actions they mention will be linked to developments near to where they are and may well be fragmentary. They are unlikely to be consulting their watches so events will tend to lack a time or duration. While their information is vital for building a picture of events, it has to be collated, connected and put in context to make a viable whole. What follows is what I believe happened based on this evidence. I have not used parts of some accounts if they seem to be unlikely, contradicted by other accounts or even probably mistaken. I am also doing what, as a historian, I am most reluctant to do: using probability and gut feeling when the sources are lacking to complete the story. I hope to make it clear when I take this very controversial course and the reader can decide whether it is justified or not.

I believe that there were in fact two attacks on Kalidjati that day, separated by only a few minutes: the first one from a small force of Japanese infantry that had infiltrated the north side of the airfield and the second and larger one involving AFVs and a motorised column from the main road from Soebang in the north-east corner of the airfield. It is this later attack which one hears the most about but this action alone does not explain the accounts of eye-witnesses. The most likely explanation is that the Japanese had planned a synchronised attack by forces on two sides of the airfield, a theory put forward in Earle's account,[187] and that one of these was compelled to begin a little early for some reason. Their usual *modus operandi* was to out-flank the enemy and here at Kalidjati they knew the layout of the airfield from aerial photographs, copies of which had been distributed to the attacking forces. These would have probably been supplemented with up-to-date information about anti-aircraft gun numbers, positions, etc. As the Bofors gun could be used in an anti-tank role, it would be very rash of any commander to rely on a one-column assault with light tanks and lorries through the main gate onto an airfield with these weapons all around the perimeter and possibly warned of their approach, yet this is what the RAF and Dutch accounts seem to suggest – or do they?

It appears that around 1000hrs 'remote but clearly audible firing could be heard'[188] by Zomer in his HQ near the main gate at the north-east of the aerodrome. This coincided with a telephone call from ML Command, possibly from Colonel Kengen, OC ML, intended to reassure Zomer that Kalidjati was in no immediate danger. The furious officer:

'held the receiver outside the window and then shouted in the mouthpiece, "That's the Japs, damn it, we are not firing ourselves, for heaven's sake, listen."'

There are two possibilities for the source of this firing, which was prior to the main attack that RAF and Dutch sources agree happened at around 1030hrs. Either Zomer could hear Prummel's latest detachment in action against the enemy on the Soebang road or the noise came from the infiltrating force north of the airfield that may have been ordered to open the offensive earlier than had been planned as a result of the main force encountering the Dutch (their mobile communications would have allowed them to pass the order) or perhaps because it had been spotted by someone from 49th Bty, resulting in a fire-fight. The distant firing could not have been the Japanese attacking Whistondale's car as all the Dutch timings suggest he was way down the road by then and had run into the enemy long ago.

---

[187] Macartney-Filgate, op. cit., p30: 'It is evident that the enemy had synchronised the approach of the various attacking parties with great precision.'
[188] Boer, op. cit., p268

Maj-Gen Sitwell gives the time of the attack in his reports as 'about 1000 hours'[189] and this fits with Earle's account.[190] I believe that prior to this the infiltrating Japanese force moving westwards from the main Soebang road had come across C Troop's No 1 Gun at the extreme north of the aerodrome behind Battery HQ, probably finishing their belated breakfast prior to moving out to form a roadblock.[191] Jack Gunn's account suggests that the gun crew were caught unawares by this force and slaughtered to a man by bayonet or sword before they could reach their weapons or raise the alarm. The enemy then moved on towards A Troop HQ, somewhere between No 1 Gun and Battery HQ. The attack on the Troop HQ possibly did not go so smoothly for some reason and it may be that this was the firing that Zomer and the RAF heard, both having HQs at the gate to the east of here.

Rev Godfrey, then waiting at Battery HQ, writes of hearing rifle and machine-gun fire which he first says came 'from the direction of the drome entrance' which was east of him. However, he then goes on to say that some men:

'seized their rifles and made a dive behind the bungalows towards the direction where the sounds were coming from'

and 'behind' was north, the direction of No 1 Gun and A Troop HQ! Very shortly after this, Major Earle arrived on his motor bike, having seen the Japanese armoured column approaching from Soebang, and:

'charged into the B.H.Q. building shouting the while "To the rendezvous".'

Earle himself reports that:

'enemy rifle and machine gun fire opened up from the scrub on at least two sides of the aerodrome'

at almost the exact time he got back to his HQ, whereupon he ordered his battery to move to the rendezvous. The light tanks appeared on the airfield very shortly afterwards. The Padre does not mention seeing them at all during his speedy departure westwards in his personal truck together with his driver, Loftus, and one of the BHQ cooks:

'Looking out on to the airfield as we turned into the main road there was nothing to be seen save some small bushes on fire but the sounds of firing from unpleasantly close quarters continued.'

---

[189] TNA: CAB 106/39 and WO 32/12105 as a draft despatch and WO 106/5983 and WO 106/2562 as a revised 'report' version. The information on Kalidjati is the same in the main text of all of these.
[190] Macartney-Filgate, op. cit., p30
[191] I have been told that it was very late to be eating breakfast but L/B Halford and some of his comrades in 12th Bty were also doing just that when the Japanese attacked. (Rev Godfrey, op. cit., p27)

This would have been the small arms fire that he had heard earlier rather than fire from the AFVs or he would certainly have commented on it.

In a post-war letter to the War Office Casualty Branch, BQMS Webster explained that A Troop HQ, 'a private house on the west side of the aerodrome', was cut off as the Battery evacuated the airfield 'and word could not be sent to them'. The building was:

'seen to be fired upon and then attacked by bayonet charge by Japanese infantry'[192]

with the loss of life of all within it (around eighteen men), both THQ personnel and ORs awaiting removal to hospital for malaria and other medical issues.[193] I suggest that this enemy detachment was now beaten back for a very short while by men from 49th Bty as in Jack Gunn's account: 'we were reformed by officers who led us back and we took it back again'. As this was the only time that Jack Gunn's battery was in action as infantry against the Japanese, it would have been the time he recalled using a bayonet. When I asked how he could do it, he replied that it was very easy when the man coming at you also had a bayonet and it was either him or you! What they took back was not the entire airfield but C Troop's No 1 Gun site and possibly A Troop HQ and it was at the former that their officers made them look at the corpses of their dead comrades.

There is further backing for this interpretation from the memoirs of an RAF man on the airfield. LAC Chad Middleton, one of the 84 Sqn ground crew demolition party sent to destroy the unserviceable Blenheims in Dispersal Area North, a little further west along the main road from 49th Bty's buildings, recalled how before they could set about their task:

'all hell broke loose. The Japs who had been occupying the perimeter of the airfield broke cover and in the mayhem and confusion which followed many ground gunners and other suffered horrible deaths. We were so overwhelmed that all we could do was to try to get away from this holocaust.'[194]

While Middleton's account goes on to say they made a run for, and escaped on, an Army lorry, he could not possibly have known that the casualties 'suffered horrible deaths' unless he, or someone he spoke to later, had actually seen the bodies that day. The most he could have known was that men had died. The simplest explanation for this is a successful but short-lived British counter-attack.

---

[192] TNA: WO 361/342: the information comes from BQMS Webster's letter in this file but as he himself was not actually there on the day he gives his source as Sgt R L G Brooks of 49th LAA
[193] TNA: WO 361/342: Gnr North's form and Webster's letter
[194] Shores and others, Vol 2, p296

There is also indirect confirmation for a secondary attack through the rear of the airfield in Middleton's talk of 'Japs . . . occupying the perimeter' and breaking cover and Rev Godfrey, as we shall see, talks of the havoc wrought by snipers hidden in the nearby trees. These are obviously not the same troops as the infantry in trucks who arrived with the main enemy force.

The success of the counter-attack was very short-lived: the airfield as an Allied base was doomed the moment the main Japanese column, with light tanks, armoured vehicles and infantry in lorries, arrived at the main gate. The Wakamatsu force was only around 1,200 strong in all but this was enough. There were no proper Allied infantry or defensive positions and no firepower to match that of the light Japanese tanks. There was no possibility of a defence. Dutch reports and both Maltby's printed despatch and his report to the Air Ministry agree on 1030hrs as the time for the frontal assault. This storm-surge resulted in a chaotic evacuation by every unit there that could get away. The attackers split up, their tanks and AFVs bursting through the gates onto the flying field while the infantry in lorries went west along the perimeter down the main road to Bandoeng or south down a road on the east side of the airfield itself through the offices and workshops. Whether the defenders survived or not depended very much on their own initiative and where they happened to be.

From this point on so much happens almost simultaneously that it is difficult to find a logical order to put it in and survivor accounts unfortunately do not generally give any timings. The despatch one would have expected that W/Cdr Jeudwine would have been required to write after his escape from Java later that month is not in the National Archives (or is not currently available there), like other crucial reports dealing with this incident, so I have done my best with the information I have.

Most of the survivors seem to come from those units that had retreated to or were stationed around the western part of the airfield. Transport for all the units at Kalidjati was probably lined up along here facing south on a road running between Dispersal Area West and the guns of B Troop, 49th Bty, or along the southern boundary of the flying field facing west. This allowed evacuation via a subsidiary road at the south-western corner of the aerodrome through the bush to join the main road to Bandoeng further west without blocking that road near the airfield, as in an ideal world it might bring reinforcements.

The Dutch units at Kalidjati, both ML and KNIL, were scattered over the airfield but most of the ML aircrew and some ground crew had already left the airfield by bus or truck by 1000hrs while others were waiting on the southern side of the airfield for orders to go. The KNIL AA unit, warned to move at around 0930hrs, were either on the move or ready to go as it suffered no casualties that day.[195] Their compatriots on the eastern side of the airfield would not be so lucky. Thanks to Flt Lt Verco's prudent arrangements, almost all the RAAF personnel, ground and flying, were able to get away safely in their transport on the west side of the airfield, their only acknowledged casualty being the officer who had accompanied Whistondale on his ill-fated expedition.

The two non-operational RAAF Hudsons had already flown off to Bandoeng but the two operational Hudsons now made remarkable escapes as the Japanese attacked. It is an incredible story of perseverance, initiative and courage. The vivid and detailed report of P/O Campbell Hill, observer on the crewed aircraft, survives in the National Archives.[196] He had been rudely awakened from his well-earned sleep after night bombing by Jeudwine's visit to Soebang and recalled to the airfield with the rest of the aircrew billeted there. Once at Kalidjati, they found the situation uncertain with no orders forthcoming from Gp Capt Whistondale, or, after the latter's departure, Jeudwine himself. He and his pilot, P/O Wilson, decided to find their aircraft in order to take off as soon as possible when the order to depart that they thought was crucial at this time finally came through. They drove in a lorry, gathering a crew as they went, to Dispersal Area West where they believed it would be parked up:

'as the remainder of the drome was unserviceable due to Japanese pattern bombing.'

Not only was the Hudson not there but as they turned back onto the airfield to search elsewhere they could see:

'enemy mechanised units . . . entering the gate in the North East corner of the drome.'

They then searched the southern boundary from west to east before finding their aircraft in a pen the south-east corner 'with its nose jammed right up against the back of the pen.' There now followed a considerable struggle to free and turn the Hudson while firing from the tanks and armoured cars moved from 'the other side of the drome' to 'increasing' but 'directed at nothing in particular'. Eventually the aircraft was free and the airmen climbed aboard, Campbell Hill extricating an Australian who had fallen 'up to his neck in a swamp behind the pen' and the attempt to take off began.

The main runway was out of the question as 'two enemy tanks and four armoured cars were within 100 yards' but Campbell Hill had guided Wilson into the same pen using a lorry when they had arrived at Kalidjati only a couple of days before. He therefore directed his pilot to 'a narrow track

---

[195] Boer, op. cit., p235
[196] TNA: AIR 20/5573

through the bomb craters' – and between two enemy tanks 'not fifty yards apart'. He:

'held the brake full on, opened up the throttles and away we went. We were well level with the tanks before they recovered from their surprise and opened fire.'

Even a hit from one of the tanks was not going to stop Wilson completing this hairy take off, just avoiding the trees as they sped on their way to Bandoeng.

F/O P Gibbes' escape was equally dramatic. He had taken cover in a ditch on the western side of the airfield along with Flt Lt Holland of 84 Sqn when the Japanese armoured forces opened fire towards them. Despite this, he told Holland he was going to get into his aircraft and take off and proceeded to work his way across to it, jumping in during a lull in the firing. From the description of his position on the airfield it seems probable that his aircraft had either been parked up as near as possible to Dispersal Area West and its access to the surviving runway or was in the process of being moved there when the attack occurred. Not daring to show his head and all alone in the aircraft, Gibbes set the controls for take up and finally pressed the starter buttons for the engines. Luckily both started and without stopping to warm them, he opened the throttles and took off through a maelstrom of enemy fire.[197]

The RAF were also preparing to depart but had not reached the same state of readiness as the RAAF. A group of volunteers, as we have seen, was heading to Dispersal Area North to destroy the unserviceable Blenheims of 84 Sqn and these men, we can assume, largely escaped by hitching lifts on Army trucks nearby or in the RAF transport that had been lined up along the track to the west ready to evacuate personnel when the order came. The RAF aerodrome defence party was in the trenches or pillboxes on the airfield with Coulson's men and some ground crew were still on the airfield, presumably ready either to destroy equipment or to get the surviving aircraft into the air.

Much more is known (from a British point of view) about the RAF and RAAF escapes from Kalidjati than those of other units as a number of eye-witness accounts have been published[198]. Some reports from survivors are also available in the National Archives. Most RAF pilots and some aircrew were waiting at RAF Station HQ near the main gate at the north-east corner of the aerodrome, hoping to get the order to fly off their serviceable aircraft. The Station HQ staff, of course, were still there. The orders

---

[197] Shores and others, op. cit., p298
[198] ibidem, pp295-302; Don Neate: *'Scorpions Sting'*, Air-Britain, 1994, pp60-61; Alain Charpentier, Lionel Lacey-Johnson and Geoffrey Jeudwine: *'Global Warrior'* (biography of W/Cdr Jeudwine), privately published, 1999, pp29-31, 38-39

received from HQ via Whistondale to disperse their Blenheims had been obeyed and the few that were still operational were in Dispersal Area East.

Jeudwine was in Station HQ, RAF Kalidjati, when the Japanese attack came in. The anonymous 84 Sqn account reports that immediately after the RA officer visited with the news of the Japanese advance, he ordered the Blenheims to be flown off to Bandoeng. Before this order could be put into effect, Station HQ came under rifle and mortar fire. It seems there was a mass exodus and a dash for the airfield but 'by the time the cars were half way across the Japanese had reached the entrance'[199], their infantry apparently deploying along the north and east sides followed by three tanks and two armoured cars driving onto the aerodrome itself.[200] This combination of fire from two directions plus armoured vehicles on the flying field itself made it impossible to extricate the aircraft.

However, Sqn Ldr J Tayler of 84 Sqn was one of those who had a good try at it. As he attempted to taxi a Blenheim out of Dispersal Area East, just south of the Dutch offices and workshops, a wheel got stuck in a partially-filled bomb hole. Take off was impossible and the enemy was approaching. With Cpl Jeans as their driver, he, F/Sgt Slee and Sgt Cosgrove:

'began to run the gauntlet across the southern boundary of the aerodrome in our lorry.'[201]

Halfway across they stopped to help a Bofors crew attach their gun to a lorry and the activity attracted the attention of a tank and armoured car about 300 yards away. Slee was hit but bundled into the army lorry with the gun. This careered wildly across the field and seemed to make it off safely as far as Tayler could see. He tried to distract the fire of the armoured vehicles by firing at them himself but he, Jeans and around half a dozen others were forced to take to the RAF lorry with an army driver at the wheel. Their escape was short-lived: two more tanks appeared only 200 yards away and one fired, narrowly missing Tayler but killing the driver instantly and effectively destroying the lorry. Only he and Jeans reached the safety of cover thirty yards away. They hid in the bush within half a mile of the airfield until dawn the next day, expecting a counter-attack, and when that failed to materialise they set out on foot for Bandoeng.

Escape for the RAF became a matter of finding whatever transport was available. Many reached the RAF lorries, others – like LAC Middleton - hitched lifts with the RA and a few ran into the jungle and made their way to safety from there. Flt Lt Wyllie tells in his account of his escape from Kalidjati of:

---

[199] TNA: AIR 20/5573
[200] Numbers of tanks and armoured cars depends on which version you read. Boer says six tanks.
[201] Shores and others, op. cit., p299-301

'four Jap tanks on the road on the eastern side of the field. Three were busy demolishing a row of buildings which were occupied by a detachment who had been manning the Bofors guns intended to defend the aerodrome. The fourth tank was machine gunning anything or anyone that came in their sights who were trying to get aircraft away.'[202]

He was nearby at the time trying to extricate a Blenheim from Dispersal Area East but a burst of fire from the tank made him change his mind. He and P/O Macdonald beat a very hasty retreat, meeting up with Jeudwine on the western side of the airfield.

Wyllie speaks of Jeudwine waiting with his own car near the evacuating lorries.[203] The wing commander invited him and Flt Lts Owen and Holland to join him in an attempt to draw off the Japanese using the three loaded Tommy guns he had in the back of the car. With Jeudwine driving and the three flight lieutenants firing at the enemy, they travelled up the road in the opposite direction to the evacuating trucks with a couple of jeeps in pursuit for a while before joining the squadron convoy on the main road west a little further down. The Japanese in fact did not pursue anyone off the airfield but secured the runway with their armoured vehicles.

The sad story of one RAF man, F/Sgt Slee, should help to illustrate the chaos of the evacuation. Tayler tells how he was thrown, injured but alive, into an Army lorry about half way along the southern perimeter and made it off the airfield. In his account, Wyllie says that he saw Slee 'go down about a 100 yards away from the aircraft I was trying to get started' in Dispersal Area East. The anonymous 84 Sqn report notes that:

'Among those lost was F/Sgt SLEE, who is known to have been wounded and who could not be moved.'[204]

Whatever happened to him and wherever it occurred, Slee died that day and is listed on the Singapore Memorial to the Missing with 1st March 1942 as his date of death. He was a very highly respected member of the squadron and at least three sources tried to account for his loss although their evidence is contradictory. Many of the missing of Kalidjati from all Allied forces there died without leaving anyone at all who could suggest how and where it happened.

All RAF aircraft, whatever their condition earlier that morning, were now total losses but many of the personnel managed to escape via the transport Jeudwine had ordered to be dispersed for their use on the western side of the airfield. In a narrative account witnessed later by other escapee

---

[202] Shores and others, op. cit., p301
[203] The story is in Shores, Jeudwine's biography and 'Scorpions Sting', but not in official sources.
[204] TNA: AIR 20/5573

members of his squadron, he put his losses at twenty-three though 84 Sqn's report records nineteen were lost including Kewish's party and two Sergeants who had somehow got left behind in Soebang.[205] Whistondale was of course also missing and possibly had a driver from Station HQ who would not be included in Jeudwine's figures. Maltby's accounts of the fall of Kalidjati state that the RAF defence section was completely wiped out in the attack and this has been copied by other authors. However, this must be incorrect, if only because the RAF's losses were too low for this to be the case and there is also a report from Dutch sources of some of the defence party being evacuated by truck via the southern part of the aerodrome.[206] While the defence section consisted of around thirty men, total RAF and RAAF losses, killed and missing, seem to have been in the region of twenty-two, a number of who were demonstrably not members of the defence force. The final figure of RAF/RAAF losses might be slightly higher allowing for the misreporting of dates but unlikely to be more than another five.

Only a few members of the ML remain unaccounted for out of the hundreds of Allied air personnel on the airfield on 1st March 1942. There were still officers and men on the eastern side in the offices and workshops. Strangely, the workshops of the Technical Service of the ML at Kalidjati had not been warned of the danger and were taken by surprise with a substantial loss of life. A ground crew replacing the wing of a damaged Glenn Martin were similarly surprised and killed. Zomer himself had a narrow escape into the rough ground round the airfield and took a two-day walk to Bandoeng. Most of his station staff appear to have escaped including Sgt F Stapel, duty NCO, who managed to make a quick getaway from the ML command post across the airfield in his own car. It was very much a case, as elsewhere on the airfield, of every man for himself.

The air forces are accounted for but how did the ground force units fair? Was there any other attempt to defend the airfield? The remainder of Rugebregt's men who had not accompanied him up the Soebang road were engaged in combat with the enemy for a short while in the vicinity of Kalidjati village and Prummel could not extricate them. They suffered some losses. However he had better luck with the remaining part of his KNIL defence detachment (less than eighty men by now) that had remained on the south side of the airfield where their vehicles were located. They do not seem to have been involved in any of the fighting but, with Prummel, they helped parties of survivors, mostly RAF station staff, 12th Bty and ML air base staff, south through the jungle to safety.[207]

---

[205] TNA: AIR 20/5573
[206] Boer, op. cit., p270
[207] ibidem, p271

Both British and Dutch ground forces were not only scattered over a wide area but also lacked communication between their various parts. Their commanders could do little either to co-ordinate a defence or to help some parts of their unit and luck alone determined their fates. There are only two accounts of the overall defence of Kalidjati, both in the official Australian War History:

'The joint British and Dutch aerodrome defence force, in which the Bofors gun crews were conspicuous, went into action at close range. But the enemy had now brought up tanks and armoured cars and it was obviously only a matter of time before the small defence force would be overwhelmed. They continued to fight with great determination and though few, if any, survived, their gallant stand gave one crew time to reach one of the remaining Hudsons and Flying Officer Gibbes, who had been unable to find a crew, time to race to the other.'[208]

And:

'The defenders, mostly British anti-aircraft gunners armed as infantry, fought bravely until they had been practically wiped out.'[209]

The pilots of both Hudsons lived to tell the tale so we can assume that they gave information to their superiors about the defenders' actions that gained this praise and as the Australians had been mainly on the west side of the airfield, they would have been in an excellent position to judge the behaviour of the RA units in that area. However there is further information at a more detailed level of the actions of 49th Bty and 12th Bty that day in other sources.

The gun crews of 49th Bty were still with their guns round the perimeter of the airfield and the convoy, which the Padre tells us was formed up outside Battery HQ, would have been composed of the other elements of the Battery. Transport for the gun crews themselves – and the three-ton trucks that towed their guns – would have been adjacent to the guns. Now we come to the problem of which two guns were intended to be deployed for the roadblocks as these at least would be starting to move. It would seem probable that they would be taken from C Troop as the guns from this troop were spread so widely that they could not have been linked by GL radar. Following on from this, it would seem likely that Lt Bagnall was Troop Commander C Troop and for that reason did the recce for road block positions with Earle. Rev Godfrey's account speaks of 'one gun at least being lumbered [sic] up for its new job'. This could have been No 2 Gun C Troop from the eastern side of the airfield, which may have been pulled out and waiting at BHQ for its infantry platoon and instructions on its next position. The other gun was probably No 1 Gun, whose unfortunate crew

---

[208] Australian Air War History, Chapter 22, Loss of Timor and Java, p441
[209] Australian War History, Land Warfare, Chapter 22, The End in Java, p499

fell victims to the surprise ambush, but this is conjecture on my part as I have found no information on the point.

Most of the Bofors guns were still in their pits as the enemy stormed across the flying field making for A Troop's guns on the southern perimeter. There was time neither to extricate them nor to change their trajectory to deal with the imminent threat. A Troop had already lost men both in the air raids a few days before and when their Troop HQ had fallen earlier in the day and they now lost many more. In the Padre's words, 'very few of them succeeded in making a get away' as the Japanese attacked their guns, adding 'to this day there are still fifty of them missing and unaccounted for'.

Eyewitness accounts from the south side of the aerodrome report that the fire from tanks and AFVs seemed to be random rather than specifically aimed at a particular target. It would seem the reality was that some of the armoured forces had headed in direction of A Troop guns (as the Padre saw) but were actually intent on securing the runways, preventing any destruction of fuel, ammunition or other materiel and keeping heads of gunners down and/or forcing them to leave their guns. Loss of life to A Troop was inevitable as they tried to extricate themselves and their guns but they were probably not deliberately singled out.

Gunner Roberts' description of the loss of much of A Troop in his reply to War Office post-war enquiries is best read in his own words:

'The only news I can give you about my mates in Java is that I never saw them after March 1.2.1942 [sic] when the Japs took the aridrome we were defending ... When the Japs took our Aridome we lost nearly all of A Troop we that got away never seen enemy of them again'.[210]

It is in the ORs' returns to the War Office about the missing that the most human responses to the lost occur.

One of A Troop's guns might possibly have been brought into action if Rev Godfrey's account is correct but for the 'reluctance' of its crew:

'At the corner of the drome, as we passed it, a gun with lorry had drawn up and the sergeant was on the ground shouting to his men, who seemed to evince considerable reluctance, to get out and get the gun into action. The gun was one of A Troop's.'

Given the force they could see heading at them from across the airfield one can well understand that the gun crew did not see any future longer than five minutes for anyone who played the hero in this situation. What happened to this gun and these men is unknown.

---

[210] TNA: WO 361/342. The spelling is taken from the original

B Troop got away most of their personnel but not their guns, according to the Padre, who tells of the Troop Commander (Lt Stubbs):[211]

'flying down to the gunsites on his motor cycle telling them to get out quick. "What about the guns, sir?" said the sergeant[212]. "Oh ---- the guns."'

Which was, of course, totally contrary to the ethos of the Royal Artillery yet by acting as he did Stubbs saved the lives of most of his men, though sadly for many their fate was a more lingering death in a POW camp. Nevertheless, it was a chance to fight again. Stubbs was sent to hospital later that evening with a severe leg burn; Jack Gunn told me it was from a motor bike exhaust. Perhaps he had seized Earle's bike from outside BHQ as he returned from the recce and caught his leg on the hot exhaust as he tried to start it quickly to extricate his men. We will never know.

The rest of the attacking force that entered via the main gate pushed down the east side of airfield, aiming at the Dutch office and workshop area and taking in Dispersal Area East, where many aircraft besides 84 Sqn's Blenheims were parked, and probably C Troop's Battery HQ. As we have seen, Ft Lt Wyllie recalled tanks demolishing the buildings the gunners used. The men here mostly had time to see the Japanese advance and either evacuated by truck or:

'jumped straight into the jungle which bordered the drome on three sides and after various adventures succeeded in rejoining us twenty four hours later at Tjimahi'.[213]

One of those who escaped into the jungle was Bdr F R Judge, who later gave some information to the Padre relating to the possible fate of those who did not make it off the airfield.

The convoy which Rev Godfrey tells us was drawn up in front of BHQ did not get away without difficulty. Two lorries with a gun attached from one gun site, possibly as I suggested earlier No 2 Gun C Troop waiting near BHQ ready to move out to defend a road block, was attacked by Japanese snipers 'concealed in the trees'. They not only punctured the tyres of the rear lorry that was pulling the gun but also hit the two men sitting nearest the back, Gnrs A Couchman and W O'Sullivan, killing them instantly.[214] Survivors in the remaining lorry managed to join the back of the convoy but the gun was lost. Lt Banner was about to leave with Gnr L Gray in 'a utility van' as the Japanese approached when he realised Gray was unarmed and sent him to BHQ for a Tommy gun or rifle. He 'waited until

[211] Godfrey does not name Stubbs. He is named as OC B Troop in Sgt Hoye's letter in WO 361/342
[212] Possibly Sgt P J Hester, see WO 361/342, Sgt Hoye's letter. Quote is from Rev Godfrey, p19
[213] Rev Godfrey, op. cit., p19
[214] Macartney-Filgate, op. cit., p30

he could not stay longer' but Gray did not return. As BHQ was now under rifle fire he presumed him to be killed and joined the exodus.[215] Capt Newman, who had been in bed in the building suffering from severe malaria, 'narrowly escaped falling into enemy hands.'[216] Another lucky officer to escape from there had been 'trying to get through on the telephone' but seeing the Japanese armour and infantry arrive:

'hopped into a ditch till they had gone by and then . . . made off through the jungle, after first ascertaining that the whole of the drome was in enemy hands.'[217]

The Battery had been spread all over the airfield and in the end escaped or died by the random chance of war. Macartney-Filgate tells us four guns made it off the airfield of the ten 49th Bty had there but the full extent of the personnel losses were not clear until a rendezvous and roll call later that day. In the meantime, the survivors and guns joined the retreat west and south-west from the airfield along with lorries and cars bearing the RAF, some of 12th Bty and Dutch service personnel, both ML and KNIL. Rev Godfrey crisply recalled:

'Ours were not the only vehicles on the road, there were R.A.F. as well and the "infantry" in their lorries all proceeding along in no sort of order whatever. It was what one might reasonably call a rout.'

There is still one unit which still needs to be accounted for: 12th HAA Bty. Information here is much more difficult to find. The 'Missing' file produced for the battery post-war by the War Office Casualty Department lacks the number and quality of survivor accounts of the corresponding one for 49th/48th LAA. 12th Bty were either in the trenches immediately to the north-west and the south-east of the flying field or in mobile units deployed by Coulson. Men from one or other of these detachments were being formed up to provide infantry support for Earle's two guns. Boer records that two of its platoons 'were packing their gear and loading their trucks' preparatory to defend the proposed roadblocks when the Japanese attack came in but has no detail of the action. I have no information on where this might have been taking place or which troops formed these parties.

Survivors' accounts are very fragmentary but one thing became clear the same evening: Major Coulson was missing. Driver J Metters of 12th HAA reported post-war that he was 'Killed in a Motor Bicycle accident' beside which has been written:

---

[215] TNA: WO 361/342: Webster's letter again. He had the information direct from Lt Banner.
[216] Macartney-Filgate, op. cit., p31
[217] Rev Godfrey, op. cit., p20. The officer is not identified but by a process of elimination Lt Perry is a good possibility.

'This is not correct. Maj. Coulson was last seen alive and unharmed trying to start his MK when the Japs were advancing. He is pres K.I.A.'[218]

One of the Padre's informants from the battery, L/Bdr Halford, who spoke to him a year later in a POW camp, told him that though he had not personally seen his major killed, some of his comrades had seen it happen. This may have happened at 'the X roads' (presumably by the main gate of the aerodrome) where Halford remembered seeing a machine-gun post being wiped out and a bombardier of 49th LAA killed by a Japanese tank. Maltby, in his post-war report to the Air Ministry, recorded that:

'When last seen Major Coulson and the combined military and R.A.F. defence forces were actively engaged in opposing the Japanese attack.'[219]

Whatever happened and wherever it happened, Coulson was never seen again. He was Mentioned in Despatches post-war for his service in Java, presumably his part in the defence of Kalidjati.

One of his lieutenants, Lt J E Adams, was also missing. His possible fate will become clearer shortly but men listed as missing with him included Sgt J J Keevil, L/Sgt T H Wilson and Gnrs R T Deacon and J Hanson. Metters claimed to have seen Keevil, and also Gnrs J C Lowes and W A Todd, dead at Kalidjati. Lt D H Dewar reported that Gnrs H Burdett, J B King, T H Higginson and T Gardner from his platoon were missing after they:

'jumped on board a lorry which was subsequently machine-gunned and halted by a Japanese tank'

during the attack on Kalidjati. Was this the lorry Sqn Ldr Tayler mentions in his report? Who can say? A pencil-written addendum on another page of the missing file describes Gardner not only as missing but as 'left wounded'. With Coulson dead, command of the survivors of 12th Bty passed next day to Lt B R Emmett. He does not seem to have left a report of the action but did inform the War Office post-war that Gunner H Huridge was:

'lost with others in his section under Lt J. Adams 12/6 Regt on Kalijak [sic] aerodrome Java 1.3.42'.[220]

As there is no surviving account of what happened to 12th HAA we can only surmise on likely possibilities based on where the men were deployed. A number were manning the trenches in the north-west part of the flying field. It is probable that most of these managed to escape, along with the RAF in the pillboxes there, possibly with 49th Bty. The bulk of Coulson's men would have been either in the trenches at the south-east corner near his HQ or in his mobile reserve which was likely to have been nearby or at

[218] TNA: WO 361/248: no. 28A: Driver Metters' information
[219] TNA: AIR 23/2123, Appendix "H", para 14
[220] TNA: WO 361/248

least on the eastern side of the airfield. As we have seen, these areas were hard-hit in the main assault and it was probably here that the majority of casualties occurred. They would have had little idea of their immediate surroundings as they had only arrived after dark the night before and this would have hampered both defence and escape attempts. Was there a stand and an attempt to fight back as Maltby suggested? The Australian accounts confirm it is highly possible and as we have seen there is other evidence both to back this up and to suggest an abortive British counter-attack but neither can be proved without further information coming to light.

Certainly the final death toll for the battery was high, especially given their depleted numbers when they arrived: two officers and forty-one other ranks. Some of the survivors managed to get away by truck and others escaped through the bush around the site, several taking a number of days to find their way back to Allied lines. Halford told Rev Godfrey that he and thirty others got away on a lorry after two hours 'in the woods' and managed to re-join his unit. Many men from all units on the aerodrome waited there until the firing ceased before attempting to escape through the jungle and some managed in the meantime to catch glimpses of activity on the airfield. Bdr Judge of 49th/48th LAA told the Padre later that:

'After all firing had ceased on the drome for two hours or so, he and those with him in the jungle heard a single volley of firing from the drome.'

Rev Godfrey put this together with a report of Lt Adams of 12th Bty being seen marched across the airfield with his hands above his heads and drew the conclusion that:

'after questioning all the prisoners who had been rounded up were shot.'

What is certain is that the men who were left behind, whether free, captured or wounded, were never seen alive again. An aerial reconnaissance as darkness fell that evening found no sign of any activity, Allied or Japanese, at Kalidjati. Meanwhile, the sorry refugees from the disaster were in full retreat to back to Bandoeng.

The 49th Bty convoy had made its rendezvous 'some distance beyond Poerwakate'[221] on the main road to Bandoeng from Soekamundi. There followed a weary journey through 'the mountainous country which lies between Batavia and Bandoeng'.[222] Needless to say, the three-tonners once again gave trouble as gun-tractors and, to the Padre's horror ('an act of criminal folly'), two guns were eventually abandoned from his section at the rear of the column as they could not be dragged up the steep inclines. Earle immediately sent an empty lorry back for one when the convoy joined

---

[221] Macartney-Filgate, op. cit., p31
[222] Rev Godfrey, op. cit., p18

up again and the loss was discovered. The second was rescued by the 48th's RHQ column on the move from Batavia when it passed the spot a few hours later. Nevertheless, in spite of dumping as much equipment and stores as possible, it was 1730hrs before the battery reached Tjimahi Barracks where they spent the next few hours.

Here a roll call 'in drenching rain'[223] revealed the terrible scale of the battery's losses, though returning stragglers would reduce the number of missing slightly over the next few days. The only officer missing was Lt Mounsdon but the final total amongst the ORs was a devastating fifty-nine, 55 listed as 'missing' and four known to be dead. By the time Earle had despatched his wounded and sick to hospital, including two further officers, Capt Newman (with very bad malaria) and Lt Stubbs (with a severe leg burn), his battery was reduced from around a theoretical 288 ORs plus 8 officers to a combined 155 officers and men. What could morale have been like, standing there on parade in the pouring rain on a humid tropical evening, almost no food all day and so many comrades suddenly lost in what to most would have been a baffling and bloody inferno that came from nowhere? Their losses were the worst of any British unit at Kalidjati and 49th Bty had already buried four men in the previous eight days of fighting, with at least four others injured enough to be listed as 'Wounded in action'. The other two batteries in the regiment lost only ten men killed in action or dead from wounds between them in the entire defence of Java. But war does not stop for serving units. Having been fed and issued with new rations, the depleted battery departed 'shortly before midnight' for Tjikembar aerodrome near Soekaboemi, about sixty miles west of Tjimahi.

It was a bad day for the RAF and a terrible one for the Royal Artillery but just another dismal and forgotten story of the Abandoned Army.

---

[223] Macartney-Filgate, op. cit., p32

Eleven: Bandoeng and capitulation, March 1942

So much for what happened at Kalidjati but what happened at the various Headquarters in Bandoeng that made them order their units to stay there in spite of the very real threat from the Japanese invasion? To understand this, we need to go back to what was happening in Bandoeng on 28th February 1942.

Just before 1300hrs that day, AVM Maltby sent a telegram flagged 'Most Immediate' to the Air Ministry in London headed 'Following for Chiefs of Staff'. In it he outlined the British forces still in Java: '200 Army and about 2400 R.A.F. unarmed' and 'fighting forces remaining' of '5500 Army and 200 R.A.F. arms available for all'. He interpreted the orders he received from Wavell before his departure as:

'to fight it out but to evacuate units and personnel including fighting units when fighting equipment expended and no more forthcoming'.

While acknowledging that any evacuations would have a 'deplorable effect upon Dutch and upon own forces still fighting' he still hoped to evacuate as many as possible should the Dutch agree and if the shipping was available. This last was a major problem: he had only enough shipping potentially for the unarmed forces at his disposal and none for the 'half to quarter remaining fighting forces' that 'may eventually require evacuation'. While recognising the dangers of sending ships into the area he asked: 'Can you assist – will understand if you cant.'[224]

At the time that this telegram was sent, Maltby did not know that the Japanese had split their invasion force into three and that they would wreck the defence plan for Java by landing at Eretan Wetan and taking Kalidjati almost immediately – and make any evacuation impossible. It was received by the Air Ministry just before 1900hrs on the 28th and the response drafted by Air Chief Marshal Sir Charles Portal, Chief of the Air Staff, was duly circulated the next day with a request for any amendments to be suggested as soon as possible as it was 'clearly most desirable' to send a reply to Maltby that day.[225] If necessary a meeting of the COS could be arranged after dinner to discuss any problems with it.

It sounds thousands of miles from the realities of war in Java, which of course it was. The draft telegram, with three minor tweaks, was approved and, with a Time of Origin of 1820hrs, 1st March, was sent off to Maltby the same evening. It dispelled any last illusions of relief:

'Following from Chiefs of Staff. We entirely approve your intentions and

---

[224] TNA: CAB 121/697
[225] ibidem

agree that so long as Dutch continue effective resistance there is no alternative but that all British personnel having arms must fight alongside them. The world, and particularly America, is watching to see whether we can emulate McArthur's men.

2. If Java is eventually over whelmed we know all British ranks would wish to accept whatever the fortune of war brings them. Some parties may be able to retire inland and maintain guerrilla warfare in company with Dutch. Others cut off may be forced to surrender through having expended all means of resistance. Yet others may find means of getting away to continue fight elsewhere.

3. We are sure you realise that to send special shipping and attempt organise last minute evacuation would entail unjustifiable loss of shipping besides raising acute difficulties of the kind you mention. We are very conscious of the hard trial in front of you but are sure that the honour of the British services vis-à-vis our Allies is safe in your hands and in those of all ranks serving under you.'[226]

I am sure that neither Jack nor many of his comrades would have wished 'to accept whatever the fortune of war' brought them. I am equally sure their opinion would have been that if the COS felt a 'hard trial' was necessary, they should undertake it themselves. On the other hand, I do not believe that the COS had the least understanding of just what an unspeakable experience the Allied prisoners of war in this theatre would face and how many would not survive it.

The reference to 'McArthur's men' is very interesting. General Douglas MacArthur had been commander of US Army Forces in the Far East (USAFFE) since July 1941 with around 22,000 troops (later reinforced to just over 30,000), both local and US, under his command. However, years of lack of investment in all branches of the American forces in the area plus an unpreparedness for enemy attack following Pearl Harbor combined to enforce a speedy retreat of his land forces following the Japanese invasion of Luzon, the main island of the Philippines, which started on 21st December 1941. The air force had already been largely destroyed in bombing raids. Shades of the British in Malaya! However, instead of surrendering as Percival had done in Singapore, the US forces were now holed up in the Bataan peninsula on the west of the island and holding out against the Japanese. MacArthur himself was not with them. He, his family and his closest staff were hiding out in tunnels below the island of Corregidor in Manila Bay and would be spirited away to Australia in early March to allow him to take up the position of Supreme Commander Allied Forces, South West Pacific Command, which Roosevelt had offered him in

[226] TNA: CAB 121/697

February when it had been relinquished by Wavell as the Allies restructured their approach to war in the Far East.

His men were not so lucky. The forces on Bataan were forced to surrender on 9th April 1942 but it was the defiant spirit that they were showing the enemy prior to then that the COS wanted to see from the British forces in Java. But Java was not a Bataan. Java was both too large an island for the available troops to defend and blessed with a number of suitable invasion beaches. Nothing would change those facts however determined and motivated its defenders might have been.

By the time this telegram reached Maltby in the evening of 1st March, the situation on Java had changed dramatically. The enemy were now ashore and had not only taken Kalidjati but were threatening Batavia and Bandoeng. It is undeniable that the Allies were caught on the hop by the Japanese putting troops ashore at Eretan Wetan but what was the response to this at AHK and JAC? Why had both headquarters tried to assure the commanders at Kalidjati that they were not in danger?

In his post-war report to the Air Ministry, Maltby recalled being in the combined air operations room in Bandoeng on the night of 28th February/1st March and consulting with Maj-Gen van Oyen, commander of JAC and the Allied Combined Operations and Intelligence Centre (COIC), at around 0200hrs about 'the advisability of withdrawing squadrons to aerodromes further back.'[227] Van Oyen was against this on three counts. The first was incomprehensible, given the size of Java:

'If squadrons withdrew to aerodromes south of the hills they would be severely handicapped in opposing the landings.'

It would be true to say that if all the aircraft at Kalidjati withdrew to Andir, that airfield would be overcrowded and present a magnificent target for any Japanese aerial attack – Singapore Island all over again. Distance itself was not a problem: the Blenheims and Hudsons had plenty of range to attack the invading forces from any airfield on Java. It would have been more accurate to say that there was no obvious place to send the British bombers that would have been suitable for them and for which AA defence could be promptly provided.

With any knowledge of the situation on the ground, arguments number two and three were equally flawed. Van Oyen claimed that although the Dutch detachments defending the river crossings between Kalidjati and the invasion point were weak, Soebang had a garrison of 1,000 men with a dozen armoured cars and a 'Dutch battalion at Cheribon was being ordered

---

[227] TNA: AIR 23/2123; Appendix 'H': Capture of Kalidjati Aerodrome – 1st March 1942

to stage a counter attack against the landing.' Not being aware of the inadequacies of these forces and the problems they faced, and probably without any real concept of the distances involved, Maltby accepted his advice and duly instructed Whistondale when communications were restored at 0700hrs to 'conceal aircraft and prepare for further operations later in the day.'

Why did van Oyen give the advice he did? There were two other invasion forces to keep surveillance on and react to. Where Kalidjati was concerned, he had no local information to work on. The intense tropical storms that had disrupted communications at Kalidjati also kept his telephone connections with the area out of operation until 0700hrs, by which time the Japanese had captured most of the villages in the immediate coastal strip and almost as far south as Soebang. He would get no information from them and had to rely on reports from the land forces further east around Cheribon and from over-flying aircrew. One source was too far from the action to know and the other would be neither accurate nor informative, based as it was on snatched views over a beach heavily defended by enemy AA fire and any chance sightings of forces on jungle roads. It seems probable that COIC, which fell under van Oyen's command, decided it was unlikely that the Japanese would manage to land many of their troops by daybreak (0530hrs)[228] therefore there was still time to re-assess the situation later and evacuate and destroy the airfield if necessary. Once again the Allies had badly underestimated the enemy. By the time the first fighter attack went in soon after dawn, both Japanese assault detachments were well on their way and the bombs and strafing fell only on the rear echelon and beachhead headquarters.

The obvious solution was aerial reconnaissance but the one attempt at this was a total fiasco. Four Curtiss-Wright CW22 Falcon aircraft of the ML's 1st Reconnaissance Afdeling ran into such intensive AA fire when they approached the landing beach in the early morning that they aborted their mission[229] and no further attempts were made at this stage. The RAF had no specialised reconnaissance aircraft on Java. The operations of the JAC and the KNIL units in the area were therefore based on guesswork, as were the assurances given to Zomer and Whistondale that Kalidjati was not in danger. Having carried out night-long attacks on the approaching convoy, the squadrons at the airfield were stood down around dawn and the offensive was then taken over by the fighter squadrons and a Dutch bomber squadron based elsewhere. This continued throughout most the day.

The various HQs at Bandoeng had much to occupy their minds besides a single airbase, however strategic its position. There was one Japanese

228 Boer, op. cit., pp251-2
229 ibidem, p261

invasion force making good progress towards the civilian capital, Batavia, and another heading for the large naval port of Sourabaya. While the former had both Schilling's KNIL forces and 'Blackforce' to offer protection, the latter had very few resources to defend it. Therefore it was probably nearly midday before they really understood the threat to Kalidjati, let alone knew about its fall. The arrival of the evacuated Glenn-Martins at Andir aerodrome two miles south-west of Bandoeng at around 0800hrs would not necessarily have been unexpected as it would have been seen as merely as a precautionary measure by Zomer. He tried to tell ML HQ at around 1000hrs that the Japanese were attacking but there does not appear to have been any reaction to that. The real confirmation arrived with the two Hudsons flown off as Kalidjati was attacked; these must have landed at Andir around 1100hrs. Most non-flying ML, RAF and RAAF aircrew and ground crew trickled into Andir during the afternoon and made their reports, as appropriate, to ML Command or to Maltby at his BRITAIR HQ, with these both passing the information on to JAC.

A telegram from Sitwell to the War Office, timed at 1115hrs on 1st March, sent the first news of the fall of Kalidjati back to Britain. It was a brief addition to the third paragraph of his telegram and comes under the misleading heading 'EAST JAVA':

'ERETAN. Enemy with light tanks attacked KALIDJATI aerodrome (? about) (?11)00 hours. Situation obscure but 4 Bofors and portion of 15 Light A.A. Battery R.A. got away and now moving to Tjikembar.'[230]

From the layout of the telegram it seems likely that this was an addition as news arrived of the disaster. Previously the text had been a description of deployment of forces but from here on it deals with current fighting on Java, a factor not mentioned before. However, the time of despatch given on this telegram is obviously wrong, as it mentions enemy movements up to noon on the 1st and the movement of an AA battery to Tjikembar, which did not happen until the evening of that day. It also did not reach the War Office until 1140hrs the next day.

As well as the situation being 'obscure' and the time being uncertain, it appears that it was unclear at British HQ Java which RA units were at the airfield. Earlier in the telegram it correctly lists 49th Bty at Kalidjati but with 15th HAA Bty 'employed as infantry' whereas 12th Bty was at the airfield while 15th were at Tjililitan with 242nd LAA Bty. When the report of the attack is added, the 15th is suddenly a LAA unit – a fate which has already befallen the HQ of 77th HAA Regt at Tjilatjap in the paragraph before. The overall impression is one of confusion amongst Sitwell and his staff. Was this simply because command of the AA units had been handed over to van Oyen and JAC? A possibility, yet as RA staff officers with

---

[230] TNA: WO 106/3302

relatively few resources under their nominal command they should have known which batteries and regiments were LAA, which were HAA and where they were.

Whatever the ins and outs of this, Sitwell obviously got some sort of message around midday about the attack on the airfield, possibly via some of the survivors of 12th HAA. A stream of refugees from the airfield started to arrive in and around Bandoeng about then and some men from 12th Bty, unencumbered by their guns unlike 49th Bty, were among these. It is likely that they returned to Tjimahi Barracks, which they had left the day before to deploy to Kalidjati, to report to the newly-promoted Lt-Col E J Hazell, now commanding 6th Regt in place of Baillie. How coherent the reports were it is impossible to say. It could have given no comfort to Pearson, who probably reached Tjimahi in the early afternoon at about the same time as the first part of 48th's HQ convoy, having failed in his desperate efforts to reach 49th Bty that morning. Perhaps he feared that the problems he had previously noticed within the battery would resurface and make it unable to deal with the crisis it faced but it seems clear that the attack was so sudden there was no time for anything other than instinctive responses. 49th's arrival in the late afternoon would have been a relief in spite of its awful losses and would have allowed him to question Earle thoroughly on what happened. A report would have been forwarded in due course to Sitwell and JAC but no report from either Pearson or Earle survived the fall of Java.

Two commanding officers, Whistondale and Coulson, did not make it out and it took Zomer and Prummel a couple of days to get back but Jeudwine, like Earle, would have made a report personally to his HQ that day. This no longer exists, presumably lost with all other records in Java. Nothing approaching a full picture could have been presented to AHK and JAC before the evening of 1st March and even then the accounts they received were probably extremely confused. To be fair to the reporting officers, they must have been in a state of shock after what had happened and not very clear themselves on the whole affair. The information supplied by any of the surviving servicemen of both the British and Dutch forces was obviously confused and confusing but it was enough for JAC to move their attacks to the roads leading away from the coast and at around 1400hrs Maj-Gen J J Pesman, Commander of Bandoeng Group of the KNIL, was ordered to use his mobile unit to retake Kalidjati and hold it.

Van Oyen was having huge problems. He was in overall charge of Allied air forces, the intelligence service and the anti-aircraft defences on Java – a vast portfolio under the circumstances of 1st March. He had made a number of wrong assumptions that morning, admittedly based on the fact that he had no current information to work on, and had given the wrong advice to

Maltby when he asked whether Kalidjati should be evacuated. All this had led to the airfield still being occupied and operational when the Japanese attacked. Its loss allowed the enemy into the heart of Java within striking distance of Bandoeng, effectively destroyed the British bomber force on the island and also gave the invader a fully-operational aerodrome with fuel, AA defences and workshops intact. It was a major disaster that van Oyen would not wish to be associated with. As the news of the loss of the airfield sank in during the day at the HQs in Bandoeng, it became more and more obvious that unless this could be recaptured, the defence of Java could be very short-lived indeed.

Other events were also putting him under considerable strain. Lt Col E L Eubank, commanding USAAF forces in Java, had pulled his squadrons out and evacuated them to Australia from late on 1st March in spite of van Oyen's opposition. A formal complaint followed[231] but this could not bring back the American fighters and bombers, though Eubank was right in thinking that to stay would simply mean his aircraft would be destroyed on the ground as well as in the air. For the beleaguered Dutch on Java it would have been a devastating blow.

When Sitwell and Maltby got reports from their returning officers and worked out what had happened on the airfield, you would expect them to hot-foot it round to van Oyen to demand how they could have possibly been misled into leaving their forces at Kalidjati. After all, the RAF had now lost all its bombers and the RAAF effectively so, while 49th LAA Bty had ceased to be an active anti-aircraft battery, having only three guns and lost nearly half its complement dead, missing, injured or sick. Just at this moment something happened that diverted attention away completely from van Oyen and his mistakes and threw the British into the mire instead. Early on 2nd March the daily KNIL bulletin published a report in English that said:

'in no uncertain language that the british [sic] defence-forces on Kalidjati were put to rout leaving their arms undemolished, that these facts were wired to Washington to the Dutch Delegate to the Chiefs of Staffs with the order to have these facts brought to the attention of General Sir John Dill.' [232]

Now the boot was well and truly on the other foot. Maltby and Sitwell were not only faced with an allegation that British forces had shown cowardice in the face of the enemy but this report had gone international at the highest level, striking a blow at Britain's reputation amongst the Allies. Any thoughts either of them might have harboured overnight about having it

---

[231] Boer, op. cit., p252. Field Marshal Sir John Dill, representing Great Britain in the Allied Joint Staff Mission (JSM) in Washington.
[232] Mackay, op. cit., p69

out with van Oyen now disappeared as they struggled to counter this black propaganda. According to both Sitwell and Maltby, the report came from the intelligence branch of Dutch GHQ, presumably COIC, whose boss was van Oyen. As the loss of the airfield was likely to prove so critical in Java's defence, van Oyen had an excellent reason to wish to shift the blame for its fall onto others. He also had the authority to put the report in the bulletin. Whichever way you slice it, van Oyen had the seniority to okay a report like the one that appeared and good reasons to publish it. It was published in English in the KNIL newssheet, which makes me think that, besides shifting the blame for his own mistakes, he also wished to warn the Australians that they could not trust the British. I am sure Maltby also believed he was behind it but Sitwell blamed in turn Dutch Fifth Columnists and various Dutch officers until way after the war, but oddly never van Oyen.

Sitwell naturally protested about the report and Maltby, as Senior British Officer and Senior Air Officer, had his own concerns. They accordingly decided to have a combined court of enquiry to investigate the fall of Kalidjati and the behaviour of British personnel. The report from this, entitled 'Report on Kalidjati Incident' and dated 5th March 1942,[233] was sent to London before Java fell. Unlike so many other things and people at this time, it actually arrived but interestingly never seems to have got any further than the Air Ministry. A minute in the file containing this report actually has the instruction:

'V.C.A.S. does not wish a copy of this to go to the War Office.'

The reason for this is quite clear. While asserting that there was no foundation in the reports of British cowardice, such blame as was allocated fell on the unfortunate Major Earle, a junior officer without adequate resources or intelligence who was left out of the loop on communications from outside the airfield. He was considered:

'at fault in moving both guns and ground defences at the same time. He should have arranged to cover his retirement and has been censured for this.'

That he did this as the result of enemy action rather than as part of an organised plan was apparently irrelevant. The whole focus was on what happened on the airfield itself and in the surrounding area, but not why. The question of possible mistakes at HQ level was not examined as the allegation had been cowardice in the face of the enemy. Earle was nominally in charge of the aerodrome's defences so the buck stopped with him.

---

[233] TNA: AIR 2/7730

Oddly the contemporary RA sources I have used do not mention this court of enquiry. As they seem oblivious of its existence and because it would be extremely inconvenient to pull serving officers out of the line in such desperate circumstances to hold one, I am inclined to believe that it never happened, at least not in any formal sense. It was vital for Dutch-British relations, not to mention British-Australian relations, that the whole affair was papered over and put to bed as quickly as possible. There is nothing like a quick report agreed by all parties to do this, and I believe that it suited van Oyen and his political masters as much as the British in Java and elsewhere to do this. By not examining what happened off the airfield at Headquarters level, both sides to could agree that it was a fair assessment of the situation. In the end there was still a war to be fought and the British, the Australians and the Dutch were the only ones to fight it on Java. Case closed.

The War Office had attempted to put in a word for the gunners while the situation was still very uncertain:

'Pending detailed report our presumption is that bulk of garrison fought it out until overrun by tanks, remainder untrained in infantry role were powerless to counter attack and could not have saved aerodrome.'

It seems that there were already mutual recriminations between the War Office and the Air Ministry for the final sentence reads:

'Unfair to attribute loss of aircraft wholly to failure of garrison since landing on preceding night gave warning.'[234]

The last information the War Office had of the situation there until the report came in suggesting cowardice in the face of the enemy was Sitwell's sketchy report of 1st March about what had happened at Kalidjati. No-one from the War Office appears to have made any enquiries about what had happened at the airfield and Sitwell had apparently made no effort to inform them further. The War Office had no way of knowing at this stage that over 100 RA personnel were killed or missing, though the NEI Dutch had warned in a telegram that 'The casualties are not yet fully known but are heavy in relation to the strength.' Ignoring these ominous warnings, the War Office seems to have made no further enquiries, though realistically it was only a day or two until Java surrendered so the time for this was limited. The main concern had been cowardice on the part of British troops and this had been disproved. Extensive losses were not a problem – Java was lost anyway.

As far as the COS were concerned, Java was definitely the past. In fact, when you look at the printed minutes of the COS cabinet committee it is

---

[234] TNA: WO 106/3302

clear that Java has been written off and the focus of their attention is on the 'live' war situations elsewhere – except for a vague outline interest in how the defeat is progressing and a more acute one in how the Australian press is taking it. All that was needed to stabilise the situation where the Allies were concerned was a telegram giving an account of the 'joint enquiry' and its findings and a promise that a written report followed by mail, along with a climb-down by the NEI Dutch, with the comforting assurance that all these clearly demonstrated the earlier report was without foundation.[235] The Americans were assured that it was all a mistake and by 7th March, with surrender on Java only hours away, the Allies were once again united in their resolve.

While the Allies outside Java might have written the island off, the Allies inside Java were still fighting desperately. The Australian War History[236] sums up the situation beautifully:

'In retrospect it can be clearly seen that from the time the Japanese Navy and Air Force gained mastery of the seas round the Indies and of the air above, no reasonable hope remained of successfully defending Java.'

That point had been reached by 1st March even before the Japanese had effectively defeated the only available defence plan by their initial landings in three different places. Nevertheless, all Allied forces fought on desperately for a few more days.

An official Dutch account surviving in the National Archives gives the impression that until around noon on 1st March the commanders of Allied forces in Bandoeng were assessing the situation with the aim of reorganising forces to deal with the most important developments.[237] At this point the loss of Kalidjati was seen as a crucial blow to any defence attempts for Java and over the next three days desperate attempts were made to retake both the airfield and the vital town of Soebang nearby. Maj-Gen Pesman, Commander of Bandoeng Group of the KNIL, was ordered at around 1400hrs on the 1st to use his mobile unit to retake Kalidjati and hold it. The tanks were available immediately but the motorised infantry required would not be ready until the next day.

The attack on the 2nd, made through the Tjiater Pass, met with well-organised resistance around Soebang and though a few tanks got through, overall the attempt failed. However, rumours had reached Bandoeng that it had succeeded. Major Graham, commanding 95th LAA Bty, asked permission for a party of his men to go in and recover 49th LAA's missing guns, while Macartney-Filgate and Lt-Col Hazell proposed sending a joint

---

[235] TNA: CAB 121/697
[236] Australian War History, Land campaigns, Chapter 22: 'The End in Java', p506
[237] TNA: CAB 106/134

force to reconnoitre and if possible recapture the aerodrome. Sitwell immediately contacted Dutch HQ, who confirmed that the battle was still undecided. An officer's reconnaissance patrol from the two AA regiments found the Dutch troops still eleven miles from the airfield but unable to penetrate further.

However, it was so important to regain control of Kalidjati that a second attempt was made on 3rd March, using men from Maj-Gen Schilling's force in western Java. It would be cruel to call this a fiasco, though that is the most appropriate word. The troops had been travelling for hours and had barely fed. On the road east from Poerwakarta from around 10am until nightfall they were attacked unceasingly by Japanese aircraft using both machine-guns and bombs. To use the words of the report, they 'got disorganised' and were forced to retreat. It was now impossible to get the airfield back and it was used regularly by the invaders against its previous owners.

The Dutch forces had never had sufficient training nor been numerous enough to defeat the Japanese on their own. The idea had always been that the other Allies would make up the shortfall. Schilling and Blackburn had taken up positions following their combined plans based on an attack coming from the west coast and this attack had of course materialised. Schilling had then had to detach some of his force to attempt to take back Kalidjati and Blackburn had also been asked to take part in this offensive. He recalled post-war that he had been requested on 2nd March to leave a skeleton force to hold his defensive positions at Leuwiliang and take the rest of 'Blackforce' to Poerwakarta as the whole of the Bandoeng plateau was now in danger. There was no mention of Kalidjati.

Blackburn was an experienced soldier. He consulted his maps and found that Poerwakarta was 'roughly 200 kilometres from where I was then sitting'.[238] Schilling was unable to tell him the exact position of the enemy in that area or give any details of the proposed counter-attack. Blackburn quickly weighed up the situation. If he took part, his force at Leuwiliang could be fatally weakened. The earliest he and his men could get there, given the terrain and transport available, would be dawn the next day and that was without much rest. Neither he nor his officers knew the ground and would need time to reconnoitre. The whereabouts of the enemy was apparently unknown and the torrential monsoon rain that appeared to be set in now for the next few days would make the task much harder. He gracefully declined the invitation to get sucked into such a hopeless plan and his refusal was accepted. He now turned his attention to doing what he could in the west.

---

[238] TNA: CAB 106/139

Schilling and Blackburn had drawn up plans before the invasion based on where they thought the enemy would land and what the strengths of the Allied force were. These plans saw 'Blackforce' in the role of a striking force attacking the invaders whenever and wherever possible, especially in their rear as the enemy approached Batavia. The first two days of war destroyed this dream of a mobile fighting force. Firstly, the Japanese moved far quicker than anyone anticipated. Secondly, the need to defeat the invader north of Bandoeng and take back Kalidjati necessitated taking troops from Schilling, which left Blackburn with more static defences to fill. Thirdly, the local Dutch troop commanders, wrongly believing the Australian commander was moving his forces to fight near Poerwakarta, blew up the strong modern bridges he relied on to move his mobile forces, especially the few light tanks of 3rd Hussars at his disposal. Blackburn would have to come up with a new plan to deal with the current situation and do it very quickly.

Having checked out the notes on Japanese tactics issued to him by 1st Australian Army Corps, he decided that defence in depth was the best way of defeating the enemy's normal encirclement manoeuvres, with part of his force remaining mobile in armoured vehicles and trucks to intervene where necessary. His artillery, 2nd Battalion, 131st Field Artillery, US Army,[239] would be placed to cover his main position and its flanks but was to hold its fire until it got a direct order from him or another senior officer to maximise its surprise element.

'Blackforce's first major action took place on 2nd March at the demolished bridge at Leuwiliang. The Japanese forces, unaware of the presence of the Australians, spent several hours examining the bridge and its surroundings before Lt-Col Williams of 2/2 Pioneer Battalion gave his men the order to open fire on them. This came as a bolt from the blue and appeared to inflict considerable casualties, including members of a staff party who were caught out in the open and apparently all killed. The next 48 hours were a story of relentless action as the Japanese attempted to turn Blackburn's flank on the line of the river. 'Blackforce' fought back with everything in their armoury, including at last the American field artillery, which did sterling service against the enemy mortars, thus slackening off the pressure on the centre of the position.

The line held but this situation could not last as everywhere else the Dutch forces were now in retreat. On 4th March, Blackburn was asked to fall back to hold open the road and railway line from Batavia to Buitenzorg, as these would allow troops in the Batavia area to move back to Bandoeng. Blackburn took up a suitable position and held up the enemy forces until 6th March. Once in captivity, he discovered that the Japanese had thrown 'a

---

[239] E Bty remained near Malang with KNIL East Java forces.

complete, fully-equipped' division at his position at Leuwiliang and had suffered over 500 casualties. 'Blackforce's casualties were less than 150. Incidentally, Blackburn's command had been supplied by the excellent system set up and personally supervised by Capt Johnstone, late in charge of 48th LAA Regt's RASC platoon. By the time Java capitulated, his organisation would be providing such necessities of life as he could lay his hands on to many other units.

Meanwhile there was a major change in the RA structure on Java. On 2nd March, quite unexpectedly, Maj-Gen Sitwell was apparently:

'not satisfied with the way the command of the A.A. units was functioning under the existing arrangements' and 'accordingly reformed the nucleus A.A. Headquarters as the 16 A.A Brigade placing Lieutenant-Colonel PEARSON, commanding the 48 Light AA Regiment, in command of all the anti-aircraft troops with acting rank of Brigadier.'[240]

It is hard to see his reasoning behind this appointment. The regiments answered through him to van Oyen and this only added an extra level of command. Pearson would be lost to 48th LAA and would also have to find his own staff, as Sitwell would presumably keep his. Pearson did in fact take two officers from 77th HAA a day or two later for this purpose. Perhaps Sitwell hoped that this might render him militarily unnecessary and thus free for a last attempt at escape from Java. The only other explanation I can see is that, possibly, faced with the complaints of aggrieved commanding officers who, due to mistakes or indecision at HQ, had effectively lost a battery or had had batteries needlessly moved miles, he may have felt it would do them good to have to face what he had to face in dealing with the NEI Dutch commanders. In this respect, and with the bad feeling stirred up by the loss of Kalidjati, he might have considered Pearson would be more diplomatic than Saunders. The other two regimental commanders were out of the picture. Hazell was too junior and Humphreys was at Tjilatjap.

Now Blackburn was ordered to retreat to a position to the east of Bandoeng, not in front of it to continue offensive action as he had previously planned with Schilling. At dawn on 6th March, Sitwell warned him in a confidential memo that the resistance of NEI forces was likely to cease very soon and that he would then me responsible for the rations and maintenance of 'Blackforce' as British HQ was leaving the area.

The Dutch had been involved meanwhile in fierce fighting in and around the Tjiater Pass south of Soebang from 5th March. Though reinforcements were poured into the area and further back around Lembang, the enemy tide could not be stemmed. On 6th-7th March, non-stop bombing prevented supplies getting through to the troops. The Allies no longer had an air force

---

[240] TNA: WO 106/2562

to counter this and morale quickly drained away. The loss of Kalidjati had slashed the time Java could be defended from the invader and surrender was now only a matter of hours, rather than days, away.

What then had happened to the remainder of the Allied air forces and AA regiments? While aerial attacks had been limited on the day of invasion itself, the next week was an incessant battering of the Allied forces from the air by the Japanese. By the time of the invasion, RAF fighter aircraft were down to one composite squadron, 232(F), flying Hurricanes and based at Tjililitan near Batavia. Their airfield was defended by 242nd LAA Bty, 48th Regt, until faced with the prospect of being caught as Kalidjati had been, aircraft and anti-aircraft guns were withdrawn to Andir on 3rd March. That day the Dutch announced that they intended to declare Batavia an 'open city' to avoid unnecessary deaths there and all remaining British units, RAF and RA, including 239th HAA Bty, began their withdrawal to the Bandoeng plateau, along with the retreating KNIL.

The batteries of 77th HAA Regiment, the only 'heavy' anti-aircraft force to still have its weapons, were split on the island on 1st March.[241] 239th Bty had remained near Batavia, moving away to Andir around the time of the invasion. The other two batteries, 240th and 241st, had travelled east to defend the port of Sourabaya. 240th Bty and RHQ had been ordered back to defend the port of Tjilatjap on 26th February but were only moving in there as the invasion began. The battery became fully operational on the afternoon of 2nd March. Meanwhile 241st Bty was ordered to join them on 1st March but on its way, 2nd Lt H J S Pearson, with four guns and 47 men, was turned back to Sourabaya by the Dutch. The rest arrived in Tjilatjap on the morning of 3rd March but did not go into action until 1700hrs on the 4th as an alternative site had to be found to that originally planned. In spite of all their efforts, the port was bombed beyond use by the Japanese air forces.

21st LAA Regt's batteries meanwhile were dispersed between Tasikmalaja, Tjilatjap and Jogjokarta, all on the south side of Java with RHQ in Bandoeng. Over the next few days until the Dutch surrender on 8th March, they gradually came together in the area around Tasikmalaja as the remains of the British and Australian forces headed south.

On 3rd March, 242nd and 49th LAA Btys, 48th Regt, were ordered to move from Tjililitan and Tjikembar to Tjimahi to reinforce the AA defences at Andir which was under unceasing enemy attack. By now, all such marches had risks of serious air raids and 242nd's lengthy trek was a concern to 48th LAA's new commander, Macartney-Filgate, but they got through without loss. On 5th March, 49th Bty lost its three remaining guns and became an

---

[241] TNA: WO 106/2539

infantry unit under Lt-Col Hazell with the remains of 6th HAA and other gun-less RA units from Sumatra.

At a conference on 5th March, ter Poorten had told the British commanders that as soon as the Japanese passed the outer defences of Bandoeng, he would declare it an 'open town' to protect civilian lives. He also told them that Dutch HQ could not operate from anywhere other than there because of difficulties with communications so effectively that would be the end of resistance on their part. There would be no guerrilla war as they could not trust the native population. At midnight on the night of 5th/6th March, a Regimental Commanders conference was held at the former Abdair HQ at which it was announced that the RAF was withdrawing from Bandoeng the next morning. 48th LAA Regt and 239 HAA Bty were to follow them at noon. All British troops on the Bandoeng plateau, except 'Blackforce', were now to withdraw in convoy to Tasikmalaja some seventy miles to the south. This was to move off at 2pm with 49th LAA forming the rear-guard in its new infantry role. Nothing happened to upset this plan and the British withdrawal south began.[242]

The Dutch were in an impossible position. By 7th March they were definitely losing the fight to defend the road leading from Soebang to Bandoeng at Lembang, in spite of pouring whatever reserves they had available into this sector. Their troops were constantly bombed and strafed and had shortages of all kinds. No air support was available. The units retreating from Batavia were only just beginning to arrive back and they were exhausted. Bandoeng itself was full of civilian refugees not only from other parts of Java but also from outlying portions of the NEI. It was clearly only a matter of hours before surrender and the government of the NEI was very well aware of how the Japanese treated people who resisted them. A civilian massacre in Bandoeng must be prevented at all costs. Bandoeng must be declared an 'open town', like so many others in Java.

Maj-Gen Pesman was ordered to attempt to negotiate the surrender of his exhausted men but the Japanese rebuffed these advances. Nothing less than the personal appearance at Kalidjati aerodrome of the Governor-General and his C-in-C would do and if they had not left for that rendezvous by 10am on 8th March, 'Bandoeng would be annihilated by bombing'.[243]The Japanese C-in-C gave them only one option, unconditional surrender, and they had to accept this. It was the only possible course under the circumstances. Under this, all forces fighting under Dutch command also surrendered, which of course included all British, Australian and American forces still on Java.

---

[242] Macartney-Filgate, op. cit.
[243] TNA: CAB 106/134

Meanwhile those other Allied forces were moving around in the hill country south of Bandoeng, hampered by rumours, lack of communications and supplies, and increasing hostility from the Dutch inhabitants. The area should properly be called 'mountainous' rather than 'hilly'. 48th LAA Regt used a road with a one-in-four descent and sharp bends that put a terrible strain on the unfortunate drivers of the heavily-loaded three tonners towing a Bofors. Eventually they reached Tasikmalaja, where the regiment and its vehicles were hidden from enemy aircraft by roadside trees and scrubland. Here on the evening of the 7th Rev Godfrey was called upon to conduct a funeral service for a man from 77th HAA Regt (possibly Gnr William Moreton, 239th HAA Bty) who had been crushed to death on the march the previous day. There was no cemetery available so a grave was dug on the racecourse occupied by his battery. Rev Godfrey recalled:

'I think that funeral somehow summed up and symbolised the ending of a chapter. The swiftly gathering darkness, the few guns pointing dejectedly up into the sky, the blank hopeless looking faces of officers and men, and the splash as the body, tied up in sacking was lowered into its waterlogged grave.'

While their commanders were well aware that the Dutch must surrender before long, they were not yet ready to give up the fight. Early on 7th March, the guns of 21st LAA were still firing at enemy aircraft: a 'final, pathetic, swan song' in the Padre's words. At 9.00am that day, Brig Pearson called a meeting of regimental commanders, in this case the colonels of RA AA regiments, at Tasikmalaja. He had received orders for a defence of the area while Maj-Gen Sitwell made a reconnaissance of the hills around Tjisomboet:

'with a view to a further withdrawal to that area and later, presumably, to the coast under cover of a protective screen provided by 'Blackforce'.[244]

Saunders, with 21st LAA Regt and 239 HAA Bty, 77th Regt, would be in command of all AA defences. Hazell was in charge of the 'infantry': his own 6th HAA survivors and 49th LAA Bty, 48th Regt. Macartney-Filgate would be in command of the 'field guns and anti-tank guns' of 95th and 242nd LAA Btys, 48th Regt, with the rank of CRA for the area. 'What a prospect!' declared Rev Godfrey. 'It was a plan worthy of a Don Quixote!'

It was never put into action. There was a busy day of planning by the regimental and battery commanders, followed by a change of orders at 9.00pm. Now 48th Regt, less 49th Bty, was to meet up with 'Blackforce' and use their Bofors as anti-tank guns in a fighting rear-guard as British forces retreated to the Tjisomboet area. After giving the appropriate orders to the

---

[244] Macartney-Filgate, op cit.

batteries, Macartney-Filgate and his adjutant, Captain Williams, made a night journey over the precipitous roads of the pitch-dark countryside to meet up with Blackburn and 'Blackforce', only to be told by the Australian brigadier at 3.00am that the Dutch had surrendered at 6.00pm the night before. The terrible communications had prevented him from spreading the news. It was all over.

Evacuation was not an option. Tjilatjap, the only Allied-held port of any size, was in ruins and anyway, there were no ships to take them away. Failing this, many had hoped that some form of guerrilla resistance might be run from hideouts in this unforgiving landscape of steep hills and deep valleys with a much worse road system that that found in the north of the island. The Dutch had not been keen on this idea as they not unnaturally feared Japanese reprisals would fall on helpless civilians. The British still looked at the situation carefully. Churchill had sent Lt-Col L van der Post to the island to set up some kind of resistance movement and he arrived at Wavell's HQ around 18th February but there was not enough time to do anything properly, not to mention the difficulties with supplies. It was this sort of difficulty, especially non-existent medical supplies in such a hostile climate, which forced the Allied commanders to decide against guerrilla action. The other deciding factor was that the Dutch had surrendered on behalf of all the Allied armed forces so anyone still bearing arms need not be granted the comparative safety of a prisoner of war on capture. Nevertheless, van der Post[245] and others did set up groups of varying size which lasted for few weeks, some ending in the massacre of all members.

British forces now started to converge on the town of Garoet and its immediate vicinity. It took a while for formal ratification of the surrender order to come through and in the meantime, a confrontation took place on 8th March between Lt-Col Saunders of 21st LAA and A/Cdre Silly, RAF. Saunders had set up the guns of 78th Bty at Tasikmajala airfield but found that his battery there had been stood down on orders of a senior RAF officer. Saunders naturally told his major that the only person he should take orders from was him and went in search of this defeatist officer. Silly's response to Saunders was that he was Senior British Officer on the airfield and he had around 500-600 unarmed RAF personnel either there or arriving shortly and he did not want to risk their lives. Under pressure from Saunders he admitted that he did not know if there had been any kind of surrender signed or even agreed yet but thought there had or would be. The argument obviously got so heated at this point that he eventually gave Saunders a signed chit timed at 1500 ordering him not to offer any resistance to Japanese land or air forces. Saunders preserved it all through captivity to be able to write it out word for word in his damning post-war report. He now decided to take the men under his command to join the

---

[245] TNA: CAB 106/85

other British land forces around Garoet. At 1815hrs that evening while still some miles from his destination, he was informed of the Dutch capitulation. Having settled his regiment at their new bivouac site, he drove off to a meeting with Sitwell where he had the surrender confirmed to him.

Now the end had truly come. The Dutch had surrendered. Evacuation was impossible. So was guerrilla warfare in unknown territory with few supplies, few medicines and few communications where the local people spoke an unfamiliar language and the continual monsoon rain soaked everyone and everything. No options were left. The commanders of the other Allied forces on the island signed formal surrenders on 12th March. Jack Gunn had received his last pay the day before: 5 guilders.

Twelve: The end of it all

The first part of the capitulation period was as chaotic as the brief war had been. Most Allied servicemen on Java became POWs fairly quickly but not W/Cdr Jeudwine or Lt Banner. Mary Pearson's dilatory suitor did not survive to make his peace with her. He and three NCOs from 49th Bty made their way to the coast and paid Javanese boatmen to take them to freedom. Unfortunately these men set upon them with knives and Banner and one of the NCOs, Sgt E Beardwood, were killed. The other two, BQMS F H Webster and Sgt R L G Brooks, held them off with their revolvers and managed to reach land just off Java. It was already occupied by the Japanese and they became POWs,[246] both surviving to be liberated later and tell the tale. Banner and Beardwood were 'Mentioned in Despatches' post-war 'in recognition of gallant and distinguished services in the field'.[247]

Jeudwine was more fortunate. On 3rd March he and his squadron's aircrew were ordered by Maltby to make their way to the southern port of Tjilatjap in the hope of evacuation, leaving the rest of the squadron in Bandoeng. The port was in chaos but they found two lifeboats, only one of which was serviceable. Jeudwine decided to take 'those with a knowledge of sailing, preferably Australians'[248] with him on the venture, the remainder staying behind at an agreed rendezvous in the hope he could send back a ship to collect them when he reached safety. Twelve men crewed the lifeboat, christened 'HMRAFS Scorpion' after the Squadron's crest: Jeudwine himself, Sqn Ldr A K Passmore and his crew, F/O C P L Streatfield (who could navigate by the stars), and P/O S G Turner, an Australian officer, P/O M S Macdonald, and seven non-commissioned Australian aircrew. On 22nd April after an epic voyage of 47 days and around 1,500 miles, they reached northern Australia. Sadly but not surprisingly the submarine sent to pick up the men waiting on Java - including Jeudwine's two crewmen - found no-one at the rendezvous. They had gone into captivity ten days before on 20th April.

Captivity was inevitable for most of the Allied personnel on Java, senior officers, junior officers and ORs alike. It is not the purpose of this book to cover this period but it is useful to know some details just to round off the story. The ORs from the various RA units tended to be moved together to new destinations, unless they were in hospital when taken prisoner or left behind in a camp because of illness. Many men from 49th Bty, Jack Gunn amongst them, ended up in the ORs POW camp at Kuching in Borneo, labouring in the docks or on the airfield there. In late 1944-early 1945, the

---

[246] TNA: WO 361/342 and WO 208/4287
[247] Supplement to the London Gazette, 5 December 1946
[248] David Russell, Jeudwine's rear gunner, quoted in 'Global Warrior', p34

Japanese drastically cut the rice ration issued to the prisoners and as this was their main source of food, the number of deaths from starvation as well as tropical diseases, mistreatment and injuries rose rapidly.

Jack told me that men would swap their last mouthful of food for a cigarette and that some men younger or fitter than him died in the squalor of the camps. He himself focussed on his dreams of the future to keep him alive: the perfect garden he would make after the war, the food he would eat, and above all going home to his wife Sue. He decided they would have a daughter, Jacqueline. Captivity had changed his priorities - he now wanted a family very much. He thought constantly of Sue, seeing the sun set and thinking she would be seeing it before long and watching the moon rise and imagining her soon doing the same. He hung on and hung on until the Australians arrived on 11th September 1945 and liberated his camp, just three days before the Japanese would have marched the survivors into the jungle and killed them. Of the 2,000 British servicemen who went into the ORs camp at Kuching, there were not enough fit to make up a working party of thirty men.[249]   And there were hundreds dead. 49th Bty now numbered 115 from the original 288 ORs who had sailed from the Clyde. Two officers were also missing. The losses from its sister batteries, 95th and 242nd, were equally bad, though only a handful of these had been killed in action, yet the official regimental history of the RA in the Far East gives 48th LAA Regt's losses as 165, less than 49th Bty on its own.[250]

It was time for Jack and the other survivors to start on their journey home. He was first taken on board an Australian hospital ship, HMAHS 'Wanganella', and told his in-laws in a letter home dated 21st September that he had weighed 7 stone 6lbs when released. 'Tubby' Gunn had almost disappeared! He eventually travelled back on the liner SS 'Ranchi'. However, if you read her passenger lists in the National Archives, the only trace you will find of her carrying troops on this voyage is a note about the burial of one who died on the ship. It would not have mattered to Jack. It angered him that the Malayan planters he met on board who had no respect for him and his comrades after all they had suffered to try to help them. However, the most important thing was he was going home - and the first sight of the white cliffs of England as they sailed up the Channel brought tears to many a man's eyes.

Jack reached England on 24th November 1945 but quite a number of FEPOWs had made it back before him. While soldiers usually travelled by sea, some RAF personnel managed to get lifts back by air. Russell,

---

[249] Agnes Keith, 'Three Came Home', p194
[250] Gen Sir M Farndale, op. cit., p338, Annex D. Farndale's information on 48th Regt is similarly misleading: 'Formed July 1940. Disbanded Feb 1942. Lost in Java in 1942.' (op. cit., p443) He does not even give the dates for the invasion of Java and its fall in his chronology, pxv

Jeudwine's gunner from 84 Sqn, luckily survived the war but his navigator, Sgt G Palmer, did not. However, it is unlikely that any of the survivors of 84 Sqn met up with their former CO again as he had died in an air accident in October 1945 as they were travelling back. It was one of those stupid, avoidable things that should never have happened. After escaping from Java and serving with both the RAF in the Middle East and Bomber Command in Europe, Jeudwine was promoted to Group Captain in August 1944 and posted to command RAF Little Staughton in August 1945 'with instructions to close the airfield'[251]. He was killed here on 19th October 1945 during a flight in a Hawker Typhoon.

The Typhoon has almost iconic status in British aviation lore yet the terrible truth is that it was not a world-class tank-buster - it was a deadly machine plagued by a number of unsolvable faults that killed more of its pilots than the enemy did. Perhaps the worst thing of all is that the RAF knew this only too well from the very beginning, though on the positive side the type was retired from active service at the earliest possible opportunity.[252] When Jeudwine announced to his Engineering Officer one morning that he was going to take a Typhoon up when an oil leak was fixed to 'try some aerobatics', that officer rightly queried the wisdom of this, being of course fully aware of its deadly foibles. These included losing its tail in flight (never fixed, despite propaganda during the war and since) and blowing its engine in sharp dives, an unfortunate trait well known to, and utilised by, the Luftwaffe! Jeudwine's response to this sound professional advice was to say 'it will handle just like a Hurricane'. If only! Early in his afternoon flight the aircraft, like many another of its type, went into a spin from which it did not recover and flew into the ground. Needless to say, he died in the crash.

The survivors from the British forces on Java went their own ways. Major R Earle, commanding officer, 49th LAA Bty, stayed in the Army. Bombadier Jack Gunn went back to civilian life, having been quickly discharged with a glowing reference:

'Military Conduct: Exemplary. Testimonial: . . . From his documents he has shown himself willing – reliable - hardworking; adaptable and has initiative and leadership'[253]

He went home to Sue, who was, like him, in very poor health. She had tried desperately to keep The Business going during his absence but wartime shortages, the difficulty of getting suitable help and the constant questions from the people she met every day - 'Have you heard anything from Jack? Is he alive? Is he still missing?' - were a perpetual strain. Eventually she

---

[251] *'Global Warrior'*, p132.
[252] I am greatly indebted for this information to Jack Livesey who has kindly put his comprehensive (but so far unpublished) research on this aircraft at my disposal.
[253] From Jack Gunn's service record, 1st January 1946

was forced to sell up, then broke the base of her spine. He had altered, she had altered. It was the terrible situation many returning servicemen faced but their marriage survived. And he did have a daughter Jacqueline, the first of his four children.

Jack, like most other demobbed soldiers, set out rebuilding his life, finding a job, starting a family, tending his garden and allotments and all the day-to-day activities he had dreamed of in the camps. He could not hold a job down at first as, like many another FEPOW, the injuries and tropical diseases he had suffered continued to plague him, but he worked hard and persevered and won through. He joined the Post Office in 1950 and worked his way up from an ordinary postman to Inspector by the time he retired in 1974. He was enormously proud of the Post Office and his career there. He died of cancer in November 1994, aged 80. He had told no-one of his pain. It was his secret alone, like so much of his war service.

So much for the men who escaped from the fall of Kalidjati but what do we know of the fate of the men who were left behind? They were certainly never seen alive again. It was not unknown for Japanese first-wave troops to kill their enemies rather than to take prisoners and this was most probably what happened to these unfortunate men. A POW camp holding around 400 RAF and RAAF personnel was established at Kalidjati on 28th March 1942 and lasted about six months. While the aircrew were extensively and brutally interrogated, the others were set to work on and around the airfield.[254] In May 1942 some of these POWs found 'several bodies of British soldiers (unrecognizable save for their black army boots)'[255] in a ditch near the entrance to Dispersal Area East and RAF men who had been at the camp later told L/B Halford of 6th Regt:

'that over 50 bodies had been found in and around Kalidjati. In the ditch where many bodies were found were a Major's crown and five pips.'[256]

While there is no mention of this in the file relating to the mistreatment of POWs at Kalidjati, it seems pretty certain that the prisoners there found at least some of the bodies of those missing and presumably buried them. From the evidence found in the ditch it seems likely that the bodies had included those of Major Coulson and Lts Adams and Mounsdon. Whatever had happened, the Allied servicemen left at Kalidjati when the storm hit were dead. The unidentified bodies, with others found round the airfield, were reburied in mass graves in Soebang from where they were disinterred

---

[254] TNA: WO 325/69: Kali Jati Camp, Java: ill treatment of POWs. (Title on cover: 'Kali Jati Massacre')
[255] Rev Godfrey, op. cit., p19-20. A map showing the location at which the bodies were found is included in his memoirs.
[256] Rev Godfrey, p27

after the war. One hundred and thirty one bodies were reburied in Jakarta Ancol War Cemetery in Djakarta.

After the war, however, it was necessary to account for all the missing. This was the task of the War Office Casualty Branch. As this was long before the days of computers, everything was done manually with limited staff dealing simultaneously with many different units and huge numbers of cases and working as quickly as possible to get things settled. Files containing the information they received, working notes and odd memoranda of decisions on 'presuming' dates of death survive in the National Archives, organised by unit (e.g. 49th/48th LAA Battery).

The department had a system for the Far East 'missing'. It relied where possible on the versions of Part II Orders that were kept in most POW camps. They were generally considered (though drawn up while in captivity) to have been produced with a degree of rigour that made them a fairly reliable source of information if nothing conflicting was produced in researches.[257] Further information came from released POWs. Some could not, or did not want to, help. It may seem strange to us that men could claim they knew nothing of their comrades' fate but we cannot understand what they must have gone through. Once the Casualty Branch felt it could establish a date of death with reasonable certainty, it would 'presume' death on that particular date and pass on the information to the next of kin (who had had a 'missing' warning) and to the CWGC, which then marked graves or memorials accordingly.

The Casualty Branch began sending letters to returned 49th Bty POWs from the very beginning of December 1945 and replies were promptly received that largely corroborated what the Part II Orders had set out and also sorted out some of the anomalies. The process of 'presuming' and deciding on dates of death may well have finished as early as 23rd February 1946, judging from administrative notes within the file, by which stage there were fourteen men still unaccounted for.

And now a mystery, for those of you who like mysteries. Some of these files for RA units in the area are very scrappy with little concrete information and often as little guesswork to make up the gaps. The file for 49th LAA Battery RA, on the other hand, is both full and informative. Amongst those replying to queries were Major Earle, the unit's commanding officer, QMS H Bates, 48th Regt's Artillery Clerk, RSM Holland, BQMS Webster, and a number of gunners. They not only filled up the forms on the list of missing that they had been sent but also provided graphic accounts of what had happened to the missing or the dead. Every bit of information in the file leads to the conclusion that an officer and over fifty men died on 1st March

---

[257] TNA: WO 361/248. Memo numbered '23'.

1942 when the Japanese took Kalidjati. Yet when you consult the Commonwealth War Graves records for these men, you find that it lists one officer and eleven ORs from 49th Bty killed on 1st March 1942 with 50 ORs from the battery killed on 21st February 1942.

There is another source of statistics for the batteries losses: the last commander of 48th LAA Regiment, Lt-Col Macartney-Filgate. Firstly he drew up a list of the regiment's casualties for his memoirs. These was written while he was a POW so the list was probably compiled in 1942-3 like them and deals only with the period up to the surrender in Java. Once back home, he spent several years gathering information from which he drew up lists setting out what happened to every man in the regiment who went out to the Far East and sent copies of these lists to Rev Godfrey in April 1949.[258] There is a separate list for the ORs of each of the three batteries, 49th, 95th and 242nd, and another for HQ, based on the original lists of those going abroad. Each man is listed by his service number, original rank, surname and initials with a separate column for the cause, date and place of death if the man died. If he survived this column is left empty. The opening paragraph of his covering letter described what he had done:

'I have now completed, so far as is humanly possible, the casualty list of the 48th Light A.A. Regiment. It has been a long and depressing business, but I have been anxious to verify a number of doubtful cases so far as I could, and it is only now that I feel confident that the final result is as accurate as can be achieved. I have received the most friendly co-operation from R.A. Records, in the course of which I have been able to correct some of their facts just as they have been able to correct several of mine.'

Not only was his final list the definitive one as far as both he and the RA were concerned but also it sounds as though there had been few differences anyway between his list for 48th Regt and the RA's. If any man alive knew what had happened to the personnel of 48th LAA Regt, that man was their Colonel who had put so much time and effort into finding his missing men. One thing that is very clear from both his memoirs and his lists is that 50 ORs of 49th LAA Bty did not die on 21st February 1942.

Naturally I have queried the discrepancy with the CWGC, especially as the missing from 12th HAA Battery who died at Kalidjati have been given 1st March 1942 as their date of death even though the records in their cases were much less clear. The Commission insists that the dates given are the dates given to them by the War Office (although there is nothing in file WO 361/342 dealing with the missing of 49th LAA Bty to confirm this). As I am not a relative of any of the men, the matter must rest there.

---

[258] These and the covering letter are now deposited at IWM London, ref: Private papers of Canon R C R Godfrey: IWM Documents 7879.

How could such discrepancies occur? Why were so many of the casualties from the fall of Kalidjati were given a 'presumed' date of death a week before they actually died? It was inevitable that the odd mistake would happen given the volume of work and the probability of staff switching from list to list and unit to unit and occasionally misreading handwriting as well but the mistakes, as we have seen, go further than this. Was there a conspiracy to cover up the losses at Kalidjati that day? Failing any indisputable evidence to the contrary, I believe it was clerical error within the Casualty Branch, that a list with mistakes in it was typed for the CWGC. There would be neither time nor reason to read through the entire file to double-check. Even if someone had realised something was wrong, it can be simpler to go along with an administrative mistake, in spite of the anomalies it might throw up, rather than try to sort it out. Basically, it is reasonable to suppose that a faulty list was sent accidentally to the CWGC and they constructed cemeteries and memorials from this.

However, the most important objection to any attempted cover-up is who would want to do it and why? It would take a very senior officer to over-rule the Part II Orders on which the casualty lists relied so heavily. Did anyone have a motive? All my research leads me to conclude that the answer is no. The War Office knew little about what happened at Kalidjati – probably did not even know exactly where it was – and cared even less. To be blunt, the loss of a hundred men here or there was negligible as Java was known to be indefensible and the aerodrome had been the RAF's or JAC's responsibility. It was the fortune of war. An acceptable loss. The taking of Kalidjati was not a problem but the British campaign in Java overall was.

There were very strong reasons post-war for concealing the truth about what had happened in Java in 1942. It was vital to conciliate both the Australians and the British public. The Australians wanted an inquiry into what happened in the Far East during the war.[259] There was no disguising the fact that the early months of the campaign had seen a series of knee-jerk reactions to crises, a large number of which occurred because both Britain and the USA had mostly ignored the region in the interwar years and failed to put the money, men and materiel into a coherent defence policy there. This had resulted in a great number of Australian deaths, both in battle and in captivity, for no appreciable gain. While the focus of their ire was undoubtedly Malaya, they had also lost two experienced infantry battalions in Java. If there was an inquiry that involved the NEI as well, the Australians were bound to find out about the chaotic lack of organisation there. This could be politically disastrous.

---

[259] TNA: PREM 8/757: Minute: 3rd October 1947: A Henderson, Secretary of State for Commonwealth Relations to the Prime Minister (Clement Atlee). The original call for this had been in January 1946.

The strength of public feeling in Britain about the Far East debacle of 1941-2 was another major factor. Publication of the despatches of the senior officers in the area, Brooke-Popham, Maj-Gen C M Maltby (Hong Kong), Wavell, Percival, Maltby and Admiral G Layton, had been held up until 1948 for various reasons, mostly political. Australia was not the only member of the Empire or Commonwealth likely to feel aggrieved about what happened in the Far East and all the published despatches were first run past such member states as might have had issues with them, in addition to the tour they made of government departments and the Cabinet.

Questions were asked in Parliament as publication of these despatches was delayed again and again. The pressure from MPs in areas where the losses were greatest was very strong and totally lacked subtlety. In the House of Commons on 28th October 1947, R R Stokes, MC, Labour MP for Ipswich, asked the Rt Hon Emanuel Shinwell, Secretary of State for War:

'Is the Minister aware that many of my constituents are very fed up with this intolerable delay? We lost more than two battalions of men from my neighbourhood, and we are after the blood of the person who landed troops who had no possibility of fighting at all.'[260]

Stokes had already been told in June 1947 that the despatches would be published by the end of the year and all these delays must have fuelled public anger and suspicions. East Anglia as a whole was particularly badly hit by the collapse out east, in infantry battalions and units from the Royal Engineers and RA, 48th LAA Regiment included.

Basically at the end of the war no one in authority wanted to reopen a can of worms that would not reflect well on senior officers and politicians of the time. The War Office could not contest the fact that although units were put into the area, the Java campaign was never properly organised and inadequate in all directions: no GHQ, lack of all military necessities, the ineffectual Sitwell left nominally in charge and no interest shown after it was seen to be indefensible. This may have been realistic in wartime but was likely to be dynamite in a post-war world where Singapore was a scandal. With this in mind it is interesting to see what happened to the report that Sitwell submitted in February 1946 as his despatch for publication as GOC Land Forces in Java.

Sitwell, to his credit, pulled no punches. He made no bones about the problems facing the NEI armed forces in Java in personnel, training and equipment and the very real problems they had with communications. Of more obvious interest to a British audience, he set out his operational orders, his lack of signal communications which undermined any chance of

---

[260] TNA: PREM 8/757

real control of what he described as his 'token force'[261] and this force's dire shortages of all necessary equipment and stores. Point six in the list of instructions he received on taking up his post was that he 'could expect no help from outside whatsoever for a very long time.' In short, by page seven of the thirty-five page report, no reader should have been in any doubt that this was an abandoned rump of forces, left behind to save face rather than achieve anything much.

In spite of this, copies of his draft were at first widely circulated to various departments within the War Office, to the RAF and Royal Navy, to the Foreign Office, the Dominions Office and the Cabinet Office, as was standard practice for despatches to be published.[262] The covering letters ask for comments and any additions or corrections the recipients may feel are necessary before publication. The response varied from the Foreign Office's total acceptance without any requested changes to a detailed grid from sources in the War Office outlining nearly fifty proposed changes, some quite lengthy, and including input received from Maltby and from the Admiralty. Interestingly, one that regularly occurs is to avoid making derogatory statements about the Dutch with the advice, as a general comment, that:

'A published Despatch must not contain any passages likely to offend Allied or Imperial susceptibilities.'

Whatever might or might not have been decided about the suitability of Sitwell's report and the amendments it might need, a new perspective was introduced when M.O.1. (Records) to the Historical Section, Cabinet Offices, War Office Library, asked for more information on 15th October 1946. This was necessary 'to check this despatch before publication.' A burst of memos over the next nine days revealed that none of the War Office departments contacted had any relevant information to check it against. The nearest they got seems to have been the report on the fall of Sumatra submitted by Lt-Col Baillie after he was sacked by Sitwell in February 1942, a copy of which appears in this file although it had nothing to do with Java. There are no reports in the file from officers who served in Java, although by that time the War Office should have received a number of these, nor any indication these were requested to provide the necessary information.

Now things went sharply into reverse. From a rush to publish a despatch on 17th October 1946, by 30th January 1947 moves were afoot to downgrade it to an unpublished report. Three reasons were advanced for this. Firstly, Sitwell's force was below the one division or its equivalent required for a

---

[261] TNA: CAB 106/39, p3. See appendix for his Order of Battle figures
[262] TNA: WO 32/12105. This charts the progress of his report from arrival of the original draft onwards

despatch. Secondly, it was 'of very little general interest' and thirdly, there were 'many indications' that it was inaccurate, being written four years after the operation and with few records available either to Sitwell or the War Office. While lack of records was not a reason for the RAF discounting Maltby's report, it is undeniable that there are errors in Sitwell's. For example, he described 48ᵗʰ LAA as having only two batteries in his Order of Battle, possibly underestimating his British contingent by several hundred officers and men. Such a basic error would make anyone wonder what other less obvious mistakes there were. It did not reflect well on Sitwell himself and his probable competence as GOC Land Forces.

It is amazing that no one thought of these objections until a year after Sitwell first submitted his despatch and after it had been round a multiplicity of departments both inside and outside the War Office. Did the queries in October 1946 make someone look at the whole report more closely and recognise that in light of the growing clamour for an explanation of what happened in the Far East, this was definitely not the sort of thing to be put in the public domain? Letters were sent to all departments concerned informing them of the decision not to publish. A chance for the deficiencies in the British Army's Java campaign to come to light was effectively closed down. Even if this was not deliberate, the effect was the same as if it had been.

Sitwell, now serving in Egypt in his substantive rank of Colonel, was naturally very annoyed, as without his despatch no record would appear in public of the land forces' contribution to the Java Campaign. He was crispy informed that the decision was made and would not be changed but offered the sop that as a Report it would:

'be available to the Official Historians to whom it is anticipated it will be of considerable value.'

And that was that.²⁶³ A version of Sitwell's original draft, rearranged and with minor changes, was placed in War Office records as his report.²⁶⁴

In the end, the truth about the Java campaign and the fall of Kalidjati was hidden by two simple expedients. Firstly, the lack of a published despatch from Sitwell, a fact that impacted on the public understanding of both events, and secondly, Maltby's printed despatch. This was a 'Report on the Air Operations during the Campaigns in Malaya and Netherlands East Indies from 8ᵗʰ December, 1941 to 12ᵗʰ March, 1942'.²⁶⁵ As such, it naturally focussed on the RAF's role in the conflict and the activities of the land forces are of peripheral interest. As AVM Pulford had died, it included

---

²⁶³ TNA: WO 32/12105
²⁶⁴ TNA: WO 106/2562 and WO 106/5983
²⁶⁵ TNA: CAB 106/86. Printed in the London Gazette, 26ᵗʰ February 1948

what he would have covered in a post-war despatch and consequently the joint report stretched to sixty-eight printed pages with appendices, much of which relates to Malaya. Of the rest of the report, eight pages are dedicated to a 'Summary of Operations based on Sumatra' and thirteen to a 'Summary of Operations based on Java'.

Anyone hoping to understand the strength and deployment of British land forces in Java from this despatch would be both disappointed and misled. While the components of 'Blackforce' are set out in some detail, the RA Anti-Aircraft regiments and batteries are dismissed with:

'Certain British A.A. batteries were concentrated on aerodrome defence in Western Java as follows:'

What follows is the number of Bofors guns at Tjililitan and Kalidjati airfields with no indication of their regiments or batteries but does add that 15th HAA and 12th HAA were deployed to these aerodromes as infantry on 25th and 28th February respectively. Maltby also reports that there were no HAA guns for these two airfields. This of course is all perfectly true but what he fails to make clear is that there were in fact elements of five RA regiments, both LAA and HAA, on Java but any of these that did not provide cover for RAF airfields were naturally irrelevant to his report.

From the RAF perspective, the Java campaign was not a problem in itself because its organisation and administration of its forces there were as good as could be expected given the circumstances and because they had been under the command of JAC after the departure of ABDACOM, as had the RA units of the British Army. This meant that all faulty decisions at ultimate command level were Dutch mistakes. However, there were two major issues relating to the loss of Kalidjati aerodrome. Firstly, as well as being Senior British Officer in Java, Maltby had also been AOC RAF/RAAF and some might think he had not shown sufficient grasp of the situation on 1st March 1942 in this latter role. Perhaps he should have looked more closely at the threat to Kalidjati from the Japanese invasion, taken a forceful line with van Oyen and ordered his squadrons out very early in the day, which would, incidentally, have freed the RA batteries to leave too. His lack of action led directly to the loss of the RAF/RAAF bomber force on Java. Secondly, appointing Whistondale as station commander RAF Kalidjati was a terrible but predictable error of judgement. He had shown himself to be an incompetent station commander on a previous occasion and should never have been appointed to the position again. He was clearly out of his depth when the crisis came and his ill-planned and ill-fated disappearance from the airfield, whether to look for the Japanese or to collect his kit, left all British forces there, army and air force, in limbo.

These two points were dealt with swiftly and efficiently by Maltby in his despatch by placing his emphasis on the top of the command structure and away from his men on the ground. At a stroke Maltby shifted all the blame onto the Dutch – no worries about offending an ally amongst the RAF! Whatever his officers on the ground did, any mistakes they made, could never have changed the outcome – it was all van Oyen's fault as his, Maltby's, superior officer. He had failed to correctly assess the danger to the airfield and its occupants and order suitable action. The buck should stop with him! And technically Maltby was right.

Maltby recorded the evacuation of Dutch aircraft in a way that might make the reader believe, wrongly, that all the Dutch air personnel at Kalidjati left early in the day. The failure of Dutch forces to stop the Japanese advance is noted, followed by the briefest of descriptions of the successful enemy attack on the airfield:

'About 1030 hours the aerodrome was overrun by Japanese light tanks supported by infantry in lorries – part of the force which had landed at Eritanwetan some hours earlier - and the aerodrome was captured. . . . the aerodrome defence party, a combination of Army and R.A.F. personnel, put up a stout fight and covered the withdrawal of the ground personnel of the squadrons, the majority of the Bofors guns adopting an anti-tank role. It is believed that there are no British survivors of the aerodrome defence party. The Japanese appear to have given no quarter.'[266]

There is no indication of the size of the defence forces, the make-up of the Army component or their losses, jointly or severally. It is, after all, an RAF despatch. The whole episode is neatly wound up with the paragraph:

'It has been impracticable as yet to obtain a clear picture of what exactly happened at Kalidjati. Surviving British witnesses of consequence are few. Much still remains unsatisfactorily explained. It is hoped that time may reveal the full facts.'

And that is that. The 'inquiry' he had held is not mentioned but it is irrelevant now as it was limited to a discredited charge of British desertion of the airfield. There cannot be an inquiry into why Kalidjati fell as the British forces were under Dutch command and Maltby has now explained the reasons for it anyway. As to what happened on the airfield itself, he has effectively dismissed any sensible chance of this being discovered, although clearly there were a number of surviving officers and men who could offer information. Case closed.

It was the final step in a damage limitation exercise by the top ranks of the Army and the RAF. Basically, nobody who mattered cared about what had happened either at Kalidjati or in Java and they didn't want any inquiries into it. That would have given Lt-Col Saunders a platform for his excoriating criticisms, not to mention Lt Col Macartney-Filgate, Captain Johnstone, RASC, and others, and was to be avoided at all costs. Longer

---

[266] TNA: CAB 106/86: paras 540 and 541

term, no reports from the officers of 48th LAA (Pearson, Macartney-Filgate and Earle) could be available for public scrutiny in the National Archives. Cover-up achieved.

In the final analysis, who was responsible for what happened? At the highest level, the blame for the fate of all British forces in Java must fall on their government for the political decision to send them there and then deciding, for political reasons, against withdrawing them while there was still time to do so. The War Office also has responsibility for the failure to make proper preparations for all British land forces in a country that could not possibly be expected to provide for them and leaving them with negligible leadership and resources when it became obvious that Java was indefensible.

Where Kalidjati is concerned, responsibility also lies with the Dutch, who were in overall command in Java. It was inevitable that it would fall at some time and, after the Japanese landed at Eretan Wetan, there was precious little chance of the small ill-equipped Dutch forces within striking distance doing anything to prevent an attack. It should have been obvious to HQ that there was also absolutely no prospect of the forces available at the airfield defending it successfully. With the advantage of hindsight it is very clear that the order to destroy the airfield and evacuate both aircraft and personnel should have been given very early on 1st March. Had Zomer started carrying out demolitions when he first proposed to do so, the Japanese would have had to spend a couple of days at least repairing the aerodrome and bringing in supplies. While it could not change the inevitable, it might have lengthened Java's survival as an Allied outpost.

Why did the Dutch fail to give the order? I believe they were, simply, totally out of their depth. The Dutch commanders had no training or experience for what confronted them. They delayed and were indecisive and this proved to be fatal, yet to be fair, they had very few forces for the mighty task they were faced with and these were poorly equipped with bad communications. Their failure then and afterwards was, as the Australians concluded in their War History, a foregone conclusion. The Fifth Columnist allegations are, I believe, an uninformed smear to try to account for what was a quite inevitable defeat. The alliance between the Axis powers and the Japanese is not a good enough reason for this. The Nazis ordinarily would not have made an alliance with Japan – it ran counter to their racial theories – though it does make sense on the basis that 'my enemy's enemy is my friend'. Any Nazi sympathiser in the NEI with any brains at all would have known that the Japanese would not see them as anything other than an enemy and would, I believe, have felt the same about the invaders. British reports demonstrate that, almost without exception, the Dutch gave them all the help they could from their very limited resources up to the point that they suspected the British might cut and run. It is hardly surprising that attitudes changed then.

Realistically the RAF, and Maltby as its local commander, must take a large part of the blame for the disaster that followed for failings at both top and local level. In the latter case, some responsibility must also lie with the senior officers on the aerodrome. Earle and Coulson reported to Whistondale and ultimately came under the same Dutch command structure as Zomer, yet all of these failed them. Whistondale, as we have seen, should never have been in charge there. While Zomer seems to have been more competent, he did not keep either the RA units or some ML ones on the airfield informed of developments on 1st March and many died as a result. It seems strange too that, after his confrontations with Whistondale, he did not follow his own advice and pull out all Dutch personnel from the aerodrome.

Zomer returned to the airfield very early on 1st March knowing that the Japanese convoy was approaching Eretan Wetan and briefed to demolish and evacuate Kalidjati[267] should the need occur. When he told Whistondale to act on his own initiative it was surely an outburst of pure frustration after a week of dealing with the man. He undoubtedly did his best to help the British forces on the base but if he was infuriated by their behaviour so, I believe, were many of his compatriots. In the end it affected the ability of the units there to act together efficiently.

Were there problems between the two nationalities sharing Kalidjati? There was certainly poor communication but I think it went much further than this. Java was Dutch territory and the British, although the bigger imperial power, were here as guests. It was extremely unlikely that any of the British would have spoken Dutch and they needed to be provided with all the necessities of life. Although the Dutch had done the very best they could, it is possible that their allies were less than grateful. Did their forces seem to be patronising or to throw their weight around? The RAF bomber squadrons arrived with aircraft, many of which became unserviceable, and were duly evacuated. Their station commander was clearly out of his depth. Why had the runways, grass strips, not been repaired after the air raids that had stopped a couple of days before? Was there some kind of stand-off at Kalidjati?

As it was, the fate of the airfield and its occupants depended on their own actions and those of their officers. Any inexperience amongst the RA batteries is largely irrelevant in this case. Earle and Coulson had no reliable intelligence on which to base their actions however experienced they and their men might have been. They would have had to be extremely lucky or had supernatural powers to have come up with a good defence plan given the information at their disposal. Had there been a parachute assault, as at P I in Sumatra, it is just possible it could have been held temporarily with

---

[267] Boer, op. cit., p261

the resources available but a land assault supported by light tanks was way beyond their capabilities. If they did not instinctively provide a coherent and comprehensive defence, the blame must be laid at the door of the senior officers who left them there in an impossible position.

Why has the fall of Kalidjati been forgotten? The simple answer is because very few people knew much about it in the first place. Very few of the officers and men of 49th LAA Bty would have known how badly they had been let down by senior officers at HQs both on and off the airfield. They probably died either on 1st March 1942 or later believing they were just unlucky and caught on the hop by the Japanese. No-one said anything because they didn't realise that it wasn't just chance and that they could have been extricated before the storm hit. Also, everything happened so fast that no one person had a clear idea of the overall event. Even the senior British officers on Java had only a minimal idea of what happened there. I would love to be able to believe that there was a massive conspiracy of silence about the incident but actually I don't think that is true. Pearson's and Macartney-Filgate's reports have probably not been released because, with the information they had on Kalidjati to add to all the other failings, they were just too damning on the situation in Java generally.

Why has the Java Campaign been forgotten? Well, it has in Great Britain but not in either The Netherlands or Australia. Look for their writings on it if you don't believe me. For us it just seems to have been too far away and too insignificant after the enormity of the fall of Singapore. Yet the serviceman out there, Earle and Jeudwine, the 'Regulars', Mounsdon, the agricultural college graduate, Jack Gunn, the oil and hardware merchant, were real people with a life that existed outside the battlefield every bit as much as those who died or were made captive at Singapore or Hong Kong. They should be every bit as unforgettable.

Did the 7,000 British, Australian and Indian Army and the 5,100 RAF personnel abandoned on Java in the face of an unstoppable Japanese advance make a crucial contribution to the final Allied victory in the Far East? I would love to believe that the sacrifices they all made were vital but, realistically, I very much doubt it. Should there have been a post-war inquiry into the loss of Kalidjati? The answer has to be no. The British forces in Java had been operating under Dutch command when the Japanese invaded therefore it fell outside the scope of a British inquiry. Any joint inquiry of both nations would have been forced to conclude that it was simply a mixture of human error, inadequate defence forces off the airfield and being taken by surprise on Kalidjati itself. However, I do believe that there should have been an inquiry into how British forces sent to Java were organised, supplied and led as that was not only scandalous but a wholly British affair.

Does what happened in Java in February-March 1942 still matter and who cares? Does what happened at Kalidjati seventy years ago matter today? There was probably a massacre but who cares after all these years? We all should. Again and again we hear people demanding both in war and peace that 'something must be done' about a particular event or situation. The campaign in the NEI in early 1942 was a knee-jerk political and military decision, taken as a response to a seemingly unstoppable Japanese advance. 'We must do something' was the order of the day and that 'something' was to commit British and Australian units to the defence of the NEI with no possibility of evacuation if, as actually happened, it was found to be indefensible. They were not properly equipped and had no command structure to support them in a foreign country with which they had little previous contact and where they did not speak the language. They were dependent on local resources for many essentials both of warfare and of life itself and these resources were very limited. Many of the officers and men in the British RA units had little or no experience of warfare. They were conscripts in a mostly conscript army, not the volunteers our soldiers are today. There was a sprinkling of World War I veterans and a number of Regular soldiers and officers, but not all Regulars take instinctively to wartime service; it calls for different qualities. In the Far East in 1941-2, the Japanese moved so quickly that there was no time for anyone to 'learn on the job'. You had just one try at it.

A public outcry for action or political face-saving should not mean deploying our armed forces without a valid exit strategy or due consideration of what is practicable. God knows men never learn from history in the ordinary way but surely stories like this should make us all think. And, in the final analysis, all men and women who put their lives on the line for their country should be remembered with gratitude and pride.

Appendix A: British forces on Java, 1st March 1942

Approximate Order of Battle (Army)
(CAB 106/39: Sitwell's report: pp4-5)

English

'B' Squadron, 3rd Hussars (Light Tanks)

77 H.A.A. Regiment: H.Q. and three batteries

21 L.A.A. Regiment: H.Q. and two batteries – one of four troops and one of three

48 L.A.A. Regiment: H.Q. and two batteries less two guns*

> All A.A. Regiments above with Signal, R.A.S.C. and R.A.O.C. sections attached.

6 H.A.A. Regiment: H.Q. and two batteries (personnel only).

35 L.A.A. Regiment: two batteries (personnel only) under command of O.C. 6 H.A.A. Regiment.

Allied Military Hospital at Bandoeng

Miscellaneous base administrative units (personnel only) such as Base Ordnance Depot, Detail Issue Store, Security Sections, NAAFI, etc.

Total: 3,500

*48th LAA Regt actually had three batteries, while both 6th HAA and 35th LAA batteries were considerably reduced from their war establishment.

Australian

Infantry Brigade Headquarters

An Australian Machine Gun Battalion

An Australian Pioneer Battalion

Field Company R.E.

Reserve M.T. Company (All personnel of a low medical category)

Miscellaneous small units consisting of Guard Platoons etc including some deserters from Singapore whose value was very doubtful.

Indian

Miscellaneous M.T. drivers, clerks etc.

Total: 2,500

Grand total: 6,000

RAF numbers on Java, 8th March 1942
(AIR 23/2123, Maltby's report, Para 608)

In Tjikadjang area, in the hills, armed – 2,200 (approx.)

Tasik Malaja and other areas, in the plains, unarmed – 2,500 (approx.)

Stragglers, detached and in hospital – 400 (approx.)

Total – 5,100 (approx.)

Appendix B: Death roll, Kalidjati Aerodrome, Feb-March 1942

49th LAA Bty, RA: 21st – 28th February 1942

Bown, Albert, Gnr, 1833315, died 21.02.42

Gafney, William George, L/Bdr, 6010593, died 21.02.42

Mayhew, Bertie Daniel, Gnr, 1520583, died 21.02.42

Parsons, Ernest Frederick George, Gnr, 1736040, died 26.02.42

49th LAA Bty, RA: 1st March 1942

(*CWGC's date of death: 21.02.42. ** CWGC's date of death: 24.02.42)

Akhurst*, Arthur Albert, Gnr, 1736248

Allen*, John Andrew, Gnr, 1759303

Barr*, William G, Gnr, 1679353

Bettison*, Eric, Sgt, 1468013

Braddock*, William Herbert John, L/Bdr, 1611811

Cassels*, William James, Gnr, 1822293

Convine*, Sidney Robert, Gnr, 1605764

Couchman, Albert, Gnr, 1734192

Creasey*, Edward, Gnr, 1758844

Dix*, James Albert, Gnr, 5824077

Farrant**, Leonard Henry, Gnr, 1549844

Foster*, Harry Arthur Charles, Gnr, 1592967

Franklin*, Alfred, Gnr, 1759234

Freeston*, Ronald, Gnr, 1653738

Gardner, George, LBdr, 1602188

Garrett*, Wilfred Bertram, Gnr, 1548968

Garwood*, Cyril George Roy, Gnr, 1653644

Gissing*, Harold George, Gnr, 1653703

Godden*, Jack, Bdr, 1652709

Goodfellow*, George Frederick, Gnr, 1653715

Gray*, Leonard, Gnr, 1653676

Green*, George William, Gnr, 1609561

Greening*, William Albert, Gnr, 1690756

Hamilton, John James, Gnr, 1490118

Hands, Alfonso Parry, Gnr, 1773592

Harris*, Harold Alexander, Gnr, 1626511

Hazelton, George Ernest, Bdr, 1486768

Hellingsworth*, James Robert, Gnr, 1653790

Hillier*, Frederick George, Gnr, 1598598

Homer*, Arthur, Gnr, 1759274

Humphrey, Percy, Gnr, 1696705

Jenner, Albert, Gnr, 1801512

Joyes, Arthur Edward, Gnr, 1483043

Keogh*, John, Gnr, 1710460

Lakin*, Herbert, Gnr, 1809127

Little*, Arthur, Gnr, 1689612

Little*, Ernest William Edward, Gnr, 1696730

Littlejohn*, Henry Charles, Gnr, 1696731

Maltz*, David Geoffrey, Gnr, 1796891

Moodey*, Harold, Gnr, 1572811

Mounsdon, Richard Keith, 2nd Lt, 198831

Nairne*, Alfred Albert, Gnr, 1801532

Nicholls*, Leonard John, Sgt, 1548115

O'Sullivan, William, Gnr, 1487414

Partridge*, John, Gnr, 5620258

Pearson, Ellis James, Gnr, 1548933

Pennell*, Robert Rowland, Bdr, 1478339

Perry*, Elijah, Gnr, 1734090

Prew, John, LBdr, 1801670

Royle*, Thomas, Gnr, 1809101

Russell*, William Henry, L/Bdr, 1520204

Sargent*, William James, L/Sgt, 1486775

Shaw*, Thomas, Gnr, 1803910

Silk*, Charles Horatio, Gnr, 1827634

Simpson, Leonard, Gnr, 1828554

Speedie*, John, Gnr, 1769254

Staplehurst*, Arthur, Gnr, 1639474

Stewart*, John Leslie, Gnr, 1696804

Warrington*, Frederick Arthur, Gnr, 1801705

White*, Thomas, Sgt, 1678851

12ᵗʰ HAA Bty, RA: deaths, 1ˢᵗ March 1942:

Adams, John Edgar, Lt, 151925

Bond, Clifford George, Gnr, 1817015

Burdett, Harry, Gnr, 1502840

Carr, Frank, Gnr, 1676375

Coleman, John Joseph, Gnr, 847816

Conquest, Bertram Edward, Gnr, 1502871

Cook, Thomas Joseph, Gnr, 1600635

Copeland, Herbert Lawrence, Gnr, 1760369

Corlett, John, L/Bdr, 815098

Coulson, Nevil, Major, 67887

Crutchlow, Noah, Gnr, 1502883

Deacon, Richard Thomas, Gnr, 7144475

Deeprose, Reginald Alfred, Gnr, 1797526

Fairs, Maurice Richard, Gnr, 988051

Forrest, Arthur Stanley, Gnr, 1738779

Francis, George, Gnr, 1580883

Fry, William Henry, Gnr, 1811648

Fryer, Harry, Gnr, 822003

Gardner, Thomas, Gnr, 4447406

Gore, Albert Edward, Gnr, 1817395

Hanson, John, L/Bdr, 847784

Harris, Raymond John, Gnr, 1811608

Higginson, Thomas Henry, Gnr, 860867

Howard, William, Gnr, 872438

Huridge, Harry, Gnr, 1427260

Hurlstone, John Joseph Patrick, Gnr, 850383

James, Glyn, Gnr, 1817116

Johnston, William James, Gnr, 3239062

Keevil, Joseph Jesse, Sgt, 805169

King, John Barr, Gnr, 1518879

Kistell, William Bosanko, Gnr, 1591078

Lowes, Joseph Cuthbert, Gnr, 848602 (CWGC: 24.02.42)

Nicholls, Thomas William, Gnr, 1580671

Pigott, Cyril, Gnr, 1748911

Rennardson, Arthur William, L/Bdr, 1749003

Reynolds, Leslie Charles, Gnr, 1514294

Stanton, Alfred Arthur, Gnr, 1745269

Tart, Joshua, Gnr, 822311

Todd, William Alfred, Gnr, 1435926

Trickett, Jack, Gnr, 1580908

Underhill, George Henry, Gnr, 782342

Unterman, Francis Rene, Gnr, 1427564

Wilson, Thomas Henry, L/Sgt, 842112

RAF/RAAF personnel: deaths, 1st March 1942:

Bott, James Edwin Warwick, F/O, RAF, 84718, 84 Sqn (CWGC: 05.02.42)

Cary, Norris Robert, Cpl, RAFVR, 968737?, 84 Sqn

Daniels, George James, LAC, RAF, 638546, 84 Sqn

Edwards, John, LAC, RAF, 652344, 84 Sqn

Finlayson, William Murdoch, A/C 2nd Cl, RAFVR, 1341365

Forby, Jack, A/C 1st Cl, RAAF, 39764, 1 Sqn

Fretwell, Albert, LAC, RAFVR, 746615, 84 Sqn

Kewish, Douglas William, P/O, RAAF, 401128, 84 Sqn

Matthews, George William, Cpl, RAFVR, 756632, 84 Sqn

McBride, Alfred Henry, Sgt, RAF, 358842, 84 Sqn

Mohr, Reginald Daly, Sgt, RAAF, 400019, 39 Sqn

Ogburn, William Henry, LAC, RAFVR, 920019, 84 Sqn

Reid, John Ruskin, Sgt, RAAF, 400261, 84 Sqn

Richards, Robert, F/O, RAFVR, 39301, 59 Sqn

Russell, David Geddes, LAC, RAFVR, 1007171, 84 Sqn

Russell, Samuel Kane, A/C 1st Cl, RAFVR, 1357602, 84 Sqn

Slee, William, Flt Sgt, RAF, 560903, 84 Sqn

Telfer, William Richie, Cpl, RAFVR, 974502

Tweedie, George, LAC, RAFVR, 995075, 84 Sqn

Whistondale, George Frederick, Grp Capt, RAF, 16259

This list of Air Force personnel is more susceptible to mistakes than the RA unit lists, as I have found less official information to confirm the names. It is undoubtedly incomplete. F/O Bott died on 1st March but an original wrongly-dated report was never corrected.

Maps

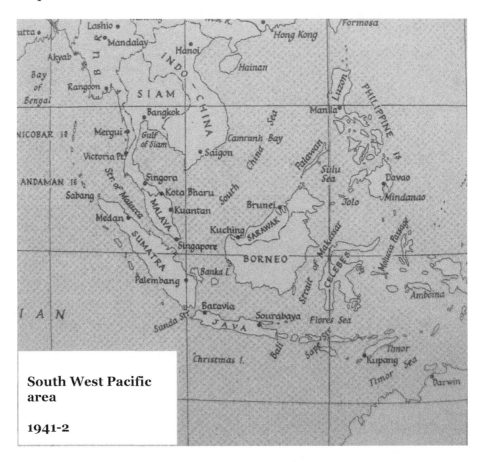

South West Pacific area

1941-2

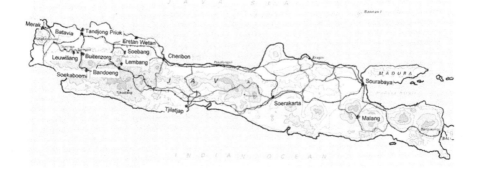

Java, 1942

Towns: •

Roads: ▬▬▬

Railways: ┼┼┼

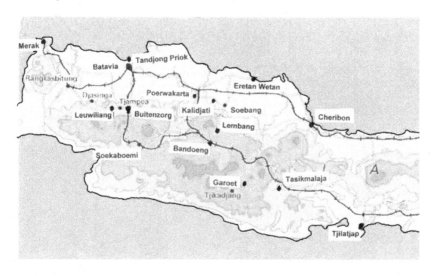

Western Java, 1942

Towns: •

Roads: ▬▬▬

Railways: ┼┼┼

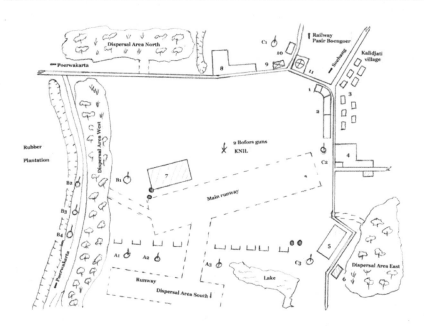

Sketch map of Kalidjati airfield [not to scale]

Key:

═══	Roads
⊔	Aircraft pen
●	Pill box
⚲	Bofors gun positions, 49th LAA Bty
⊔⊔	Ravines

1 =   ML HQ
2 =   Old hangars: ML Tech services, RAF servicing and RAF HQ
3 =   RAF ORs' camp and HQ 84 Sqn
4 =   ML offices and quarters, C Troop HQ
5 =   ML bomber hangar
6 =   KNIL defence force HQ/Coulson's HQ
7 =   'Ryan' hangar
8 =   Officers' quarters, officers mess
9 =   49th LAA Battery HQ
10 =   A Troop HQ
11 =   Hospital

Dispersal Area East: alang-alang (grass 2-10ft tall) and low shrubs
Dispersal Areas South and West: grass and low shrubs
Dispersal Area North: wooded with high trees

Bibliography

Printed sources:

'Bloody Shambles, Volume Two: The Defence of Sumatra to the Fall of
    Burma'; Christopher Shores and Brian Cull with Yasuho Izawa,
    Grub Street, London, 1993 and reprints
'Global Warrior'; A. Charpentier, L. Lacey-Johnson and G. Jeudwine,
    privately published, 1999
'History of the Royal Regiment of Artillery: The Far East Theatre 1941-6';
    General Sir Martin Farndale KCB, Brassey's, 2000
'Imperial Military Geography'; Major D H Cole, Seventh Edition, Sifton
    Praed & Co, 1933
'Scorpions Sting: The story of No. 84 Squadron Royal Air Force, 1917-
    1992'; Don Neate, Air-Britain Publications, 1994
'The Imperial Cruise'; James Bradley, Back Bay Books, Little, Brown &
    Company, 2009
'Their Last Tenko'; James Home, Quoin Publishing, 1989
'The Loss of Java'; P C Boer, NUS Press, 2011
'The Royal Air Force 1939-1945, Volume II: The Fight Avails'; D Richards
    and H St. G. Saunders, HMSO, 1954
'The Winston Specials'; Archie Munro, Maritime Books, 2006
'Three Came Home'; Agnes Keith, Michael Joseph Ltd, 1948

Official War Histories:
'Australia in the War of 1939–1945; Series 1 – Army; Volume IV – The
Japanese Thrust', (1st edition, 1957), Author: Lionel Wigmore
'Australia in the War of 1939–1945. Series 3 – Air; Volume I – Royal
Australian Air Force, 1939–1942', (1st edition, 1962), Author: Douglas
Gillison
'The War against Japan. Vol I: The Loss of Singapore, History of the
Second World War, United Kingdom Military Series'. Maj-Gen S
Woodburn Kirby, HSMO, 1957, reprint Naval and Military Press, 2004

The London Gazette:

        Supplement, 22nd March 1918: MC: Lt (A./Capt) J V Macartney-
            Filgate, RFA, Spec. Res.
        Supplement, 28th May, 1946: MID: Lt Col S R Pearson [48th LAA];
            Lt Col M D S Saunders [21st LAA]; Maj G A Moxon [15th/6th
            HAA]; Maj N Coulson (Posthumous) [12th/6th HAA]; Capt
            W L Sherrard (Posthumous) [12th/6th HAA]; Sgt J J Keevil
            (Posthumous) [12th/6th HAA]
        Supplement, 5th December 1946: MID: Lt M S Banner
            (Posthumous) [49th/48th LAA]; Sgt E Beardwood
            (Posthumous) [49th/48th LAA]

Supplement, 20th January 1948: Despatch of Air Chief Marshal Sir
Robert Brooke-Popham, GCVO, KCB, CMG, DSO, AF
Supplement, 26th February 1948: Despatch of Lt Gen A. E. Percival,
CB, DSO, OBE, MC

Original sources that proved most useful:

The National Archives, London:

ADM 199/1138: WS convoys, 1941-2

ADM 237/1600: Convoy WS 14 and DM 2, 1941-2

AIR 2/7730: Netherlands East Indies: Kalidjati Incident

AIR 20/5573: Malaya operations 1941-1942: Bomber Operations NEI

AIR 20/5578: Malaya operations 1941-1942: fighter operations [Sqn Ldr F
J Howell's report; Gp Capt H S Darley's report, Appendix 'C'; Sqn
Ldr W J Harper's report]

AIR 20/5585: Malaya operations 1941-1942: organisation reports [W/Cdr
G O Hamilton-Ross' report; Wg Cdr Briggs' report]

AIR 23/2123: Operations of the RAF during the campaigns in Malaya and
Netherlands East Indies: report by Air Vice-Marshal P.C. Maltby,
1941 – 1942

AIR 23/4830: Japanese air operations in Java and Sumatra, 1942

AIR 23/4959: East Indies Archipelago [Part 1]: List of Aerodromes,
satellites, landing grounds, emergency landing grounds, seaplane
stations, and seaplane alighting areas, 1942

CAB 106/20: Report of the action at Palembang of the 6th HAA Regiment,
Royal Artillery, and the withdrawal to Java, by Lt Col G W G
Baillie, 1942

CAB 106/29: "ABDACOM": official account of events in the South-West
Pacific Command Jan.-Feb 1942

CAB 106/39: Despatch on operations in Java, 24 Feb - 20 Mar 1942, by
Maj Gen H D W Sitwell, General Officer Commanding British
Troops in Java

CAB 106/85: The story of No. 43 Special Mission (Java 1942), Lt-Col L van
der Post

CAB 106/86: Report on the air operations during the campaigns in Malaya
and Netherlands East Indies, 8 Dec 1941 - 12 Mar 1942, by Air
Vice-Marshal Sir Paul Maltby, Air Officer Commanding Royal Air
Force in Java (Supplement to London Gazette 38216) [London
Gazette 26 February 1948]

CAB 106/133: Netherlands account of the action in Sumatra, Jan-Mar 1942

CAB 106/134: Netherlands account of the battle of Java, Mar 1942

CAB 106/139: Report on operations in Java and diary, 23 Feb - 12 Mar
1942, Brig A S Blackburn, VC, General Officer Commanding
Australian Forces.

CAB 106/140: Account of operations of Australian forces in Java, Feb-Apr
1942 [2/2 Australian Pioneer Battalion]

CAB 120/805: Records. Nominal. Army, 01 Oct 1940 - 30 Nov 1943

CAB 121/697: Situation in the Netherlands East Indies Vol. I, Oct 1940 - Oct 1945

FO 371/31812: Japanese air raids on Netherlands East Indies, 1942

MT 40/45: Movement of troops and stores: estimate of future commitments, 1941

PREM 3/326: Netherlands East Indies, Feb 1941 - Oct 1944

PREM 8/757: The publication of various despatches of Far Eastern campaigns of 1941/42 Sir R Brooke-Popham; General Maltby [Hong Kong]; Lord Wavell; General Percival [Malaya]; Air Vice-Marshal Maltby. 1947-1948

WO 32/12105: Despatch on operations in Java, 24.02.42 to 20.03.42, Maj Gen Sitwell

WO 106/5983: Narrative of operations of British forces in Java, Feb-Mar 1942 [Maj Gen Sitwell's report]

WO 106/2527: Sumatra: aerodrome defence, Jan 1942

WO 106/2539: Java campaign: miscellaneous reports, Feb 1942 [Reports of Lt Col H R Humphreys, RA, CO 77th HAA Regiment, and Capt A Johnstone, RASC, attached to 48th LAA Regiment]

WO 106/2556: Despatch on operations in South West Pacific, January 15th – 25th February 1942 by General Sir Archibald Wavell, GCB, CMG, MC, A-D-C

WO 106/2558B: Far East emergency: reinforcements, Dec 1941 - Mar 1942

WO 106/2562: Java operations: narrative by Maj Gen Sir H G W Sitwell for period Feb-Mar 1942

WO 106/2563: Java story of 21 LAA Regt, 1941-2 [Lt-Col M D S Saunders' report]

WO 106/2564: Java action of British troops, Mar 1942

WO 106/2572: Operation ABDACOM: general, Jan-Mar1942

WO 106/3302: Defence of Java, Feb-May 1942

WO 106/5983: Narrative of operations of British forces in Java, Feb-Mar 1942

WO 166/2721: War Diary of 48th LAA Regiment, 1940-41

WO 166/2796: War Diary of 49th Battery LAA, various dates 1939-41

WO 208/1611: Netherlands East Indies; Japanese invasion, demolition of installations and oil wells, and evacuation of British and Dutch troops and civilians, Dec 1941 - Apr 1942

WO 208/4287: Java, 1942-1945

WO 325/69: Kali Jati Camp, Java: ill treatment of POWs ['Kalijati Massacre']

WO 361/248: Netherlands East Indies: 12th Battery, 6th Heavy Anti-Aircraft Regiment, Royal Artillery; missing personnel

WO 361/342: Netherlands East Indies: 49th Battery, 48th Light Anti-Aircraft Regiment, Royal Artillery; missing personnel

WO 361/1280: Far East: Java; Tandjong Priok and Boei Glodok POW Camps; 48th LAA Regiment, Royal Artillery; Part II Orders, 14 Jul 1942 – 12 Oct 1945

WO 361/1450: 48th LAA Regiment, RA, nominal roll of POW deaths

WO 361/1589: Statement of W/O Wm Procter R.A.F.
WO 361/1626: RAF nominal roll of missing

The Imperial War Museum London [IWM]:

IWM Collection: Catalogue No: 2008-11-08: Gp Capt G F Whistondale
IWM Documents.398: Private papers of Lt S E Bagnall
IWM Documents.7879: Private papers of Canon R C R Godfrey:
    Journal and private papers of the Rev R C R Godfrey, Chaplain to
    48th LAA Regiment, RA
    'The 48th Light Anti-Aircraft Regiment in the Dutch East Indies,
    February-March 1942 by Lt Col J V O Macartney-Filgate MC'
IWM Documents.8116: Private papers of Brig S R Pearson
IWM Documents.8148: Private papers of Capt R A Baron Mackay

Documents, unpublished letters, photos and papers of Jack L L Gunn, in
author's possession
Unpublished research on the Hawker Typhoon, courtesy of Jack Livesey

Index

Printed in Great Britain
by Amazon

61871376R00119